Inequality, Grievances, and Civil War

This book argues that political and economic inequalities following group lines generate grievances that can motivate civil war. The theoretical approach highlights ethnonationalism and how linkages between group identities and inequalities spur mobilization and resort to violence. Although contemporary research on civil war has largely dismissed grievances as irrelevant, emphasizing instead the role of opportunities, the authors show that many alleged nonresults for grievances stem from atheoretical measures, typically based on individualist data. The authors develop new indicators of political and economic exclusion at the group level and demonstrate how these exert strong effects on the risk of civil war. They provide new analyses of the effects of transnational ethnic links and the duration of civil wars and extended case discussions illustrating causal mechanisms.

Lars-Erik Cederman is Professor of International Conflict Research at the Center for Comparative and International Studies at ETH Zürich. He is the author of *Emergent Actors in World Politics* (1997), the editor of *Constructing Europe's Identity* (2001), and the co-editor of *New Systems Theories of World Politics* (2010). He is the winner of the 2012 and 2002 American Political Science Association's Heinz I. Eulau Awards, the 2000 Furniss Book Award, and the Horace H. Rackham Dissertation Award from the University of Michigan.

Kristian Skrede Gleditsch is Professor in the Department of Government, University of Essex, and a Research Associate at the Peace Research Institute Oslo (PRIO). He is the author of *All International Politics Is Local* (2002) and *Spatial Regression Models* (2008) as well as numerous journal articles. He is the winner of the 2012 American Political Science Association's Heinz I. Eulau Award, the 2011 International Association for Conflict Management outstanding article in the field award, the 2007 Karl Deutsch Award from the International Studies Association, and the 2000 American Political Science Association's Helen Dwight Reid Award.

Halvard Buhaug is Research Professor at the Peace Research Institute Oslo and Professor of Political Science at the Norwegian University of Science and Technology. He received the 2006 Royal Norwegian Society of Sciences and Letters award for excellent research by young scholars in human sciences. Recent academic publications include articles in the *Journal of Conflict Resolution*, *Global Environmental Change*, *International Security*, *International Organization*, and *Proceedings of the National Academy of Sciences of the USA*.

Cambridge Studies in Contentious Politics

Editors

Mark Beissinger *Princeton University*
Jack A. Goldstone *George Mason University*
Michael Hanagan *Vassar College*
Doug McAdam *Stanford University and Center for Advanced Study in the Behavioral Sciences*
Sarah A. Soule *Stanford University*
Suzanne Staggenborg *University of Pittsburgh*
Sidney Tarrow *Cornell University*
Charles Tilly (d. 2008) *Columbia University*
Elisabeth J. Wood *Yale University*
Deborah Yashar *Princeton University*

Continued after the Index

Inequality, Grievances, and Civil War

LARS-ERIK CEDERMAN

*Center for Comparative and International Studies,
ETH Zürich*

KRISTIAN SKREDE GLEDITSCH

University of Essex and Peace Research Institute Oslo

HALVARD BUHAUG

Peace Research Institute Oslo

CAMBRIDGE
UNIVERSITY PRESS

CAMBRIDGE
UNIVERSITY PRESS

32 Avenue of the Americas, New York, NY 10013-2473, USA

Cambridge University Press is part of the University of Cambridge.

It furthers the University's mission by disseminating knowledge in the pursuit of education, learning and research at the highest international levels of excellence.

www.cambridge.org
Information on this title: www.cambridge.org/9781107603042

© Lars-Erik Cederman, Kristian Skrede Gleditsch, and Halvard Buhaug 2013

First published 2013

Printed in the United States of America

A catalog record for this publication is available from the British Library.

Library of Congress Cataloging in Publication Data
Cederman, Lars-Erik, 1963–
Inequality, grievances, and civil war / Lars-Erik Cederman, Center for Comparative and International Studies, ETH Zürich; Kristian Skrede Gleditsch, University of Essex and Peace Research Institute Oslo; Halvard Buhaug, Peace Research Institute Oslo.
    pages cm. – (Cambridge studies in contentious politics)
Includes bibliographical references and index.
ISBN 978-1-107-01742-9 (hardback) – ISBN 978-1-107-60304-2 (pbk.)
1. Civil war – Social aspects.   2. Equality.   3. Human rights.   I. Gleditsch, Kristian Skrede,
1971– II. Buhaug, Halvard, 1972– III. Title.
JC491.C374   2013
303.6′4–dc23   2013001656

ISBN 978-1-107-01742-9 Hardback
ISBN 978-1-107-60304-2 Paperback

Contents

Tables

Figures

Preface

Apart from acquiring real estate, there are few things that make you more indebted than writing collaborative monographs. Indeed, this book is the product not only of our own efforts, but also those of our colleagues and students who made major contributions in terms of conceptual development, data collection, software development, and analysis. In this very respect, the book falls somewhere between a co-authored book and a co-edited volume.

More than anything else, this book is the fruit of several years of intense research collaboration involving a tight network of conflict researchers in Europe. These activities started as an informal network that we labeled Geographic Research On War Network (GROWnet), which originally included colleagues at the Peace Research Institute Oslo (PRIO) and the Norwegian University of Science and Technology in Norway, ETH Zürich and University of Geneva in Switzerland, and the University of Essex in the United Kingdom, and was subsequently extended to collaborators at Uppsala University in Sweden. Within this context, we have published a large amount of co-authored research, with an author list featuring every possible combination of the three authors of this book and beyond. Some of the research paving the way for the book was funded by an ECRP grant on "Disaggregating Civil War" (06ECRPFP004) awarded by the European Science Foundation, 2007–10, through individual grants from the national research councils, that is, the Research Council of Norway (182399), Swiss National Science Foundation (105511–116795), and UK Economic and Social Research Council (RES-062-23-0259). Gleditsch also acknowledges support from the Research Council of Norway (180441/V10). As of the summer of 2012, the network received new funding from the European Union as a COST Action (IS 1102), which will allow it to expand its activities to many more partners in Europe under the heading of the European Network of Conflict Research (ENCoRe).

Sidney Tarrow played an instrumental role at a pivotal moment by suggesting that we publish our book project with Cambridge University Press, where Lewis Bateman has supported our work with both patience and professionalism. All in all, we held three book workshops at ETH Zürich on 10 November 2011, at Yale on 24 February 2012, and at PRIO on 10 March 2012. We received excellent feedback from the participants at those workshops, including Keith Darden, Hanne Fjelde, Scott Gates, Jack Goldstone, Håvard Hegre, Helge Holtermann, Simon Hug, Stathis Kalyvas, Janet Lewis, Nicholas Sambanis, Frances Stewart, Andres Vargas, Nils Weidmann, and Tore Wig. We also benefited from comments from participants at seminar presentations at Koç University on 16 April 2012 and the London School of Economics and Political Science on 9 May 2012, including Belgin San Akça, Ali Çarkoğlu, Emre Hatipoğlu, Bill Kissane, Omar McDoom, Michael Mousseau, and Jameson Lee Ungerer. In addition, Carles Boix, Michael Hechter, Erik Melander, and Camber Warren commented on parts of the manuscript.

Current and past PhD students and researchers of the International Conflict Research Groups at ETH Zürich have selflessly sacrificed large chunks of their valuable research time to provide public goods in the shape of data projects and analysis. Nils Weidmann and Christa Deiwiks volunteered their skills in terms of data management and computational and spatial analysis. Julian Wucherpfennig and Philipp Hunziker played an instrumental role in project management and econometric analysis. Luc Girardin, with the help of Sebastian Schutte and Philipp Hunziker, created the computational infrastructure that made the project possible, including the data portal GROW[up]. Manuel Vogt, Nils-Christian Bormann, and Seraina Rüegger managed the coding and updating of large data structures, all related to the Ethnic Power Relations (EPR) data set. Indeed, this book project revolves around this data resource, which originates from research collaboration involving Andreas Wimmer and Brian Min, both then at UCLA. We are grateful to a long list of experts who offered their advice regarding, the coding of countless country cases; see Chapter 4, footnote 7, and http://www.icr.ethz.ch/data. In particular, we would like to acknowledge the expert input by James Scarritt and Manuel Vogt, who helped us update the coding of Sub-Saharan Africa. Our data collection efforts were generously supported by the National Center of Competence in Research, "Challenges to democracy in the 21st century," and funded by the Swiss National Science Foundation (SNSF) and the Swiss Network for International Studies (SNIS).

At the University of Essex, we have benefited from comments and suggestions from current and former colleagues Tobias Böhmelt, Han Dorussen, Ismene Gizelis, Steve Pickering, and Ulrich Pilster. Nils Metternich and Andrea Ruggeri served as research officers on our ESF project and have become valued collaborators who have influenced the research reported in this book in numerous ways.

Research underpinning this book has also benefited greatly from brown-bag seminars and informal discussions with colleagues at PRIO under the auspices of the Centre for the Study of Civil War (CSCW). Being associated with the GROWnet, Scott Gates, Nils Petter Gleditsch, Johan Dittrich Hallberg, Håvard Hegre, Helge Holtermann, and Gudrun Østby have followed the development of this project and generously offered insightful and constructive comments and suggestions along the way. Likewise, we have benefited tremendously from input on GIS, data, and statistical methods from Jan Ketil Rød, Håvard Strand, and Andreas Forø Tollefsen. External CSCW affiliates such as Sabine Carey, David Cunningham, Kathleen Cunningham, Magnus Öberg, Idean Salehyan, and Gerald Schneider have also provided valuable comments. Finally, we would like to thank Andrew John Feltham for his excellent help managing our activities through CSCW.

It should be stressed that a lot of crucial steps were taken in connection with collaborative publications that preceded this book. Andreas Wimmer and Brian Min co-authored an article that inspired Chapter 4 (see Cederman, Wimmer, and Min 2010). Nils Weidmann co-authored the article that constitutes the initial basis of Chapter 5 (see Cederman, Weidmann, and Gleditsch 2011). Chapter 6 draws heavily on an article co-authored with Idean Salehyan and Julian Wucherpfennig (see Cederman, Gleditsch, Salehyan, and Wucherpfennig 2013), Chapter 7 builds on some of our other joint work (see Buhaug, Cederman, and Gleditsch Forthcoming), and Chapter 8 relies on material from articles that we co-authored with David Cunningham and Idean Salehyan (Cunningham, Gleditsch, and Salehyan 2009) as well as Julian Wucherpfennig and Nils Metternich (Wucherpfennig, Metternich, Cederman, and Gleditsch 2012). We are also grateful for the publishers' permission to use material from these publications.

Last but not least, we would like to acknowledge the continuous support from our partners and families who provided both intellectual inspiration and a healthy counterweight to the "workaholic" tendencies of academic life. Without their boundless patience and generous willingness to bear the burden of often-absent spouses and fathers, this book could not have been written.

1

Introduction

Do grievances cause civil war? The desperate struggles of discriminated and stateless peoples around the world suggest that the answer to this question must be affirmative, as illustrated by such cases as the Palestinians in the West Bank and Gaza, the Fur in the Sudan, the Tamils in Sri Lanka, the Karen in Myanmar, and the Kurds in Turkey and elsewhere. Indeed, the upheavals in North Africa and the Middle East in 2011 demonstrate that it is difficult to sustain regimes that exclude large parts of the population from political power along ethnic or nonethnic lines.

In stark contrast to these observations, however, much of the contemporary literature on civil war takes a very different view. Regarding explanations rooted in political and economic grievances with suspicion, leading scholars of civil war typically give short shrift to grievance-based accounts on the basis of results indicating that ethnic diversity and unequal individual wealth distributions have no statistically distinguishable relationship to internal conflict. In particular, ethnic grievances as triggers of civil wars receive little support in this literature, despite their having attracted substantial attention in qualitative studies. Arguing that grievances are the product, rather than a cause, of violence, or otherwise so omnipresent that they cannot account for civil conflict, these authors question the sincerity of political entrepreneurs' appeals to ethnic nationalism, dismissing them as the opportunistic and self-serving arguments of warlords, thugs, and criminals.

In his best-selling book *The Bottom Billion*, Collier (2007, p. 18) expresses these doubts explicitly:

So what causes civil war? Rebel movements themselves justify their actions in terms of a catalogue of grievances: repression, exploitation, exclusion. Politically motivated academics have piled in with their own hobbyhorses, which usually cast rebels as heroes. I have come to distrust this discourse of grievances as self-serving.

Along similar lines, Mueller (2000, p. 92) interprets grievances as an opportunistic cover for greedy and even criminal activities:

What passed for "ethnic warfare" in Bosnia and Croatia seems then to have been something far more banal: the creation of communities of criminal violence and predation. In the end, the wars resembled the movie images of the American Wild West or of gangland Chicago, and they often had less to do with nationalism than with criminal opportunism and sadistic cruelty, very commonly enhanced with liquor.

If ethnic conflict is fundamentally banal then it could potentially take place in any society, as illustrated by British soccer hooligans and motorcycle gangs in Denmark: "Under the right conditions, thugs can rise to a dominant role, others can lend a hand or withdraw into terrified isolation or studied indifference, and any place can degenerate into a Bosnia or a Rwanda" (Mueller 2000, p. 68).

From a less radical vantage point, most scholars who rely on quantitative evidence insist that ethnic frustrations fail to explain internal conflict. In a review of political-economy approaches to "ethnic mobilization and ethnic violence," Fearon (2006, pp. 857–8) comes to precisely this conclusion:

Cross-national statistical studies find surprisingly few differences between the determinants of civil war onset in general, versus "ethnic" civil wars in particular. Once one controls for per capita income, neither civil wars nor ethnic civil wars are significantly more frequent in more ethnically diverse countries; nor are they more likely when there is an ethnic majority and a large ethnic minority.

In fact, this skeptical attitude as regards grievances as causes of civil war and ethnic conflict is so pronounced among rationalist scholars that Horowitz (2002, p. 547) characterizes it as "antipathy to antipathy."

Challenging these nonfindings, we argue that they, to a large extent, result from inappropriate theoretical assumptions and problematic empirical operationalizations. To be sure, measuring grievances is more easily said than done. As mental states that can easily be misinterpreted, such phenomena are notoriously difficult to pin down objectively. We wholeheartedly agree with Blattman and Miguel's (2010, p. 18) diagnosis:

At present, the economic motivations for conflict are better theorized than psychological or sociological factors. Individual preferences in existing models typically include only material rewards and punishments. One key implication is that we have not derived the falsifiable predictions that distinguish between material and non-material theoretical accounts. Yet, the greater degree of existing theory on economic factors does not imply that researchers should discard non-economic explanations of conflict.

Much of the contemporary research on civil war aggregates the analysis to the country level. While expressing similar doubts about the relevance of grievances as explanations, a new wave of scholarship has shifted the attention away from entire countries to micro-level studies of specific processes of civil violence. In seminal contributions to the civil war literature, Kalyvas (2003; 2006) casts doubt on the validity of "master cleavages" as the key to such conflicts. Instead, he argues in favor of a much more disaggregated perspective that highlights mundane micro-level motivations, such as local feuds and the settling of petty grudges that have little to do with the warring parties' broader ideological justifications. Although Kalyvas remains open to the possibility of ideological preferences influencing the outbreak of conflict, and some micro-level studies leave room for the role of political grievances (e.g., Gates 2002; Wood 2003; Weinstein 2007), most authors contributing to this literature deviate from such explanations (e.g., Fearon 2006; Blattman and Miguel 2010).

Our empirical strategy differs from both the country-level and micro-level literatures by focusing on interactions between the state and actors at intermediate levels of aggregation, such as ethnic groups and rebel organizations (Cederman and Gleditsch 2009). This approach allows us to go well beyond conventional country-level studies in terms of empirical detail, while at the same time allowing us to maintain the broad horizons of a truly *global* comparison. Following in the footsteps of Gurr's (1993a; 2000b) and Horowitz's (1985) classical contributions to the literature on ethnic conflict, this is a book about the impact of political grievances on civil war in general and the conflict-fueling role of ethnic nationalism in particular. As illustrated by the revolts in Tunisia, Egypt, and Libya erupting in the spring of 2011, anger with political exclusion without reference to ethnic cleavages may lead to violence, but ethnonationalist civil wars remain arguably the most important, and also most misunderstood, class of grievance-related violence.

As a way to overcome the formidable obstacles associated with the operationalization and measurement of grievances, our strategy is to take one step back in order to detect structural situations that can be safely assumed to cause frustrations in the first place. In particular, we postulate that political and economic inequalities afflicting entire ethnic groups, rather than merely individuals, are especially likely to fuel resentment and justify attempts to fight perceived injustice. According to the terminology introduced by Stewart (2008b), such asymmetries can be labeled "horizontal inequalities" since they concern established groups, as opposed to "vertical inequalities" among isolated individuals and households. Part of the reason why grievance-based arguments have found little support in the quantitative literature is that such studies have typically measured vertical inequality, while ignoring its horizontal counterpart.

Since the most powerful counterarguments to grievance-based explanations have been backed up by quantitative indicators, this book centers on the development of better measures of inequalities that are directly linked to group-level theories of civil war. Furthermore, the problems of measuring political and economic inequalities call for new data. There is an important research tradition that relies on well-established data sources, such as the Minorities at Risk (MAR) data set. Nevertheless, these and similar data impose restrictions that make them less suitable to study the types of processes that we focus on in this book. Therefore, we build on a new version of the Ethnic Power

Relations data set that we refer to as EPR-ETH, which traces ethnic groups' access to state power (see Chapter 4). Our analysis also makes frequent use of Geographic Information Systems (GIS), which facilitate measurement of sub-national properties and configurations. In particular, we rely on a geo-coded extension to EPR-ETH (GeoEPR), which provides detailed information about the EPR groups' settlement areas (see Chapter 5). Furthermore, the EPR-ETH data include a new extension that covers transnational ethnic kin (see Chapter 6). Finally, the book also employs a mapping that codes links between the EPR-ETH groups and conflict data coded for rebel organizations. All these data resources can be accessed through our data portal GROW^{up} (Geographic Research On War: unified platform).[1]

If properly reconceptualized as group-level claims resulting from macro-level processes, such as nationalism and state formation, rather than as fixed ethno-demographic configurations or apolitical collections of individual characteristics, grievances can be systematically linked to political violence through actor-specific mechanisms. Taking this step from "factors to actors" enables us to postulate and evaluate a number of specific hypotheses concerning conflict parties' behavior under varying ethno-political configurations. Our argument does not, in any way, exclude possible effects of alternative causal mechanisms that are not related to inequalities or grievances. Rather than setting up false dichotomies that pit "greed" or "opportunities" against "grievances," our aim is to show that the latter category strongly influences the probability of civil conflict even while controlling for the former. Thus, the goal is to resurrect and refine a specific class of grievance-based explanations rather than debunking the alternatives.

The second part of our book analyzes the causes of civil war outbreak. In Chapter 4, we find that ethnic groups that are excluded from governmental influence are more likely to experience conflict than those that enjoy secure access to executive power. Recent loss of power or outright discrimination, rather than mere exclusion, tends to increase the risk of conflict even further. Our results indicate that political horizontal inequality often triggers civil violence.

Moreover, the findings of Chapter 5 demonstrate that group-level economic inequality can also lead to violent conflict, especially for groups with wealth levels below the national average, as exemplified by the Chechens in Russia and the Albanians in Yugoslavia. However, the evidence is much more mixed for groups that are wealthier than the average group. Furthermore, our analysis shows that the conflict propensity of disadvantaged and to some extent advantaged groups appears to hinge on political exclusion in the sense that economic horizontal inequality only matters where there is also political horizontal inequality.

In Chapter 6, we show that this group-level perspective also allows us to capture transborder processes involving ethnonationalist kin. Despite recent advances in this area, a central puzzle remains unresolved: namely that ethnic

---

[1] The system is available at http://growup.ethz.ch.

groups that at least in theory could count on support from large transborder ethnic kin (TEK) groups have often remained surprisingly peaceful, such as the stranded Russian populations in the "near abroad." Postulating a curvilinear, conflict-inducing effect of the TEK group's relative size compared to the incumbent, state-controlling group, we find that the risk of conflict increases within the middle range of the size spectrum. Moreover, our results suggest that the net effect, compared with situations without transnational links, is conflict-dampening for large TEK groups that enjoy access to executive power in their countries, as illustrated by the lack of conflict in many post-Soviet states. In contrast, our model shows that excluded TEK groups, such as the Kurdish minorities in Turkey, Iran, and Iraq before 2003, tend to increase the risk of civil war.

The group-level analyses are complemented by findings aggregated up to the country level in Chapter 7, including different measures of inequality and conflict. The aggregated analysis makes it possible to compare ethnic to nonethnic conflicts and the risk of conflict with excluded groups to the risk of civil war in countries without ethnic cleavages. Moreover, we contrast explanations based on horizontal inequalities to those that feature vertical inequalities. The results suggest that our group-level findings can be readily generalized from group relations to the country level, while also demonstrating the advantages of replacing conventional ethno-demographic indicators with measures that are more sensitive to the underlying political logic of ethnonationalist conflict and within-country variation.

Part III goes beyond the traditional focus on conflict onset. In Chapter 8, we examine the duration and outcome of conflicts, which allows us to consider the actual characteristics of organizations involved in conflicts and their relationship to ethnic groups, and to take seriously the possibility that ethnic groups may not be unitary actors and that rebel organizations can have a complex relationship to ethnic constituencies. We demonstrate that ethnonationalist exclusion influences not only the initial emergence of conflict but also its duration. Again, the argument is that decisions by states to exclude groups from power, rather than the mere existence of ethnic cleavages, are what make a difference for explaining patterns of violence.

Finally, Chapter 9 concludes the book. There we summarize our findings and explore trends affecting entire world regions. This analysis allows us to draw general conclusions for theory and policy, especially with respect to inclusion of ethnic groups through power sharing.

Having summarized our findings, it may be useful to anticipate the reasons why we come to such different conclusions compared with the dominant view. In fact, there are several reasons why both grievances and inequalities have been downplayed in contemporary scholarship on civil wars. To address these shortcomings, this book offers the following improvements:

• *Intermediate disaggregation rather than just individual or country-level analysis.* Most systematic studies of civil wars tend to be general but heavily aggregated, and thus lacking in empirical precision, or disaggregated but focused on single countries, and thus lacking in generality. Focusing on conflict processes either at the country level or at the level of individuals or villages, much of the contemporary literature overlooks intermediate levels of aggregation where collective grievances are directly relevant, and where inequalities are most easily detected. To fill this gap, we explore explicit relational configurations at the mesolevel of aggregation, namely the group and organization levels, before aggregating our findings back to the country level.

- *Motivational rather than merely cognitive mechanisms.* Because of the strong influence of narrowly construed rationalistic and cognitive theorizing, many popular explanations tend to overlook the role of grievances. Rather than privileging cognitive processes at the expense of emotions, our book postulates explicit causal mechanisms that show how collectively felt grievances result from structural inequalities and may produce violent conflict under specific conditions.

- *Ethnonationalism rather than merely ethnicity as a conflict cause.* The conventional literature on "ethnic conflict" tends to debate the role of ethnicity in itself, as a demographic or individualist property that can be extricated from its political context. Such reasoning loses sight of the state, which plays a central role as a prize and an autonomous actor in nationalist conflicts. Our theoretical framework centers on the *political* function of ethnicity, especially where inequality creates tensions between ethnic groups that can be exploited for ethnonationalist mobilization.

- *Theoretically relevant data and measures, rather than the standard toolbox.* Scarcity and fragmentation of appropriate data on the relevant actors have also made it difficult to measure grievances, even indirectly. Indices such as the ethnic fractionalization index and the Gini coefficient of inequality are inherently individualist and therefore offer a poor operationalization of horizontal inequalities. Based on new data and new methods, we develop alternatives to these conventional measures by analyzing group-level mechanisms explicitly.

The issue of grievances and violence may seem merely academic. Yet, very much as successful medical treatments hinge on proper diagnosis, conventional methods of conflict resolution depend critically on how the causes of conflict are analyzed. Indeed, it comes as no surprise that those who dismiss ethnonationalist claims as being both ubiquitous and irrelevant for conflict tend to be skeptical about power sharing as a method for settling conflicts and prevent renewed violence. Instead, these scholars focus on ways to prop up weak governments and to help them improve their counter-insurgency campaigns. Referring to Fearon and Laitin's (2003) influential study in an article in the New York Times, Bass (2006, p. 2) draws similar policy inferences: "The Fearon-Laitin thesis suggests that the debate over the future of fragile countries should turn from questions of ethnic demography to the need for good government, economic development and adequate policing."

In view of our findings, however, without attention to ethnonationalist grievances, such policies are likely to be ineffective, and in some cases possibly even counterproductive, especially in the long run. In very hard-to-solve nationality conflicts, interventions based exclusively on "all sticks and no carrot" policies that do not address the underlying sources of grievances will typically fail (Petersen 2011). Instead, the best way to break the cycle of violence driven by political exclusion and economic inequality is to involve groups that have been marginalized by giving them a real stake in their country's future. Indeed, some of the most intractable and damaging conflict processes in the contemporary world, such as the Israeli–Palestinian civil war, are to a large extent rooted in political and economic injustice. It is very unlikely that they will ever be resolved by shoring up the coercive capacity of the state alone unless the claims of marginalized populations are taken seriously. In the concluding chapter of this book, we will return to these important policy implications. For now, we turn to the task of preparing the conceptual ground for our empirical investigations.

PART I

THEORIES AND CONCEPTS

The first part of the book contextualizes our theoretical arguments with respect to the civil war literature. After reviewing this literature in Chapter 2, we introduce our causal mechanisms in Chapter 3.

2

Inequality and Grievances in the Civil War Literature

This chapter surveys the literature on the link from inequality and grievances to civil war violence. As will become clear, the perceived validity of such factors has remained controversial in conflict research. After considering the classical literature, as well as some of the more recent writings in this area, we turn to a critique of the literatures that inform our own theory-building efforts in Chapter 3.

Classical Contributions

Given the obvious relevance of power and wealth distributions as potential sources of conflict, it is not surprising that inequality plays a central role in classical theories of civil war and revolution.[1] In an influential article, Davies (1962) argued that revolutions were motivated by frustrations resulting from an evolving gap between individuals' aspirations and their actual economic status. Also adopting an explicitly psychological perspective, Ted Robert Gurr's (1970) well-known theory of relative deprivation characterizes various types of collective violence as reactions to frustrations stemming from unfulfilled aspirations, usually related to material well-being (see review in Brush 1996). Such a perspective differs radically from earlier sociological theories of mob behavior that explained collective violence as a societal pathology (e.g., Le Bon 1913). Instead, relative deprivation theorists argue that individuals' widespread discontent with their social situation triggers conflict, especially where modernization fuels a "revolution of rising expectations" (Davies 1962).

Although related indirectly to inequality through this psychological mechanism, relative deprivation theory does not explicitly focus on interpersonal or intergroup wealth comparisons (Hogg and Abrams 1988; Regan and Norton

[1] This section draws on Cederman, Weidmann, and Gleditsch (2011).

2005; cf. Gurr and Duvall 1973). Yet, other theories adopt a structural perspective by explicitly linking various types of inequality to structural imbalances in society, such as uneven income or land distributions (Russett 1964; Muller 1985; Muller and Seligson 1987). Partly inspired by Marxist principles, the literature on peasant rebellions explains violent collective action as a response to unequal wealth allocation (Moore 1966; Scott 1976). Frustrated with their lot, the peasant masses and other underprivileged groups are expected to take up arms as a way to seize power and redistribute wealth in their favor. Huntington (1968, p. 375) sums up the core logic of the argument:

> Where conditions of landownership are equitable and provide a viable living for the peasant, revolution is unlikely. Where they are inequitable and where the peasant lives in poverty and suffering, revolution is likely, if not inevitable. . . . No group is more conservative than a landowning peasantry and none is more revolutionary than a peasantry that owns too little land or pays too high a rental.

Relative deprivation theory remains perhaps the most prominent explanation linking grievances to conflict, but this perspective has a very mixed record in terms of empirical evidence (Oberschall 1978; Brush 1996). Early on, Gurr's frustration-aggression thesis attracted criticism from Snyder and Tilly (1972), who argued that opportunity-based mobilization, rather than grievances, causes internal conflict and revolutions. Contending that all societies contain a number of aggrieved and frustrated individuals, they did not think "there is any general connection between collective violence and hardship such that an observer could predict one from the other" (p. 520; see also Tilly 1978; Skocpol 1979). By this interpretation, widespread but diffuse anger does not suffice to spark upheavals. What is needed is a minimum level of resources and organization. Tilly (1973, p. 10) explains that

> revolutions and collective violence tend to flow directly out of a population's central political processes, instead of expressing diffuse strains and discontents within the population; . . . that the specific claims and counterclaims being made on the existing government by various mobilized groups are more important than the general satisfaction or discontent of those groups, and that claims for established places within the structure of power are crucial.

Along similar lines, a series of studies challenges earlier results pertaining to income inequality, which was usually seen to be closely connected to the notion of relative deprivation (see, e.g., Weede 1987). By the end of the 1980s, the debate about the effect of inequality and grievances on internal conflict remained unresolved, with virtually all possible causal connections – including negative, positive, curvilinear, or none – being represented in the literature (Lichbach 1989).

The mixed empirical record of the literature did not prevent major theoretical progress being made toward articulating the relationship between inequality and conflict. Much of this thinking stems from early work that broadens the narrowly materialist view of Marxist conflict theory to encompass theories that stress ethnic and cultural aspects of political competition. Among these early contributions, we find Gellner's (1964) pioneering characterization of modernity based on culturally and impersonally mediated communication as opposed to premodern structural exchanges. Also criticizing both strictly materialist explanations of mobilization processes, Michael Hechter (1978) introduced the notion of "cultural division of labor" that accounts for the emergence of grievances in cases where cultural differences coincide with occupational exclusion. While this theoretical scheme does not deny the relevance of economic forces, it accords the cultural dimension strong influence over political mobilization, which becomes especially marked when it draws on both dimensions. Based on this group-level logic, Hechter (1975) studied cases of "internal colonialism" that features the exploitation of subordinate peripheries by dominant ethnic groups, as illustrated by the relationship between the "Celtic fringe" and the English heartland. As we will see, this group-based concept of inequality anticipates Stewart's notion of horizontal inequalities to which we will return in Chapter 3.

Although often introduced as a competitor to Hechter's notion of cultural division of labor, a related explanation of ethnic conflict interprets it as a result of group competition over scarce resources. Early examples of this perspective can be found in Deutsch (1961), Barth (1969), Hannan (1979), and more recently in Olzak (2006). In these writings, competition and conflict ensue when an invading group encroaches on an established group's ecological niche (Hechter and Okamoto 2001, p. 196). As opposed to modernization theory and Marxist perspectives that expect ethnic differences to erode away with economic development, both approaches to labor markets and intergroup stratification along these lines see ethnic dominance and competition as inherent parts of the modernization process. Yet, by retaining an explicit link to production processes and resource competition, these theoretical contributions do not take the full leap to viewing power as an end in itself and say less about the role of political institutions in conflict processes. We therefore turn to Donald Horowitz's work, which explicitly advances the study of ethnic conflict in both these directions.

In what still remains a classical contribution with contemporary relevance, Horowitz's (1985) book *Ethnic Groups in Conflict* represents the most comprehensive study of ethnic conflict ever undertaken. Generally compatible with the aforementioned group-based interpretation, his book develops sophisticated theoretical arguments linking inequality and grievances to conflict through causal mechanisms that feature cognitive comparisons among ethnic groups. Building directly on Tajfel's social psychology (see Tajfel and Turner 1979), Horowitz's seminal work introduces an explicit group perspective that overcomes the individualism of Gurr's relative deprivation theory. According to his account, ethnicity serves as a metaphorical family concept that generates solidarity and intense emotions of belonging. Importantly, his theory thus fills important gaps in the causal derivations of purely structural theories. Instead of merely relying on the abstract logic of ecological competition and production forces, Horowitz uses crucial notions such as collective self-esteem and group worth that help explain why ethnic conflicts often feature intense emotional outbursts and sometimes even hatred.

As observed above, Horowitz analyzes positional power struggles that cannot be reduced to material motivations. Refusing to succumb to economic determinism, he explains how representatives of ethnic groups seek political influence for its own sake either by excluding other groups from influence or by seeking inclusion of their own group. This sense of "group entitlement" manifests itself not just in terms of resource distribution, but also in terms of cabinet seats and various symbolically charged state policies in the areas of language, religion, and culture.

Despite its general relevance, Horowitz's book primarily covers conflicts in Asia, Africa, and the Caribbean. Possibly because of this geographic focus, nationalism is hardly mentioned, although many of the conflict mechanisms discussed by Horowitz relate to ethnic competition for state power and could thus easily have been labeled in nationalist terms. Furthermore, within these specific Third World regions, the book limits itself to so-called unranked political systems, thus leaving ranked polities aside. The latter are characterized by strict and long-standing hierarchies typically imposed through conquest. Again, this possibly unduly reduces the scope of his study. Finally, despite its manifest erudition and wealth of empirical cases, Horowitz's classical study does not attempt to evaluate the effect of its postulated causal mechanisms systematically beyond case studies (usefully and often brilliantly), identifying major patterns of conflict and their causes.

The challenge of collecting systematic data on ethnic groups was taken up by Gurr in the 1980s. While Horowitz (1985) relied on erudite references to a wealth of empirical cases, Gurr's new research program launched a major data collection effort, the Minorities at Risk (MAR) data set, which quickly became the standard source of systematic data on ethnic groups. Thanks to its comprehensiveness, in terms of both geographic coverage and the number of variables included, the new data resource has spawned an entire research program that analyzes various aspect of ethnic conflict.

The first set of results was published in Gurr (1993a; 1993b). Modifying and extending his original relative deprivation theory, Gurr used his new data to study ethnic minorities' reactions to state-imposed disadvantages and discrimination. In reaction to the criticism of Tilly and other resource mobilization theorists, Gurr now stressed the role of mobilization alongside grievances as a necessary component in conflict processes. Indeed, the new results showed that "protest and rebellion by communal groups are jointly motivated by deep-seated grievances about group status *and* by the situationally determined pursuit of political interests, as formulated by group leaders and political entrepreneurs" (Gurr 1993b, pp. 166–7). The follow-up study

Gurr (2000b) broadened the theoretical framework to include "an ethiology of conflict" based on ethnocultural identity, collective incentives, capacities of collective action, and opportunities for political action. However, as suggested by the normatively inspired title of the data set itself, Gurr never wavered from the initial focus on grievances. This book and the influential article in *Foreign Affairs* (Gurr 2000b) conclude that ethnic conflict had actually started to decline thanks to a new spirit of accommodation and compromise after the Cold War.

There can be no doubt about the past and future influence of Gurr's data and analysis on conflict research. True, the exposition of his research results can sometimes be hard to grasp because of the richness of the data and Gurr's proclivity for complex causal diagrams. However, the main reason why the MAR-based research program has attracted criticism relates to the data source itself. We will come back to this issue at the end of this chapter. Together, the classical works by Hechter, Horowitz, and Gurr have laid the theoretical and empirical foundations for contemporary studies of grievances in ethnic conflict and civil war processes, including the present book.

Grievance-Skepticism in the Recent Literature

Although serving as major source of theoretical inspiration for students of ethnic conflict, these classical studies have not remained unchallenged. In the late 1990s, a team of economists at the World Bank led by Paul Collier started publishing a series of influential papers on the causes of civil war. Positioning themselves explicitly against grievance-based theories in political science and sociology, while targeting the relative deprivation theory in particular, these authors followed in the footsteps of earlier critics of relative deprivation (although typically without referring to these explicitly). As a response to the difficulties of measuring grievances directly, their approach usually relies on quantitative indicators that attempt to capture ethno-demographic configurations at the country level, for example through ethnic fractionalization or the population share represented by the largest ethnic group. Below, we will discuss the limitations of this approach.

In a much-cited article, Collier and Hoeffler (2004) claim that civil wars are caused by "greed" rather than "grievance." According to this "labor market" approach to civil wars, wars are more likely where potential rebels have especially low opportunity costs of fighting and natural resources invite warlords and their followers to enrich themselves by looting and rent-seeking. Still criticizing grievances as causes of civil wars, more recent writings by Collier and his associates weaken the stress on greed-driven arguments in favor of a broader notion of "opportunities" (Collier, Hoeffler, and Rohner 2009).

In a particularly influential article, Fearon and Laitin (2003) also argue that ethnic grievances are unrelated to political violence. Instead, they propose a theory of insurgency that hinges on state weakness, especially in peripheral areas with rough terrain. In contrast to Collier and Hoeffler's predominantly individualist and apolitical interpretation, Fearon and Laitin adopt a theoretical perspective that focuses on the role of political institutions. Yet, by adopting Collier and Hoeffler's opposition between grievances and other factors, Fearon and Laitin's theoretical approach pits frustrations and inequalities along ethnic lines against their own favored explanations, which highlight insurgency as an unemotional technology that relies on the state's weakness in peripheral areas and on the corrupting influence of oil production. Because such insurgencies tend to involve relatively small groups of fighters, the outbreak of civil war should be unrelated to social grievances in the larger population. Arguing that there is "little evidence that one can predict where a civil war will break out by looking for where ethnic or other broad political grievances are strongest" (p. 75), Fearon and Laitin warn policy makers and scholars against inferring

that ethnic diversity is the root cause of civil conflict when they observe insurgents in a poor country who mobilize fighters along ethnic lines. Instead, the civil wars of the period have structural roots, in the combination of a simple, robust military technology and decolonization, which created an international system numerically dominated by fragile states with limited administrative control of their peripheries (p. 88).[2]

Yet, already one year later, in Fearon's (2004b) much-cited study of civil war duration, ethnic grievances found their way back into the analysis, albeit in a particular context. Drawing on Weiner's (1978) classical concept of the "sons of the soil," his analysis of the duration of civil war shows that territorially concentrated and peripheral ethnic groups tend to react violently to what they perceive as incursions into their region by ethnically distinct migrants coming from other parts of the country. In most cases these typically originate from the dominant ethnic groups, therefore triggering governmental interventions on their behalf. Since such constellations are notoriously difficult to settle according to Fearon, they tend to last particularly long. Oddly enough, however, the article says little about how to reconcile the surprising finding that a particular type of ethnic grievance matters a great deal for how long civil wars last, whereas grievances are found to have no relevance whatsoever to the outbreak of conflict, as argued by Fearon and Laitin (2003). We will elaborate on this issue in Chapter 8, which explains the duration of internal conflict primarily in terms of the exclusion of ethnic groups while suggesting that the sons-of-the-soil category is a special case of ethnically excluded groups.

More recently, Fearon and Laitin (2011) devoted an entire article to sons-of-the-soil conflicts, this time also considering the issues of grievances more broadly as well as conflict onset. Attempting to account for the seeming discrepancy between their more elaborate account of sons-of-the-soil dynamics

---

[2] Apart from the work of Gurr and his colleagues that we referred to earlier, other quantitative studies have found evidence of ethnic grievances mattering for the onset of civil conflict; see Ellingsen (2000), Sambanis (2001), and Goldstone et al. (2010).

that clearly features ethnic grievances and their original grievance-skeptical position, the authors reiterate the point made in Fearon and Laitin (2003) – and by Tilly and others decades earlier – that conflict outbreaks may be unrelated to broad social grievances because of the ease with which small bands of insurgence can trigger large-scale violence. For the first time, however, the analysis leaves open the possibility that ethnic grievances may actually be at work. Although not entirely exogenous, the appearance of migrant populations competing over the same local resources as the settled population constitutes a shock to the latter, which raises the level of its discontent. Still reluctant to back down from their general skepticism as regards the role of grievance in civil war, Fearon and Laitin (2011, p. 209) now admit that "the cases we have discussed suggest that this increase in grievance can produce civil war."

The highly aggregated civil war literature, most prominently represented by Collier and Hoeffler (2004) and Fearon and Laitin (2003), has come in for sustained criticism by a new wave of scholarship that favors a radical disaggregation of the analysis down to the microlevel in order to tighten the logic of causal inference (Sambanis 2004a; Kalyvas 2007; 2008b; Tarrow 2007). However, the substantive assumptions justifying these studies are usually not all that different from those of the first wave that relied on quantitative, country-level proxies. In particular, much of the research on the microdynamics of civil war also tends to be skeptical of the role of grievances in conflict processes. This tendency is evident in Kalyvas' (2006) pioneering work. Questioning conventional macro interpretations of civil war that hinge on conflict parties' ideological goals, Kalyvas argues in favor of a much more mundane perspective that stresses private grudges and motivations. According to this view,

"political violence" is not always necessarily political identities and actions cannot be reduced to decisions taken by the belligerent organizations, to the discourses produced at the center, and to the ideologies derived from the war's master cleavage (Kalyvas 2003, p. 487).

Similarly, recent research on the individual motivations for joining rebel movements, such as Humphreys and Weinstein (2006), gives priority to material incentives. In doing so, these writers build on earlier studies that applied rational-choice analysis to attempts to overcome collective-action problems through selective incentives (Popkin 1979; Lichbach 1995; see also references in Blattman and Miguel 2010).

Of course, not all of the recent micro-based scholarship plays down grievance-related explanations. Most prominently, Wood (2003) stresses the central importance of moral outrage over governmental repression as a motivation fueling mobilization. In an effort to account for different types of violence in civil wars, Weinstein (2007) proposes a theory that differentiates between rebel organizations that recruit based on genuine grievances and those that focus on materialist, short-term incentives. It is in the latter case that the violence can be expected to become indiscriminate. Furthermore, many of the case

studies in Collier and Sambanis' (2005) edited volume that attempt to evaluate the Collier and Hoeffler (2004) model reach conclusions linking political
and/or economic inequality directly to internal conflict (e.g., see Zinn 2005
on Nigeria; Ali, Elbadawi, and El-Batahani 2005 on the Sudan; Humphreys
and ag Mohamed 2005 on Mali; and Ross 2005 on Indonesia). Exploring the
micro-foundations of rebellion, Gates (2002) provides a formal framework
that allows him to integrate non-pecuniary awards and ethnicity in his account
of rebel recruitment. Likewise, Cuesta and Murshed (2010) introduce a game-
theoretic model that traces the relationship between microlevel motivations
based on greed and grievance. All in all, however, such work remains the
exception rather than the rule. Most of the literature on the micro-foundations
of conflict is characterized by a clear effort to punctuate the "myth" of ethnic
conflict by reinterpreting such conflicts as the result of opportunities seized by
self-interested actors.

Among the grievance skeptics, the theorists of "new wars" adopt perhaps
the most radical perspective. Dismissing the very notion of "ethnic conflict" as
a cover for the criminal activities of thugs and bullies, Mueller (2004) views
internal conflict as nothing but opportunistic predation that leaves no room
for higher motives relating to the righting of wrongs, or for more general
expressions of ideology or solidarity. Anticipating Kalyvas' (2003) criticism of
theories that rely exclusively on macrocleavages, Mueller (2000, p. 63) stresses
the diversity of micromotives in civil war:

Some locals did join in the process, sometimes out of ethnic loyalty, sometimes to settle
old scores, most often, it seems, opportunistically to pursue profit in the chaos. In
many cases, the war conditions did bring out the worst in some people, and victims did
sometimes know their victimizers – though this is something that happens in most civil
wars, not just ethnic ones.

Explicitly denying that ethnic cleavages are more conflict-prone than other
divisions, Mueller views ethnicity as just one of many coordination devices
that could be exploited for collective mobilization:

Ethnicity proved essentially to be simply the characteristic around which the perpetra-
tors and the politicians who recruited and encouraged them happened to array themselves. It was important as an ordering device or principle, not as a crucial motivating
force. The same sort of dynamic could hold if the thugs' organizational principle were
class or ideological allegiance or even handedness or loyalty to a specific soccer team
(p. 62).

Similarly skeptical of ethnicity's inherent relevance in explanations of political
violence, other scholars have also questioned the raison d'être of the very
notion of ethnic conflict. For example, Charles King (2001, p. 168) agrees with
Mueller's rendering of ethnic conflict as essentially so banal that it loses all
explanatory power:

We cannot know for certain why large-scale violence, of whatever type, breaks out. Even if we could, the factors involved would probably be disappointingly banal; clashing economic interests, politicians' attempts to oust opponents, lots of young men with nothing to do and easy access to guns.

Subscribing to a similar interpretation, Gilley (2004, p. 1159) also argues that it is virtually impossible to separate ethnic from nonethnic conflicts because "[u]nlike 'class conflict' which can be proved or disproved by using pretty stable measures of the people involved (income, education, occupation, etc.), the same cannot be said of ethnicity." In this view, ethnic identities are so fluid and prone to manipulation that they cannot be meaningfully distinguished from other types of attachments (cf. Chandra 2006).

Despite their diverse disciplinary origins, these critiques of grievance-based approaches to conflict typically adhere to the same line of argumentation. In particular, they make an important assumption that is usually left untested. We refer to it as the *ubiquity-of-grievances* claim. It suggests that the outbreak of internal conflict cannot be explained through grievances because these are much too widespread to account for rare events such as large-scale political violence. As we have seen above, this argument was originally introduced by Tilly and other sociologists in the 1970s as a criticism of relative deprivation (Oberschall 1978, p. 298; McAdam, McCarthy, and Zald 1988, p. 697; Piven and Cloward 1991, p. 439). Yet, it keeps recurring as a leitmotif in the more recent literature on civil war.

Explicitly advancing the ubiquity-of-grievances claim, Collier and Hoeffler (2004) contend that since "grievances are sufficiently widespread to be common across societies and time" (p. 589) and "all societies may have groups with exaggerated grievances" (p. 564), their explanatory value remains insignificant. Reviewing the findings of studies in the area, Laitin (2007, p. 25) confirms that

ethnic grievances are commonly felt and latent; the factors that make these grievances vital and manifest differentiate the violent from the nonviolent cases. *Ex ante* measures of grievance levels are not good predictors of the transformation of latent grievances into manifest ones. And it is the factors that turn latent grievances into violent action that should be considered as explanatory for that violence.[3]

Invoking the same logic in support of his wholesale rejection of grievance-based arguments, Mueller (2000, p. 14) points out that "although expressions of hatred between groups and peoples are exceedingly (and rather drearily) common . . . violence among supposed haters is remarkably rare." This observation has major implications for conflict:

Furthermore, although there may be plenty of hate, hostility, and animosity between various peoples, warfare does not seem to correlate well with these qualities. That is, it is not notably found in the areas with the most intergroup hostility and cleavage (p. 15).

---

[3] As we have already noted, Fearon and Laitin (2011, p. 209) are still committed to this argument first advanced in Fearon and Laitin (2003).

The last part of Mueller's explanation renders explicit a second assumption that is often made together with the ubiquity-of-grievance claim, which we will refer to as the *irrelevance-of-grievances* claim. According to this view, even if the degree to which populations are aggrieved varies to some extent, this variation is not strongly associated with the outbreak of civil wars, because once we control for the "root causes" of conflict, it becomes clear that opportunist leaders exaggerate or invent their frustrations in order to pursue other, usually selfish and materialist ends. Resembling the realists' cynical view in international relations debates, this line of argumentation seeks to debunk liberal "myths" about civil war that depict rebels and revolutionaries in a romantic light. Casting the adherents of the "grievance" perspective as naive, the realist critics accuse them of "listening too earnestly to the accounts of the combatants" (Laitin 2007, p. 23): "When ethnic war breaks out, journalists congregate like ravens. They inevitably ask combatants to tell narratives explaining the killing" (p. 23). Whether appealing to either of the superpowers during the Cold War or to "world opinion" in more recent years, such scholars claim that opportunistic and self-interested rebel leaders will inevitably try to dress up their cause as a way to attract support and resources.

The quantitative civil war literature typically operationalizes ethnic grievances with aggregated demographic proxies, such as ethnic fractionalization or individual-level inequality operationalized as the Gini coefficient (Fearon and Laitin 2003; Collier and Hoeffler 2004), ethnic polarization (Montalvo and Reynal-Querol 2005), or ethnic domination measured in terms of the size of the largest group (Collier and Hoeffler 2004). These purported measures of grievances are then compared with a battery of indicators that are meant to capture explanations highlighting various aspects of self-interested motivations and resource-based mechanisms. Summing up these and other studies, Laitin (2007, p. 23) claims that quantitative data "undermine confidence in theories purporting to show that national aspirations, differences, or demographies are associated with communal violence or civil war."

Weaknesses in the Grievance Skeptics' Arguments

It is now time to question the criticisms advanced by the grievance skeptics. Our argumentation focuses on three main weaknesses in recent conflict research: namely, the bias in favor of individualist perspectives, the structuralist lack of attention to explicit motivations, and the ethnic neutrality of the state in explanations of civil war. We discuss each of these problems in turn.

Individualist Tendencies in the Conflict Literature

As we have argued in Chapter 1, conventional country-level indictors often miss the target. Quick to dismiss grievances as explanatory factors, scholars who rely on such measures often overestimate the theoretical appropriateness of their proxies. In particular, the underlying assumptions supporting their methodological decisions converge on individualist thinking that is not necessarily compatible with the "collectivist" theories that serve as the actual targets of the criticism. For example, the commonly used ethnic fractionalization index measures ethno-demographic diversity among individuals but does not correspond to any well-known theory of ethnic conflict (Cederman and Girardin 2007).[4] More generally, several authors have pointed to the weakness of aggregate proxies and the extent to which they fail to capture the theoretical positions they are meant to operationalize (e.g., Posner 2004; Sambanis 2004a; Cramer 2006; Chandra and Wilkinson 2008).

At the same time, the individualist ontology also pervades much of the more recent literature on microdynamics. In particular, this orientation goes hand in hand with a strong skepticism regarding group-level claims. Clearly, groups do not act; only members of groups do. Therefore, there are good reasons to treat essentialist claims about the unity of ethnic groups with considerable caution. In a careful critique of the macroliterature on conflict, Kalyvas (2003, p. 481) warns against reifying categories and ascribing them collective agency by default:

The interchangeability of individuals that underlies the concept of group conflict and violence is variable rather than constant. The locus of agency is as likely to be at the bottom as at the top, so civilians cannot be treated as passive, manipulated, or invisible actors; indeed, they often manipulate central actors to settle their own conflicts.

Individual decisions are just as likely to undercut the cohesion of a group as to strengthen it. In many civil war settings, individuals have to make life-and-death decisions by choosing sides between the government and the rebels. Targeting essentialist assumptions of group unity common in the international relations literature, Kalyvas (2008a, p. 1045) asserts that "ethnic defection" is much more common than normally assumed, especially in the course of ongoing conflict processes: "Even when ethnic divisions cause the eruption of civil war in the first place, these identities do not always remain stable and fixed during the conflict; if they do change, they may soften rather than only harden."

We agree with much of this criticism targeting group-level analysis. Indeed, there can be no doubt that the literature on ethnic conflict abounds with "ethnicist" interpretations that overlook internal rifts inside ethnic groups and impose ethnic cleavages on an inchoate flux of identification, let alone any coherent sense of collective agency. Ultimately, the crucial question is whether the disconnected score-settling at the micro-level adds up to any macro-level effects that deviate in any substantial way from the inferences of macro-level theorizing. Indeed, the personal quarrels and village feuds at the individual level may

---

[4] Arguing against the individualist foundations of the ethno-linguistic fractionalization index, Fearon, Kasara, and Laitin (2007) propose an explanation of conflict between pairs of ethnic groups that is based on multiplying their demographic sizes. Despite its formal interest, however, this mechanism appears to be unrelated to any known and tested theory of conflict and has never been further developed by the authors.

be nothing more than "noise" that does little to affect the logic of the main conflict cleavages. Conducting his empirical analysis based on detailed archival material, Kalyvas (2006) offers a wealth of historical evidence in support of his postulated microdynamic regularities. Yet, in the absence of systematic sampling of events across multiple countries and conflicts, it is difficult to generalize beyond Kalyvas' erudite references. Of course, Kalyvas is much too careful to fall into the trap of extrapolating from single cases, rightly cautioning against drawing sweeping conclusions about collective intentions, but other authors contributing to the microliterature have certainly succumbed to this temptation (Kalyvas 2008b).[5]

As argued by the critics of group-level analysis, the issue of whether groups can be said to meaningfully exist and engage in collective agency is ultimately an empirical question that varies from case to case. Whether it makes sense to generalize from observations of the civil wars in Greece or Afghanistan depends very much on the scope of the comparison. However, some scholars, in particular anthropologists, have taken their meta-theoretical quest to constructivist extremes that deny the very usefulness of the notion of ethnic groups (Jenkins 1997). As the most articulate proponent of this radical position, Brubaker (2004, p. 4) elaborates on the problems associated with group-level theorizing:

Groupness is a variable, not a constant; it cannot be presupposed. It varies not only across putative groups, but within them; it may wax and wane over time, peaking during exceptional – but unsustainable – moments of collective effervescence. Ethnicity does not require such groupness. It works not only, or even especially, in and through bounded groups, but in and through categories, schemas, encounters, identifications, languages, stories, institutions, organizations, networks, and events.

Continuing his antiessentialist reasoning, Brubaker offers recommendations for theory-building in the area of nationalism and ethnic politics:

Ethnicity, race, and nation should be conceptualized not as substances or things or entities or organisms or collective individuals – as the imagery of discrete, concrete, tangible, bounded, and enduring "groups" encourages us to do – but rather in relational, processual, dynamic, eventful, and disaggregated terms (p. 11).

Taking a further step toward de-essentializing the theorization of contentious politics, Brubaker arrives at the logical endpoint of his argumentation: not only should "groups" be dropped from social-scientific theories, but also the very notion of "identity" (Brubaker 2004).

In our view, such radical theoretical advice goes too far. Brubaker's perspective is doubtlessly useful for case studies of fluid micro-level situations where identities are acutely contested as well as macro analysis of the *longue durée*

---

[5] In an explicit quantitative test focusing on the Israeli-Palestinian conflict, Miodownik, Bhavnani, and Choi (2011) find empirical support for Kalyvas' main theory about the intensity of violence as a function of the distance from each side's base.

inspired by process-theorists such as Norbert Elias ([1939] 1982).[6] Yet, this does not imply that group-level assumptions should be abandoned for all types of analysis. In particular, where the time spans are more limited and the ideological "glue" of ethnonationalist politics generates considerable group cohesion, the assumption of stable group identification makes a lot of sense.

For the situations studied in this book, group-based approaches are likely to apply particularly well because the threat and escalation of conflict tend to reinforce collective identities and group cohesion (Coser 1964). In his path-breaking theory, Simmel (1955) argues that such pressures may even bring groups into being where they did not exist in the past. While political violence clearly accelerates identity formation, it is important to realize that such processes are often set in motion well before the outbreak of large-scale political violence. For this reason, Brubaker (2004, p. 19) may slightly overstate his point when he calls for "sensitivity to the variable and contingent, waxing and waning nature of groupness, and to the fact that high levels of groupness may be more the result of conflict (especially violent conflict) than its underlying cause" (see also Kalyvas 2008a). Indeed, gradually escalating, nonviolent conflict typically precedes violent phases and there is no reason to believe that the former cannot also contribute to the crystallization of the identities and boundaries of ethnic groups. Yet, rather than speculating about the sequence in purely theoretical terms, we offer a systematic test of to what extent specific preconflict configurations involving ethnic groups can be used to explain conflict duration in Chapter 8. Without ruling out the possibility of reverse causation, we suspect that the strongly constructivist interpretations that doubt whether ethnic groups and their grievances actually predate or preexist in conflict processes have been exaggerated, especially given the relative inertia of ethnonationalist constellations (Calhoun 1997, p. 32). To see this point, one does not have to subscribe to the opposite, radically essentialist claims of Kaufmann (1996), who insists that conflict "locks in" ethnic identities to such an extent that they can never change again. Ironically enough, hard-liners advocating uncompromising and repressive state policies are only too happy to lend an advertently, and sometimes even intentionally, helping hand to entrepreneurs engaged in ethnonationalist mobilization against the incumbent government (see also Chapter 3).

Without accepting the unity of ethnic groups as an ontological certainty, then, we adopt a cautiously pragmatic position. Our starting point is a Weberian conception of ethnicity that views it as any subjectively experienced sense of commonality based on the belief in common ancestry and shared culture (Weber 1978, pp. 385–98; see also Cederman 2013, p. 533). Ethnic groups, then, are cultural communities based on a common belief in putative descent. Rather than assuming that ethnic groups remain constant over long historical

---

[6] For an argument on how to endogenize macro-level identities in international relations, see Cederman (1997).

periods, we treat them as sufficiently stable to enable us to exogenize their
properties in the shorter time scales that are relevant to onset analysis. In Parts
II and III, we offer empirical support for this level of theorizing. If our postulates are borne out by empirical evidence at the macro level, we cannot be
certain of being right in all respects, but we certainly have good reasons to
doubt that micro-level dynamics are so powerful that they distort or dominate
higher-level conflict processes.

Opportunity-Driven Structuralism at the Expense of Motivation

It may seem paradoxical that conventional approaches to civil war suffer from
an excess of both structuralism and individualism. However, this apparent
paradox dissolves once one realizes that structural theories are very much
compatible with a focus on individual decision making as long as strong,
uniform assumptions are made regarding the main actors' preferences. Indeed,
the individualist thrust present in recent scholarship on civil wars can be partly
traced back to economic theories of individual incentives and rentseeking. The
persistent unwillingness to accept grievance-based accounts of internal conflict
reflects a deep ontological belief in actors' selfish and unsentimental pursuit
of their narrow material interests. This is what we have already referred to as
"antipathy to antipathy" (Horowitz 2002).

Nobody has brought this reasoning to the point more cogently than Mancur
Olson (1965), whose radically individualist thesis questions the viability of
group-level motivations of any kind, especially those that draw on ideology or
other nonmaterialist ideals. According to this view, rather than contributing to
a group's agenda, most individuals will shun the risks of armed conflict while
hoping to get a free ride on the risk-taking of others (Tullock 1971). This crass
perspective has influenced several generations of conflict researchers, as we
have seen, starting most prominently with the school of resource mobilization
in the 1970s.

In principle, the focus on organizational and logistical obstacles to collective
action is clearly a sound one, but it has led to unreflective theorizing (see the
critique in Kalyvas and Kocher 2007), and to an almost total abandonment of
collective grievances as a possible cause of mobilization and conflict:

In the 1970s, resource mobilization and political process theorists stopped asking why
people felt frustrated enough to engage in collective protest rather than organize through
conventional political channels, and instead asked when and how they secured the
resources to combat their exclusion from those channels (Polletta and Jasper 2001,
p. 286).

Until recently, most of the social movement literature has been dominated
by notions of "opportunity structures" at the expense of an explicit analysis of actors' reasons for fighting and of the role of emotions in mobilization
processes, but grievances are often present in accounts of "framing" and "narratives" (Opp 2009, ch. 6).

In many respects, the most recent waves of political-economy scholarship resemble this originally sociological perspective. Keen to employ objective indicators in their quantitative analysis, these researchers are less concerned with the precise motivations of the actors in question. Instead, conflict is explained as an outcome of particular "technologies" of combat that become effective under objective circumstances that relate to the availability of natural resources or the power projection of the state or rebel organizations. Indeed, the most prominent proponents of the greed-based interpretation of civil war have retreated to a completely open-ended position that privileges "opportunities" over "motives": According to Collier, Hoeffler, and Rohner's (2009) "feasibility hypothesis," it can be expected "that where a rebellion is feasible it will occur" (p. 2).

However, the stress on "opportunities" is not the only reason why actors' behavioral motivations have fallen by the wayside. Recent theories of ethnic conflict, in particular, have opted for an explicitly cognitive viewpoint that serves to inject a healthy dose of scientific thinking into a field that has tended to generate more heat than light. Inspired by cognitive psychology and rational choice theory, this quest to "demystify" and to "sanitize" cruel acts of political violence offers a certain comfort to external observers by rationalizing them in terms familiar to mainstream political science and neoclassical economics.

The last few decades of conflict research, especially in the field of international relations, have been profoundly influenced by both cognitive psychology and rational choice theories. In fact, theories drawn from these literatures were engaged in a heated debate concerning the best way to conceptualize nuclear deterrence during the Cold War (Achen and Snidal 1989; Jervis 1989), but have more recently had a strong influence on explanations of ethnic conflict in the post–Cold War period (e.g., Stein 2002). Such studies often rely on Tajfelian Social Identity Theory as a source of inspiration, which leaves some room for emotions in its stress on group members' need for self-esteem (Tajfel and Turner 1979). Yet, more recent developments in social psychology have consolidated the dominance of cognitive interpretations at the expense of motivational and emotion-based explanations of conflict (Hale 2008). Applications of rational choice theory to ethnic politics have further reinforced the centrality of cognitive mechanisms in conflict research. Ethnic identities are seen as convenient "focal points" that serve as coordination devices in mobilization processes (Hardin 1995), as convenient boundary markers that support distributional claims (Posner 2005), or as cost-reducing arrangements that boost interethnic trust (Fearon and Laitin 1996).

The downside of these efforts seems to be a strangely unemotional and bloodless rendering of conflict processes that are totally divorced from the hatred and resentment witnessed by countless qualitative accounts of conflict (cf. Horowitz 1985).[7] Again, there has been a widespread tendency to set up

---

[7] For these reasons, one should be careful not to draw too far-reaching inferences from experimental studies that have become popular in the conflict literature. Obviously, there is only so

a theoretical straw man, in this case associated with "ancient hatred" interpretations of ethnic violence (Petersen 2002). Having dismissed any reference
to emotions in conflict analysis as belonging to the domain of sensational-
ist journalists and uninformed politicians, these mainstream analysts quickly
dump the emotional ballast in favor of less troublesome factors that fit the
well-tested tools of political analysis. But such heavy-handed criticism risks
throwing out the motivational baby with the primordialist bathwater. Emotions are not inherently irrational and they matter hugely in politics, especially
in heated conflicts that have the potential to erupt into large-scale violence
(Petersen 2002; Mercer 2005). Ultimately, the behavioral effect of emotional
mechanisms remains an empirical issue and it is therefore a mistake to rule
them out by theoretical fiat.

Critique of the Ethnic Neutrality of the State in Explanations of Civil War

Apart from individualism and insufficient attention to explicit motivations,
a third tendency in the contemporary conflict literature contributes to the
analytical neglect of grievances. Although civil wars take place in situations that
confront incumbent governments with political organizations that challenge the
government's claim to sovereign rule, the state is often strangely absent from
explanations of how ethnicity matters for conflict. Some accounts accord the
state a much more active role in conflict processes, but treat it as an ethnically
neutral "arena" that does not have any particular stake in clashes involving
ethnic groups other than attempting to provide law and order more or less
effectively. The use of demographic proxies as measures of "ethnic grievances"
reinforces the apolitical rendering of ethnicity that fails to account for it as an
explicitly political relationship of power. Ethno-demographic measures, such
as fractionalization and polarization, are blind to politics and cannot therefore
capture the conflict-causing effect of politicized ethnicity. For example, Fearon
and Laitin's (2003) approach to civil war accords the state a central role in
their main conflict-inducing mechanism. Yet, their notion of state weakness
is entirely orthogonal to ethnic politics. Instead, ethnicity enters their analysis
separately as a measure of societal diversity along ethnic lines.

In other cases, especially those characterized by state failure, the state is not
merely neutral, but even absent, as in Posen's (1993) theory of the "emerging
security dilemma." Drawing on the notion of anarchy from international relations theory, this well-known explanation of internal conflict stipulates that
state collapse opens the doors to interethnic fighting. Similarly, theories of
"new wars" that play down the extent to which civil war features actors with
explicitly political agendas tend to assume anarchic conditions (Mueller 2004;
for a trenchant critique, see Kalyvas 2001).

much an experimenter can do to emulate the social context and emotional stakes of real conflict
within the walls of a laboratory.

We argue that these theoretical shortcomings stem from a tendency to highlight ethnicity in ways that neglect the role of nationalism. At least since the second half of the nineteenth century, most conflicts involving ethnic categories concerned politicized ethnicity rather than ethnicity per se. Indeed, the key to politics in the modern world hinges on the control of the state. In his sustained criticism of "stateless" theories of ethnic conflict, Brass (1991, p. 250) reserves a central place in conflict processes for the modern state:

> The state is itself both a resource and a distributor of resources. It is not an abstraction, but a set of repressive, allocative, and distributive institutions and decisionmaking bodies. Its functioning is facilitated and the potential for violent conflict in the struggle for control over it is reduced if the state operates behind a veil of legitimacy and if contestants in the struggle for control operate according to widely accepted rules.

As long as the focus is mainly on short-term material incentives, such as oil and diamonds, or more generally on individual opportunity costs, it is easy to lose sight of the profound importance of securing access to executive control over the state. Of course, in clientilist regimes, state power often entails material wealth, but in the era of nationalism, controlling the state can also be an end in itself (Horowitz 1985; Wimmer 2002). As we will argue in the next chapter, those who are excluded from influence over governmental decision making, and forced to live under undignified "alien rule," are the most likely to rebel against the status quo. Therefore, attempts to reduce ethnicity to apolitical ethno-demographic measures, such as fractionalization or polarization, will always fail to capture the arguably most important class of grievances, namely those relating to uneven distribution of political power along ethnic lines.

Data Problems Afflicting the Recent Grievance Literature

Before introducing our own theoretical framework in the next chapter, we end the current one with a critical discussion of the data-related challenges that confront recent studies positing a link between grievances and internal conflict. If the grievance skeptics' arguments succumb to theoretical pitfalls, the empirical message of the grievance proponents has been muddled by serious data problems, most of them related to the original design of the Minorities at Risk project that we introduced earlier in this chapter. By focusing on the notion of minorities "at risk," that is, minorities that are already discriminated against or otherwise disadvantaged, this data set breaks new ground as regards political relevance, but unfortunately at the price of introducing potential selection bias. While the sample includes some "advantaged" minorities, it remains incomplete since Gurr and his colleagues do not include many powerful groups, some of which may decide to challenge the incumbent government (Cederman, Wimmer, and Min 2010).

Of course, selection bias only applies in relation to specific research questions and is not an inherent property of data sets, as noted by Posner (2004)

and Hug (2013). To the extent that researchers focus on ethnic group characteristics that are unrelated to grievances, such as whether they are religiously
or linguistically defined (Chai 2005) or Saideman's (2001) explanation of why
some groups receive external support and others do not, the issue of selection bias do not necessarily pose problems (see the discussion in Hug 2013).
More importantly for our purposes, most MAR-based research that evaluates
the effect of discrimination and grievances at the country level escapes this
dilemma since it treats such variables as independent or explanatory factors
aggregated to the country level rather than outcomes for individual groups.
While aggregation to the country level may generate bias due to nonrandom
measurement error (Hug 2013), which may or may not be a problem with
respect to MAR's sampling, the main conclusions of important studies such
as Regan and Norton (2005) and Goldstone et al. (2010) are not likely to be
affected by the known problems relating to selection bias.

In an early challenge to Collier's greed-based perspective, Regan and Norton
(2005) base their analysis on discrimination aggregated to the country level.
In confirmation of Gurr's updated relative deprivation perspective, they conclude that grievances play an important role in accounting for the outbreak of
different stages of internal conflict while finding no support for Collier's radical interpretation. Because of its highly aggregated nature, the article cannot
offer a definitive adjudication between competing causal mechanisms, but its
theoretical framing is very insightful and has inspired the current book.

Framing their work, as we also do, in direct opposition to both Collier and
Hoeffler (2004) and Fearon and Laitin (2003), Goldstone et al. (2010) represents an impressive attempt to highlight the importance of discrimination as a
major predictor of a broad set of politically unstable situations, including civil
war. This study is especially innovative since it adopts an explicitly predictive
framework and focuses on out-of-sample evaluation. It is by now well known
that influential models in the quantitative civil war literature are guilty of considerable over-fitting in-sample and therefore serve as particularly poor tools of
out-of-sample forecasting (Ward, Greenhill, and Bakke 2010). In their pioneering study, the team led by Goldstone found that a model that includes political,
institutional variables related to regime type, infant mortality, conflict-ridden
neighborhoods, and, for our purposes most importantly, state-led discrimination of ethnic groups, performs especially well. As regards the latter indicator,
Goldstone et al. report that

countries with high levels of state-led discrimination against at least one minority group,
according to the Minorities at Risk political or economic discrimination indicators,
faced roughly triple the relative odds of future civil war onsets than those without such
discrimination (p. 197).[8]

---

[8] It should be noted that this central result anticipates our own analysis, regarding both the effect
of political discrimination and exclusion (see Chapters 4 and 7) and economic inequalities (see
Chapters 5 and 7).

Again, the discrimination data are pulled from MAR without causing any serious inferential problems relating to a skewed selection of cases since the entire analysis is conducted for entire states. In contrast, scholars who have been tempted to extract more detailed information from this data set about the workings of conflict-inducing mechanisms at the level of ethnic groups are less immune to the problem. This certainly applies to some of the conclusions in Gurr's own work, but it is probably fair to say that a majority of the MAR literature continues to struggle with the built-in limitations of "minorities at risk" as the main units of analysis. As we have seen, in these cases, the risks to causal inference can be potentially quite serious as reported by Hug (2003; 2013) and Fearon (2003).

We suspect that these data-generated difficulties constitute one of the major reasons why students of ethnic conflict and civil war have remained skeptical as regards the validity of explanations prominently featuring inequalities and grievances. Rather than merely using countries as units of analysis as a way to protect our analysis from threats to causal inference, we prefer to evaluate grievance-related explanations at the group level for theoretical reasons already stated earlier in this chapter. Fortunately, the Ethnic Power Relations data set, which we will introduce in Chapter 4, allows us to have it both ways.

After this methodological and empirical interlude, however, it is time to return to the main theoretical task of making sense of inequality and grievances in processes that generate internal conflict. This is an urgent task, because we have criticized the empirical literature mostly on conceptual and theoretical grounds, arguing that the main reason why the grievance-skeptics have not been able (or willing) to find support for the explanations they criticize is mainly related to their use of theoretically inappropriate indicators. As argued in Cederman and Girardin (2007), we need to move our theorizing beyond "off-the-shelf" measures that tap into various ethno-demographic aspects of societies, such as ethnic fractionalization, since these fail to do justice to the political logic of ethnonationalism and thus reduce grievance-based explanations to theoretically irrelevant straw men.

3

From Horizontal Inequality to Civil War via Grievances

What would it take to show that grievances actually do cause political violence? In Chapter 2, we noted that it is difficult to measure grievances directly, at least if the empirical scope encompasses a large number of cases. Therefore, we opt for an indirect approach that identifies conditions under which grievances are likely to emerge. In particular, we posit that inequalities among groups correspond to such situations, and proceed by investigating whether they are related to the outbreak of civil war in the empirical chapters to follow. In this chapter, we propose a combination of theoretically grounded mechanisms that together constitute a causal pathway that connects inequalities with violent conflict through grievances. Without a direct test of the grievance mechanisms themselves, it is all the more important to bolster their credibility by showing that they can be derived from conceptually coherent and empirically validated theories.

The main goal of this chapter is to construct a theoretical scheme that explains how inequalities cause violent conflict. Before doing so, however, it is appropriate to briefly introduce two key types of inequalities and their historical origins.

Vertical and Horizontal Inequalities

Our first task is to conceptualize inequality as a structural, asymmetric condition governing social relations among actors. Given Charles Tilly's role as a prominent critic of grievance-based theorizing in general, and relative deprivation theory in particular, it may seem surprising to use one of his works as an initial source of inspiration for our theorizing. Yet, Tilly's (1999) provocative book on *Durable Inequality* is a useful conceptual starting point because it helps overcome the problems afflicting the conventional conflict literature.

More specifically, it addresses head-on the three main weaknesses that we identified toward the end of the previous chapter.

First, Tilly's approach to categorical inequalities distances itself explicitly from individualist interpretations that view "inequality and poverty as outcomes of individual-by-individual competition according to widely shared standards of merit, worthiness, or privilege" (Tilly 2006, p. 4). According to Tilly, such a view "obscures the significance or organized distinctions and interactions among members of different categories" (p. 4).

Second, this contribution deviates from Tilly's earlier writings by focusing much more consistently on the role of exploitation in social processes. This perspective makes it straightforward to derive motivations stemming from frustrations with such situations. In this sense, Tilly's theory "builds a bridge from Max Weber on social closure to Karl Marx on exploitation, and back" (Tilly 1999, p. 7).

Third, and finally, Tilly's book incorporates an explicitly institutionalist perspective that can be characterized as an "organizational view of inequality-generating mechanisms" (Tilly 1999, p. 8). Organizations, rather than spontaneous and "societal" competition, impose structure and reinforce asymmetric distributions of power and wealth. As we will see, this aspect allows us to appreciate the central role played by the state in conflict processes.

All in all, Tilly's *Durable Inequality* advances a sweeping and general approach to the emergence of inequalities. Most centrally, Tilly argues that the most durable inequalities in social systems emerge along categorical distinctions, such as gender, ethnicity, or citizenship, rather than along more gradual differences pertaining to individual attributes. Embedded in social relations, especially within organizational structures, categorical inequalities are produced by a set of mechanisms, most prominently by "exploitation" and "opportunity hoarding," and then further cemented by "emulation" and "adaptation." Echoing Marxist theory, Tilly (1999, p. 10) defines exploitation as a situation where "powerful, connected people command resources from which they draw significantly increased returns by coordinating the effort of outsiders whom they exclude from the full value added by that effort." Similarly, opportunity hoarding corresponds to settings where "members of a categorically bounded network acquire access to a resource that is valuable, renewable, subject to monopoly, supportive of network activities, and enhanced by the network's modus operandi" (Tilly 1999, p. 10).

More recently, Stewart (2008b) and her colleagues have developed the notion of "horizontal inequalities," which proposes a more narrowly applied conceptualization of inequality than that implied by Tilly's categorical inequalities, while linking it specifically to conflict among identity groups. Contrasting this concept to vertical or individual-level inequalities, Stewart (2008a, p. 3) defines horizontal inequalities as "inequalities in economic, social or political dimensions or cultural status between culturally defined groups." If vertical inequality compares individuals and households without sorting them into categories, horizontal inequality compares entire group identities to each other without paying any attention to the internal diversity of each category.

As does Tilly's approach to categorical inequalities, Stewart addresses the three weaknesses afflicting the conflict literature that we highlighted in Chapter 2. First, Stewart (2008a, p. 3) argues that, to a large extent, much of the conventional quantitative research has failed to find evidence for a positive effect of greater inequality on civil war because of its reliance on individualist, rather than group-based, measures of income and power differences:

But the majority of internal conflicts are *organized group* conflicts – they are neither exclusively nor primarily a matter of individuals committing acts of violence against others. What is most often involved is group mobilization of people with particular shared identities or goals to attack others in the name of the group (Stewart 2008a, p. 11).

Second, Stewart (2008a, p. 18) stresses the central importance of grievances as motivations for violence conflict:

strong political [horizontal inequalities] mean that leaders of groups feel politically excluded and are thus more likely to lead opposition and possibly rebellion; while socioeconomic inequalities mean that people as a whole have strong grievances on ethnic lines and are thus likely to be more readily mobilized.

Third, her explicitly institutional focus pays special attention to the structure of the state and the nature of its policies:

Whether democratic or not, governments can be accommodating and inclusive making violent opposition less likely. In contrast, governments (especially nondemocratic ones) may make no attempt to meet people's demands and can react to opposition with harsh repression, which may provoke a further violent reaction (Stewart 2008a, p. 20).

Following the lead of Horowitz and Gurr, Stewart (2008a) conceptualizes horizontal inequality by considering political, economic, social, and cultural dimensions. Political horizontal inequalities entail blocked or limited access to central decision-making authority within the state. In this book, we refer to this type of power asymmetry as political exclusion. The economic dimension taps the distribution of income between groups. Social horizontal inequality measures primarily groups' uneven social access, for example in terms of education and societal status. Finally, the cultural aspect captures group-level inequalities with respect to cultural policies and symbols, including traditional holidays and religious rights.

In this book, we limit ourselves to an analysis of political and economic horizontal inequalities because they are arguably the most important causes of conflict, and certainly those that are the least difficult to measure systematically. Although these two types of inequality are often likely to be related, we follow Stewart in treating the distribution of power and wealth as conceptually separate components. Of course, this does not mean that social and cultural inequalities are unimportant in this respect. Quite the contrary, access to education (Gellner 1983) and state policies regarding language and religious rights (Langer 2005) are known to be powerful triggers of conflict. Moreover, political and economic horizontal inequalities have major consequences for, and are influenced by, cultural and social asymmetries at different societal levels. While the former pertains mostly to elite-level influence, such as the share of cabinet posts, the latter measures the economic wellbeing of an entire population.

The Origins of Horizontal Inequalities

Although our main task is to explain the effect of inequalities on internal conflict via grievances, we need to place our causal mechanisms in their proper macro-historical context. Where do horizontal inequalities come from? Group-level inequalities among humans have existed since the emergence of agriculture and sedentary habitation (Malesevic 2010) and may even be inherent to any complex social system (Sidanius and Pratto 1999). Whereas most sociological explanations of power differentials downplay or entirely ignore violence, we agree with Malesevic (2010) that historically long-standing group-level inequality to a large extent stems from warfare and domination. Since ancient times, processes of conquest and colonization have been the most important drivers of political and economic inequalities (Williams 2003, p. 59). In his multi-volume work on social power, Mann (1986) offers the perhaps most elaborate account of how warfare and domination are capable of transforming patterns of inclusion and exclusion. Stressing the autonomous role played by military power, Mann shows that political influence cannot be reduced to forces of production. By turning Marx's historical materialism on its head, this approach to stratification clarifies how military superiority produced political and economic dominance rather than the other way around.

Yet, the causal priority of geopolitical factors in the premodern world has increasingly been undermined by popular sovereignty and mass politics. Although war and conquest gave rise to major societal cleavages that are still with us today as residues of previous colonization and dominance hierarchies, nationalism fundamentally transformed the process of state formation and put an end to empire building, with profound consequences for social differentiation. In the new era of national self-determination and popular sovereignty that followed after the American and French Revolutions in the late eighteenth century, it become increasingly difficult and costly to conquer territory, let alone to control it against the will of the local population (Gilpin 1981, p. 142; Rosecrance 1986; Kaysen 1990).

While nationalism slowed down the power-driven stratification processes of the premodern world, it generated new inequalities based on processes of mass mobilization and cultural invention (Anderson 1991). In the modern world, cultural, and especially ethnic, stratification increasingly influences access to

political power. Developments in communication technology and mass liter-
acy, together with doctrinal changes pertaining to national self-determination
and popular sovereignty, paved the way for this profound transformation of
political legitimacy (Calhoun 1993).

Focusing on the emergence of party politics in Europe from the nineteenth
century, Rokkan (see Flora 1999) offers the most comprehensive account of
how this process produced power differentials that promoted some regions as
centers of power and demoted others to the status of powerless peripheries.
According to Rokkan's "freezing hypothesis," these processes involved considerable path dependence in terms of mobilization. Once mobilized as political
parties or social movements, cultural identities became organizationally locked
in, thus rendering the invention of new mobilization platforms difficult, if not
impossible.

In premodern times, human societies lacked the mass-based categorical
abstractions and means of communication to transform such macro cleavages
into mass-based political action. According to Gellner (1964), the nationalist
mode of politics centers on identification carried by a shared and standardized
high culture that replaced the direct interpersonal relations of smaller social
units, such as the village, in the premodern world. In the modern era, collective
identification with, and emotional attachment to, the abstract concept of the
nation made mass mobilization possible beyond local communities based on
direct contact.

This fundamental rewiring of social connectivity had major consequences
for geopolitics. As opposed to the "color-blindness" of traditional power politics, nationalist politics hinges on who is in and who is out. This way of
sorting people created new boundaries and differences, usually along ethnic
lines, which politicized distinctions that had previously been of no political
consequence. As argued by Tilly (1999, p. 172), in this very sense, nationalism
can be thought of as a generator of "categorical inequality" since

it asserts and creates paired and unequal categories, either (a) rival aspirants to nationhood or (b) members of the authentic nation versus others. It involves claims to prior
control over a state, hence to the exclusion of others from that priority. It authorizes
agents of the nation to subordinate, segregate, stigmatize, expel, or even exterminate
others in the nation's name.

From this vantage point, the era of nationalism could thus be likened to the
game of musical chairs. Given that there are many more potential peoples that
could claim nationhood than there are viable governance units in the modern
state system (Gellner 1983, p. 2), fierce political competition concerns who
is going to secure a seat of power. However, when the "music" stops, many
nationalities, such as the Kurds and the Palestinians, will still be left without
a seat. In other cases, several competitors will have to share a slot, a situation
that often causes tensions and possibly even open conflict.

Rather than tracing this development historically over centuries, however, this book analyzes the consequences of nationalism comparatively in the contemporary world, mainly focusing on internal conflict during the post–World War II period. By the end of World War II, the Western world had to a large extent become ethnically homogenized, while war-weariness reduced the attractiveness of exclusionary nationalism (Barkin and Cronin 1994; Mann 2005). Beyond this area, nationalist principles continued to spread to every corner of the globe, but the diffusion process was highly uneven. The uneven spread of nationalism delayed mass-level political mobilization in many parts of the world, thus creating differences in terms of both economic and political development that were often exploited by alien rulers (Gellner 1964). Viewed as an important part of this macrohistorical transformation, the decolonization process generated a large number of weak and ethnically heterogeneous states, many of which soon experienced their own serious nationality problems, rooted in patterns of political and economic exclusion along ethnonationalist lines (Jackson 1990).

Of course, the decision to exclude and dominate ethnic groups does not only depend on ideological commitments to abstract principles of nationalism. It also has more prosaic reasons, such as the desire to control wealth accruing from governmental control over raw materials and trade flows (Bates 1983). In some cases, rulers may even prefer to fight low-intensity wars with excluded groups at the periphery of the country rather than exposing themselves to the risk of being stabbed in the back by power-sharing partners through military coups (Roessler 2011). Moreover, besides nationalism, both political and economic inequalities can result from global processes relating to technological innovation and processes of globalization (see, e.g., Olzak 2006).

Conflict-Generating Mechanisms

Having conceptualized and traced the origins of vertical and horizontal inequalities, we now turn to the crucial causal link between inequality and conflict. The starting point of our account of ethnonationalist warfare builds on the realization that ethnic groups find themselves in radically different situations for various historical reasons. Whereas some ethnic groups came out on top in the geopolitical game, others were conquered and colonized early on, and therefore lost out in the competition for wealth and influence.

Our strategy is to explore the role of grievances indirectly by investigating the empirical link between inequalities and civil war outbreak at the level of groups. Of course, it is in principle possible to measure grievances directly (e.g., Petersen 2002) and to trace mobilization processes explicitly (e.g., Beissinger 2002), but such detailed analysis is beyond the scope of the current study. As will become clear below, collecting and evaluating global, comparative data on political and economic horizontal inequalities is a major challenge in its own right. Thus, we make the leap from the *explanans* to the *explanandum* in two

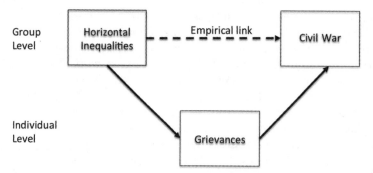

FIGURE 3.1. The causal path from inequalities to onset through grievances.

steps. The first step explains how structural asymmetries relating to political and economic inequalities generate grievances. The second step shows how grievances may trigger violent conflict, thus bridging the explanatory gap.

Building on Coleman's (1990) classical meta-theoretical approach, Figure 3.1 outlines our research strategy graphically. In order to avoid the fallacy of holistic causation, the approach calls for the specification of explicit causal mechanisms at a lower level of aggregation (Hedström and Swedberg 1998).[1] In the present context, this entails the articulation of grievance-based mechanisms at the level of (individual or group) agents, as opposed to focusing merely on the empirical link between inequalities and collective violence at the macro level.[2] That is, it entails moving from "factors" to "actors."

As argued in the previous chapter, both the assumptions of ubiquity-of-grievances and irrelevance-of-grievances should be exposed to systematic empirical tests rather than being treated as unquestioned postulates. However, it is not enough to show that there is a statistical macro link between inequalities and violence, and to demonstrate that our proposed mechanisms are plausible. We also have to establish that alternative causal pathways connecting inequalities and violence are less plausible, and that endogeneity and reverse causation do not undermine our reasoning. We will return to these issues at the end of the present chapter, and in connection with the empirical analyses in Parts II and III.

For now the task at hand is to develop the theoretical argument that explains through what mechanisms horizontal inequalities generate civil wars. In the following two sections, we will do so by first taking the step from inequalities to grievances, before connecting the latter to political violence.

---

[1] Our approach is inspired by, and has much in common with, "analytical sociology" (Hedström and Bearman 2009).

[2] We adopt this disaggregation strategy that goes from "black-box regularity to a mechanism" without making any strong, reductionist assumptions about causation being reducible to a search for "microfoundations" (see Elster 1998).

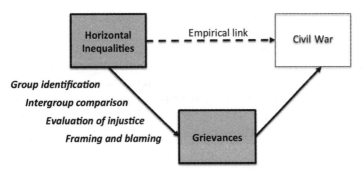

FIGURE 3.2. The causal path from horizontal inequalities to grievances.

From Inequalities to Grievances

For inequalities to be transformed into grievances, they have to be politicized. At this point we are concerned with politicization rather than with mass mobilization. We will deal with mobilization processes in the next section that close the gap between grievances and political violence. Throughout the chapter, we focus primarily on horizontal inequalities. Yet, more generally speaking, the reasoning underlying many of our causal mechanisms applies to vertical inequalities that are associated with political representation and economic interests. In Chapter 7, we will return to the link between vertical inequalities and civil war.

It is important to realize that our argument is probabilistic rather than deterministic. Not all inequalities produce grievances, and not all grievances trigger violence. Therefore, in the following, we have to keep in mind that "dead ends" of the conflict process may at any time interrupt the causal chain. In this sense, the stages of the pathway could be seen as necessary conditions rather than as contributing causes.

What does it take for skewed distributions of power and wealth to produce politically relevant grievances? As illustrated in Figure 3.2, we identify several important steps in the general causal pathway. Politicization requires a basis of identification, an explicit comparison that reveals some injustice typically through framing and attribution of blame, which in turn can be used to make explicit political claims. The remainder of this section discusses each of these steps in turn.

Group Identification

In most cases, the presence of horizontal inequalities presupposes the existence of well-defined groups, which is not a trivial precondition (Stewart 2000; Gurr 2000b). Objective group-level inequalities will hardly develop into grievances unless the groups themselves are perceived by, and identified with, a considerable part of the affected population, although articulation of grievances may help crystallize identity. This requires at least some awareness of the relevant social categories, but this awareness may not be very well developed in areas that have not benefited from mass schooling or a minimum level of development (Darden forthcoming). Furthermore, the salience of identities depends critically on the availability of relatively sharp boundary markers. The difficulties of constructing cohesive group identities based on socioeconomic classes confirm this point. Thus it is not surprising that Marxists refer to the notion of "false consciousness" in order to explain away the failures of groups to form around class interests (Brass 1991, p. 261).

Yet, this observation does not imply that the formation of ethnonationalist, as opposed to class-based, identities is a smooth and spontaneous process. As we have seen in Chapter 2, some theorists have gone so far as to reject the usefulness of collective identities and ethnic groups as analytical concepts altogether (e.g., Brubaker 2004). While it is undoubtedly true that modern politics is to a large degree group-based, and social life depends critically on social categories (Simmel [1908] 1971; Gellner 1964; Hogg and Abrams 1988), we argue that the extent to which cohesive groups can actually be said to exist is ultimately an empirical matter that depends on the specific situation. To be sure, premodern, clan-based societies, such as Somalia, represent a relatively poor fit with our group-level perspective.[3] Nor do we rule out a connection between inequality and conflict in nonethnic cases, for example, based on classes and ideology.[4] Since our goal is to evaluate the conflict-inducting effect of horizontal inequalities, however, we join Horowitz (1985), Gurr (1993a; 2000b), and others in adopting a self-consciously group-based framework, while restricting our substantive focus to groups defined through ethnic categorization rather than through other cleavages.

Categorization can happen spontaneously through bottom-up processes involving cultural innovation among intellectuals, scholars, writers, and artists. Students of nationalism have produced volumes detailing this process of "cultural engineering" (see, e.g., Hroch 1985). However, the formation of ethnonationalist identities usually involves at least some measure of organizational coordination, typically through the state. If imposed on previously ethnically "unconscious" populations, classificatory schemes, such as censuses and ethnically explicit laws regulating the use of languages and the practice of religion, help bring about identity formation (see Anderson 1991; Brubaker 1996; Martin 2001). Indeed, the more exclusionary and discriminatory such state policies are, the more directly they contribute to further cementing group identities.[5]

---

[3] In fact, the Ethnic Power Relations data set, on which we rely in our empirical analysis, lists Somalia as a country in which ethnicity is irrelevant due to the dominance of clans, which we exclude from our definition of ethnic groups (see Chapter 4).

[4] See Buhaug, Cederman, and Gleditsch (forthcoming) for an analysis of geographic inequality and the location of conflict onset; see also Chapter 7.

[5] In Chapter 2, we justified the assumption of reasonably stable group identities in conflict processes by referring to theories of reactive identity formation (e.g., Simmel 1955; Coser 1964).

Group Comparison

The further path to grievances requires a relational setting within which members of groups compare their own group's status and wealth to that of other groups. Social psychologists, especially those propounding social identity theory (SIT) (Tajfel and Turner 1979), have long argued that human beings tend to form groups based on trivial markers, which may serve as opportunistic justifications for conflict. Tajfel and his colleagues conducted a famous series of "minimal group experiments," which indicates that group loyalty quickly emerges based on arbitrary and imposed distinctions. In particular, Horowitz (1985) uses these findings as the basis of his own group-level theory of ethnic conflict. Tajfel's experimental perspective served the purpose of proving an important fundamental point about identification in social relations. Used as a conflict theory, however, social identity theory appears oddly inattentive to substantive differences relating to political or economic inequalities. In fact, it can even be viewed as a vindication of the ubiquity-of-grievance assumption: if trivial group differences are likely to escalate into competition and conflict, grievances must be truly ubiquitous and therefore could hardly explain the outbreak of conflict. Unsurprisingly, Horowitz (1985) subsequently proceeds to consider the impact of actual, rather than merely imagined, inequality on conflict, and does find a positive relationship.[6]

While constructed and misperceived comparisons may cause conflict, we posit that actual and objectively measurable differences in group status or economic development will make grievances more likely. Comparison, then, proceeds primarily based on real inequalities along ethnic lines, although perceived differences may also play a role in some cases. Rather than conforming with the principles of SIT, this logic corresponds to realistic group conflict theory, as developed by Sherif and Sherif (1953) and LeVine and Campbell (1972). This classical, but often neglected, social-psychological approach to group relations assumes that conflicting goals are central to conflict behavior. In particular, under conditions of scarce resources, out-groups appear more threatening. In the words of Williams (2003, p. 135): "Where strongly bounded ethnies act as rival collectivities (rather than mere social categories or unorganized aggregates of individuals), their *relative* positions become salient." Under such conditions, comparisons are hard to avoid: "Different aspects of group position – economic advantages, political authority, cultural eminence, generalized prestige – become central issues under differing conditions" (Williams 2003, p. 135). Ultimately, the very tangible threat of out-groups translates into

---

More specifically, Weingast (1998) applies a game-theoretic perspective to the conflict in the former Yugoslavia in order to illustrate that even a hint of repressiveness suffices to trigger interethnic polarization.

[6] See also Hale's (2008) critique of social identity theory. Yet, our and Hale's criticisms should not be interpreted as a wholesale rejection of social identity theory so much as a restriction of its substantive scope.

heightened intragroup cohesion coupled with ethnocentrism (Campbell 1965, p. 291).[7]

Evaluation of Injustice

The mere presence of real or imagined inequality clearly does not suffice to generate grievances. After all, there are countless examples featuring social actors who accept considerable asymmetries in the distribution of political power and economic wealth without becoming frustrated. Failure to evaluate the distributional situation with respect to some norms of equality typically leads them to accept the status quo, or even to ignore the issue of distribution. In the words of Williams (2003, p. 131):

Grievances are not merely expressions of deprivation and dissatisfaction. People can be deprived, disappointed, frustrated, or dissatisfied without feeling that they have been unjustly or unfairly treated – their unsatisfactory outcome may be "just the way things are" or the result of divine judgment, or a consequence of personal ineptitude. In contrast, a real grievance, regarded as the basis for complaint or redress, rests upon the claim that an *injustice* has been inflicted upon undeserving victims. Grievances are normative protests, claiming violations of rights or rules. Those who are intensely aggrieved may use the language of moral outrage.

In concrete terms, this means that someone has to identify what is unfair about the status quo. In most cases, this task falls on the group's leadership: "Without elite entry... injustices and inequalities may be accepted, cultural decline or assimilation may occur, and grievances may be expressed in isolated, anomic, or sporadic forms of conflict and disorder" (Brass 1991, p. 293).

From this reasoning it is clear that grievances may vary as much with changes in the normative framework as with the actual level of inequality. Breaches of norms may only be felt with growing relevance of a specific notion of justice. Such evaluations are likely to change over time (Parekh 2008). In general, the macro-historical process of democratization has prompted increasing pressures in favor of inclusive governance and political equality, at least at the level of individuals. Also to a large degree the product of the great American and French Revolutions in the late nineteenth century, nationalism serves as the most important source of normative evaluation in group relations. In particular, the principle of national self-determination stipulates that each nation is entitled to govern its own affairs without interference. As we have seen, wherever this principle is, or is seen to be, violated, nationalist grievances are likely to emerge.

In the empirical chapters below, we will derive a set of specific hypotheses that we evaluate systematically. Most obviously, if the incumbent elite of a state

---

[7] Indeed, if real differences do exist in a sufficient number of cases, they should leave a trace in our quantitative findings. However, we subscribe to the principles of realistic group conflict theory without, for that matter, assuming that inequalities always have to be objectively given in order to have an impact on conflict onset (see Herrera 2005). Hence, we agree with Brass' (1991) critique of attempts to reduce ethnicity to a matter of interest groups.

denies an ethnonationalist group access to central power, grievances are more likely to form (see Chapter 4). However, not even power sharing guarantees full satisfaction with the status quo. Such agreements may fall well short of the maximalist expectations of the group's nationalist ideology:

It is unlikely that grievances can simply be imaginary or invented, but the minimum level of discontent necessary for mobilization to start can be surprisingly low. Thus ethnic mobilization may occur when there is no exclusion from political participation – even when members have full access to political parties and state agencies, but feel deprived or frustrated because their policy preferences are not being granted (Williams 2003, p. 150).

Nevertheless, we postulate that, on average, grievances will be experienced roughly in proportion to the degree of violation. For example, the more harshly the government treats the group in question, the more frustrated its members will become. Furthermore, sociological theories of emotions suggest that negative emotions are especially likely to be aroused following loss of power and prestige (Kemper 1978). When the subjects blame others for their downgrading, anger and resentment increase the readiness to fight in order to change the situation (Turner and Stets 2005). Thus, we expect that the reversals of a group's status, especially political exclusion from executive influence after a long period of dominance, will provoke especially marked discontent (Brass 1991; Petersen 2002). Again, we turn to Williams (2003, p. 138) for a cogent summary of this logic:

A predictable reaction of resentment appears in those ethnies whose members feel that the collectivity as a whole is being unjustly subordinated in a ranking order. Especially sharp resentment is likely when there is an actual reversal in ranking, so that when a previously subordinate ethny acquires a dominant position we then see the familiar resentment of displaced groupings – those pushed aside, overturned, ignored, and treated with disdain by those earlier regarded as inferior.

In Chapter 4, we will test this mechanism explicitly by evaluating Hypothesis H4.2.

Framing and Attribution of Blame

Even the realization that the current order is unfair may not suffice to bring forth grievances. Indeed, our definition of grievances as a reaction to unfair treatment raises the question of who is responsible for the mistreatment. In the context of civil war, it is by definition the incumbent government that serves as target. Ultimately the representatives of the state have to be seen as sponsors and protectors of the unjust order; otherwise, grievances will not be focused and violence is thus less likely to erupt. Reminding us that "[p]olitical grievances are not like anomie, but directed against a target," Goodwin (1997, pp. 17–18) asserts that grievances may become "politicized" (that is, framed as resolvable only at the level of the state), and thereby a basis for specifically revolutionary collective action, only when the state sponsors or protects economic and social conditions that are viewed as grievous.

How do activists manage to pin the blame on the state? The classical socio-logical literature suggests that the notion of injustice is central to such efforts (Moore 1978). More recently, social movement researchers have introduced the notion of "injustice frames" that depict the members of a social movement as victims of societal injustice (see, especially, Gamson 1992, p. 68). According to Mason (2009, p. 80), framing works as follows:

To activate local social networks in support of a national movement, dissident leaders employ *framing processes* to persuade the member of local social networks to join a national movement. Framing involves identifying injustices that afflict the community and attributing them to the state or some other entity that is the intended target of the social movement. . . . Effective framing involves using traditional symbols to attract nonelites to a new set of values and beliefs about the state that will make them more willing to participate in a movement that challenges the state's sovereignty.

More generally, Benford and Snow (2000) argue that injustice frames constitute an important class of "collective action frames." Such constructs help social movements arrive at "a shared understanding of some problematic condition or situation they define as in need of change, make attributions regarding who or what is to blame, articulate an alternative set of arrangements, and urge others to act in concert to affect change" (p. 615). To be effective, collec-tive action frames need to resonate with their target audiences. According to Benford and Snow (2000, pp. 619–21), their effectiveness hinges on the inter-nal consistency of the frame itself with the goals of the social movement, its empirical credibility, and the political entrepreneurs' own persuasiveness in terms of status, moral authority, and knowledge.

Yet, while constituting a good analytical starting point, this somewhat abstract and mostly cognitive account of framing needs to be amended since it fails to do justice to the emotional aspects of action frames (Goodwin, Jasper, and Polletta 2001a; 2001b). Rather than being a matter of formal ideologi-cal consistency or general factual persuasiveness, framing in this deeper sense requires that the call to action relates directly to individual members' own life circumstances and aspirations. Successful frame-making typically relies on the construction of "political cultures of opposition" that connect popular idioms and ideological constructs to people's everyday lives in an emotionally powerful way (Reed and Foran 2002). For example, Reed and Foran explain how the Nicaraguan Revolution drew on a combination of liberation the-ology and "Sandinismo" as well as "more diffuse idioms and sentiments of nationalism, social justice, human dignity, and democracy" (p. 339). Besides being interpreted through cultural lenses, the revolutionary message needs to be "packaged" in a digestible and engaging format that can be easily dissem-inated. As Selbin (2010) explains, revolutionary and rebellions' framing does not merely depend on their structural appropriateness but also on the narrative tools invoked by the mobilizers (see also Polletta 1998). Thus, it is crucial to recognize the central role played by "myth and memory of revolution and of the power of mimesis for the mobilization and sustenance of revolutionary activity" (Selbin 2010, p. 4).

During the last couple of centuries, nationalism constitutes the perhaps most prominent master template for rebellious scripts. Despite considerable diversity as regards the specific contents of nationalist ideologies, Anderson (1991, p. 4) explains how nationalism is "modular" in these sense that it is "capable of being transplanted, with various degrees of self-consciousness, to a great variety of social terrains, to merge and to be merged with a correspondingly wide variety of political and ideological constellations." Although the recent research on emotions as the key to successful framing within social movements remains somewhat inchoate and scattered, it promises to overcome the gap between structural renderings of nationalism, as those proposed by Gellner (1983), and those that focus on the power of ideology and symbols (e.g., Smith 2009). As pointed out by Petersen (2002, pp. 57–8), considerable emotional power is implicit in Gellner's famous account of the "Ruritarians'" liberation from the "Megalomanians." In sum, these arguments articulate mechanisms that connect past exclusion and discrimination to a narrative of group identity that highlights the virtuous struggle against state oppression and unjust treatment.[8]

The power of framing becomes especially clear in its absence. Indeed, the status quo can easily be maintained by the incumbent elite if no coherent protest frame emerges. In this case the category never becomes politically relevant and the incumbent maintains cognitive dominance through Gramscian hegemony (Laitin 1986). Whether the current wealth distribution is perceived as being just or not thus critically depends on how expectations are managed through framing. In case of political exclusion and discrimination, it is usually obvious that the incumbent state elite is the guilty party. In case of economic horizontal inequalities, more elaborate arguments concerning the government's blame for underdevelopment may have to be advanced (see Chapter 5). In particular, beliefs about unfair exploitation in terms of taxation and the incumbent's extraction of the group's "own" natural resources may lead to a politicization of inequality (e.g., Aspinall 2007; see also Stewart 2008a). Weiner's (1978)

---

[8] In the social movement literature, the framing of mobilization processes belongs to one of the most intensively studied topics. Partly because of widespread grievance-skepticism as described in Chapter 2, however, analysis of collective action frames has been relatively rare in the conflict literature, although there are exceptions. For example, Kaufman (2011) offers a detailed frame-based study of the Mindanao rebellion in the Philippines dating back to the 1970s. Combining ideas from his own theory on symbolic politics, Kaufman draws heavily on the sociological literature on frames in conflict processes. For more general explanations of ethnonationalist violence highlighting the function of myths and symbols, see Smith (2009) and Kaufman (2001).

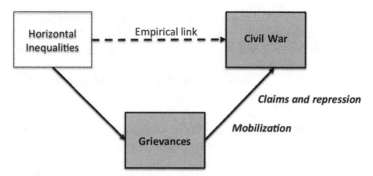

FIGURE 3.3. The causal path from grievances to civil war onset.

notion of "sons of the soil" is a special case of this important grievance process, as will be argued in Chapter 8.

From Grievances to Violence

Once horizontal inequalities have been politicized by intellectuals, prominent dissidents, and political entrepreneurs, the question arises of how such grievances can spread within the concerned populations to such an extent that they trigger large-scale internal conflict. Our argument hinges on the interaction between the challenger's mobilization and the response of the state (see Figure 3.3).[9]

Mobilization

Clearly, elite-level grievances can be articulated, and claims advanced, without their finding any resonance among the masses. This observation constitutes the core of the irrelevance-of-grievances assumption that was introduced in Chapter 2. Much has been said about collective action, and individual fears of governmental repression may certainly block any further increase in participation. Olson's (1965) theory of collective action offers the most extreme formulation of this argument. Since overcoming inequalities and establishing a new social and political order amount to public goods, free riding can be expected to be widespread, especially where state-led repression increases the risks associated with protest.

Rationalist collective action theory puts the bar very high, but it may still be possible to find successful mobilization strategies that entrepreneurs can resort to without violating the individualist axioms originally stipulated by Olson. For example, a number of conflict scholars have proposed that offering

---

[9] Obviously, the sequence of mobilization followed by state reaction is stylized. In many cases, these steps are taken repeatedly and more or less simultaneously.

material selective incentives helps overcoming the dilemma (e.g., Popkin 1979; Lichbach 1995; Weinstein 2007).

Yet, the strictly individualist perspective associated with rationalist theorizing fails to take the social context into account (Hechter and Okamoto 2001). Referring explicitly to the role played by social networks and institutions, social movement theory goes a long way toward explaining how social movements with political goals manage to overcome collective action hurdles and turn abstract claims into actionable programs that draw on considerable population support (whether direct or indirect).[10] Preexisting social networks provide a reservoir of trust that makes free riding harder and more risky because of in-group punishment (Mason 2009). In the social movement literature, such contextual reinforcement and social monitoring add up to something that has been called "mobilizing structures." According to Tarrow (1994, p. 22),

the mobilization of preexisting social networks lowers the social transaction costs of mounting demonstrations, and holds participants together even after the enthusiasm of the peak of confrontation is over. In human terms, this is what makes possible the transformation of episodic collective action into social movements.

In addition to such structures, identity formation constitutes another important resource that helps mobilization processes advance. Drawing on Harrison White's important insight, Tilly (1978) captures this logic with the notions of "catness" and "netness." This conceptualization implies that the effectiveness of mobilization efforts equals the product of solidarity of categorical identification (i.e., catness) and the density of social networks (i.e., netness). However, Tilly does not further develop the source of categorically induced solidarity. Those who have done so typically refer to the reduced transaction costs and the possibility of normative enforcement among members of the identity group in question (Goldstone 2001, p. 164; see also Opp 2009, ch. 7).[11]

The cognitive and structural focus of the social movement literature makes valuable contributions to our understanding of mobilization processes that are able to transcend the collective-action dilemma, but most of this research fails to take into account the direct impact of grievances. As has been argued in the context of framing processes, these explanations take on a somewhat bloodless and clinical flavor that seems worlds apart from the emotional heat of real-world conflict processes (Horowitz 1985). Whether based on relational or identity-based arguments, the reasoning surveyed so far attempts to steer clear from emotional effects by privileging strictly instrumental calculation and

---

[10] See also Kalyvas and Kocher (2007), who argue that collective action dilemmas do not necessarily apply in civil war settings, especially where noncombatants run a higher risk of getting killed than the rebels themselves. Although insightful, the scope of this argument is limited to particularly violent cases characterized by massive violations of human rights.

[11] For example, Simpson and Macy (2004) present a model that demonstrates the effect of collective identification on costly collective action that is validated through experiments. For a more general argument based on agent-based modeling, see Cederman (2002).

"cold" cognitive processes (Emirbayer and Goldberg 2005). In fact, this sanitized logic captures the dominant view of the literature on social movements, whether inspired by economics or sociology:

Emotions have disappeared from models of protest. When crowds and collective behavior, not social movements and collective action, were the lens for studying protest, emotions were central. Frustration, anger, alienation, and anomie were not merely an incidental characteristic but the motivation and motivation of protest. Such images were displaced 30 years ago by metaphors of rational economic calculators and purposive formal organizations, for whom social movements were just one more means of pursuing desired ends (Jasper 1998, p. 398; see also Goodwin, Jasper, and Polletta 2001a; 2001b).

Without belittling the conceptual coherence of mainstream theorizing, there are good reasons to question the absence of affective mechanisms in conventional explanations of collective protest action:

Mobilization theory based on the utilitarian rational choice model leaves one somewhat unsatisfied, because strong passions, group consciousness, ideological appeal, and appeals to solidarity in group conflict are relegated to secondary place, if they are taken into account at all (Oberschall 1993, p. 57).

To the extent emotions enter conventional explanations, they do so indirectly. Far from being emotionally neutral, Olson's (1965) classical rendering of the collective action dilemma at least implicitly presupposes that potential rebels will fear governmental retaliation (see, e.g., de Figuerido and Weingast 1999). Yet, fear is far from the only emotion that influences mobilization. Fear-based explanations need to be balanced against accounts that involve other emotions, such as anger and resentment (Petersen 2002; 2011). Indeed, the fear-resentment balance may tip over into grievance-driven collective action if grievances are strongly felt and shared, although overwhelming deterrence on the part of the incumbent elite may dampen the impact of resentment. Examples from around the world show that high-risk social movements have developed strategies of "emotion management" that serve to counterbalance the paralyzing effect of fear, for instance by evoking liberating anger and castigating free riders through shaming (Goodwin and Pfaff 2001).

Emotions provide the missing piece in the explanatory jigsaw. Failure to accord them an active role in mobilization processes makes it difficult to account for the emergence of solidarity, and how action is triggered by "moral shocks" (Jasper 1998, p. 409; although see Hechter 1987). Indeed, specific emotional patterns are associated with action tendencies that help explain why mobilization may spill over into violence (Mercer 2005; Petersen 2002). Even though organizational and cognitive factors are central to mobilization, it would be a mistake to overlook the contribution of emotionally charged grievances. Indeed, "emotional ties and investments are a potential source of power in their own right, alongside social-structural sources of power" (Emirbayer and Goldberg 2005, p. 507).

In a seminal study of the civil war in El Salvador, Wood (2003) offers especially convincing direct evidence showing how grievances can serve as the main motivation for rebels despite their exposure to extremely high risks. Her account describes how rural workers, the *campesinos*, defied a lethal campaign of violence and disappearances orchestrated by a repressive state dominated by rich, reactionary landowners. Because this study focuses on ideological, rather than ethnically, defined solidarity, it constitutes a hard test for this collective-action mechanism under extremely risky conditions. Relying on anthropological methods, including a large number of interviews with active rebels, Wood (2003, p. 18) found a very different set of motivations from Olson's free riders: "My insurgent informants made it clear to me that moral commitments and emotional engagements were principal reasons for their insurgent collective action during the civil war."

In contrast to standard approaches to collective action in civil war, Wood (2003) highlights two important aspects of her approach to the "pleasure of agency." First, she deviates from methodological individualism by assuming that affective mobilization is profoundly "other-regarding." In her view, the "reasons for which participants acted referred irreducibly to the well-being of others as well as oneself, and to processes, not just outcomes" (p. 19).[12] This is an extremely important finding as it demonstrates the limitations associated not only with rationalist theorizing, but also with individualist renderings of grievance-based mechanisms, such as Gurr's relative deprivation theory (Cook and Hegtvedt 1983; see also Chapter 2).

In this very respect, social psychology helps us appreciate the extent to which individual actors identify themselves with the group and predicate their values and motivations on the well-being of the group rather than considering exclusively their own self-interest. Of course, this process of "deindividualization" may not be perfect and does not require that all members become entirely exchangeable. Yet, a series of experiments has established that human decision making depends as much on the "group in the individual" as on the "individual in the group" (Hogg and Abrams 1988). Not unlike "sociotropic" voting (Kinder and Kiewiet 1979), according to which voters consider macroeconomic indicators rather than their own pocketbook, group-level solidarity often prevails over strictly egocentric reasoning in conflict processes (see also Hechter 1978).

Yet, it would be a mistake to reduce such collectivizing mechanisms to a purely cognitive phenomenon. As we have argued, the perception of injustice generates grievances that serve as a formidable tool of recruitment. In fact, Tilly's notion of catness is entirely compatible with collective

---

[12] This interpretation has much in common with Weber's "value rationality" as opposed to "instrumental rationality" (see Varshney 2003).

solidarity prompted by deeply felt resentment with the status quo. According to Oberschall (1993, p. 25), the microlevel assumptions that underpin this theoretical idea constitute a "multiplier effect" that creates collective grievances out of individual ones:

Members not only take offense at injuries and injustices they personally suffer, but will react to the experiences of their peers out of fellow feeling and solidarity.... A single injury is "multiplied" by the amount of group cohesion and interpersonal bonds to become a collective grievance.[13]

This formulation supports Wood's (2003) point that altruistic motives can transcend collective action dilemmas even in the face of extreme peril. Such emotional reactions become even more potent in the course of conflict processes that further escalate the level of injustice. Wood's second insight shows that, far from being constant, the level of grievances varies over time as a function of the conflict processes involving challengers and incumbents. Thus, "political culture... was not fixed but evolved in response to the experiences of the conflict itself, namely, previous rebellious actions, repression, and the ongoing interpretation of events by the participants themselves" (p. 19). Most importantly, Wood detects clear signs of reactive mobilization:

As government violence deepened, some *campesinos* supported the armed insurgency. They did so as an act of defiance of long-resented authorities and a repudiation of perceived injustices.... Participation per se expressed outrage and defiance, its force was not negated by the fact that victory was unlikely and in any case was not contingent on one's participation. Through rebelling, insurgent *campesinos* asserted, and thereby constituted in their own eyes, their dignity in the face of condescension, repression, and indifference (p. 18).

This observation leads us directly to the interactive logic of claims and counterclaims issued by challengers and incumbents. Given that grievances are inherently relational, violence-inducing mobilization processes should also be understood in a similarly relational context.

Rebel Claims and State Repression
A central task facing the rebel leaders is to turn the "blame game" into actionable claims. Targeting the incumbent government, such claims serve to correct perceived injustices. The challenger's political demands range from reforms of the current regime (e.g., more cabinet seats, transfers of public goods, or a larger measure of autonomy) to the very toppling of the government or secession from the state. In order to effect change, movements draw on collective-action repertoires that include peaceful protest, boycotts and strikes, and symbolic acts, but may also spill over into violence (McAdam, Tarrow, and Tilly 2001). As we

---

[13] Runciman (1966) introduced the notion of "fraternal deprivation" in order to overcome the individualist character of relative deprivation theory (see also Markowsky 1985).

will see, claim making may evolve over time, depending on the response of the government, in an explicitly strategic fashion.

How do incumbent state elites react to the threat of antigovernmental mobilization? Obviously, this depends directly on the nature of the claim. Democratic regimes are more likely than authoritarian ones to engage in negotiations concerning the rebels' claims as long as they entail peaceful change of the current regime. Yet, there is large variation in the willingness to accommodate group-level demands, especially if they are seen to undermine the central authority and territorial integrity of the state. Leaders of liberal democracies are typically reluctant to grant groups privileges because they believe that the individual right to vote guarantees all types of peaceful political change. Indeed, few states, democratic or not, would voluntarily accept to be dismembered through secession, although there are examples of peaceful "velvet divorces" (e.g., the breakup of the Swedish-Norwegian Union in 1905 and Czechoslovakia at the end of the Cold War). In contrast, authoritarian states, especially of the totalitarian kind, generally refuse to accept even the most modest proposals for political change while exposing peaceful protesters to the full force of their repressive capabilities.

Under what conditions is the outbreak of internal violent conflict most likely? A distinguished, state-centric tradition of theories on revolution insists that the state's reaction to challengers' claims holds the key to the answer of this question. While earlier instances of such theorizing highlight structural conditions and international opportunities, sometimes explicitly at the expense of grievances (e.g., Skocpol 1979), more recent theories of revolution factor in agency and the state's reactions to rebel movements' claims (e.g., Goldstone 1991). Here we follow Goodwin (2001), who proposes a clearly argued example of such a theoretical perspective. On this view, a specific set of policies is likely to provoke revolutionary, and, by extension, violent reactions. These relate to the state's approach to economic/social and political inequalities respectively, as well as to the government's possible resort to indiscriminate violence.[14]

The approach to economic and social inequalities is especially relevant to our attempt to make the theoretical leap from collective grievances to the outbreak of armed conflict. State elites that are perceived as the defenders of highly unequal economic and social arrangements, while systematically blocking reforms, run the risk of inviting more radical demands, thus disqualifying themselves as neutral agents working for social justice. Goodwin (1997) explains that, under such circumstances, "grievances may become 'politicized' (that is, framed as resolvable only at the level of the state), and thereby a basis for specifically revolutionary collective action, only when the state sponsors or

---

[14] Gurr (2000b) highlights two other properties of policies that relate to weak state reach and corrupt rule. The link to violence is plausible in these cases as well, but these factors are less directly linked to the grievance-related mechanisms discussed in this book.

protects economic and social conditions that are viewed as grievous" (pp. 17–18). Thus it follows that "states that regulate or abolish perceived economic and social injustices are less likely to become the target of political demands (revolutionary or otherwise) than those that are seen to cause or reproduce such injustices" (p. 17).

Second, sustained exclusion of mobilized groups from state power will also make violent outcomes much more probable, because the state's refusal to grant the excluded groups a share of power blocks peaceful avenues of political change. As it fits our own approach to exclusion, Goodwin's (1997, p. 18) argument deserves to be quoted at some length:

> Even if aggrieved groups direct their claims at the state, they are unlikely to seek its overthrow (or radical reorganization) if they manage to attain some significant share – or believe they *can* attain such a share – of state power and influence. Indeed, even if such groups view their political influence as unfairly limited, their access to state resources or inclusion in policy-making deliberations – unless palpably cosmetic – will likely prevent any radicalization of their strategic repertoire or guiding ideology. In fact, the political "incorporation" of mobilized groups – including putatively revolutionary proletariats – has typically served to *deradicalize* them.

Conversely, chronic exclusion and outright discrimination are likely to incline the movements to opt for more radical responses that may include violent strategies.

Third, states that resort to indiscriminate campaigns of repression targeting their challengers leave the movements with little choice but to respond with violent means, thus triggering revolutionary civil war. Mirroring Wood's (2003) observation about the endogeneity of grievances, Goodwin (1997) stresses that state reactions of this uncompromising nature leave the rebels with "no way out":

> Like political exclusion, indiscriminate state violence against mobilized groups and opposition figures is likely to reinforce the plausibility, justifiability, and (hence) diffusion of the idea that the state needs to be violently "smashed" and radically reorganized (p. 19).

Groups targeted in this way will have little choice but to arm themselves to protect themselves against the maltreatment of the state. Indiscriminate violence is clearly counterproductive since it tends to deepen grievances and radicalize the movement by undermining more moderate leaders. In his thorough analysis of the effect of indiscriminate violence, Kalyvas (2006) demonstrates that, although overwhelming force may crush the resistance, such ham-fisted policies of brute force typically deepen the level of grievances through emotional responses, even in those cases where they were initially held by only a small minority of a group's members.

In such situations, radical and revolutionary ideologies thrive, including exclusive and militarized ethnonationalism, because "a society in which

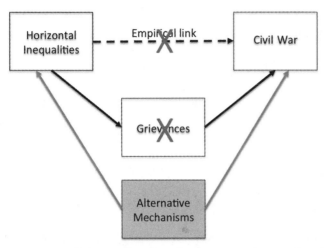

FIGURE 3.4. Grievance-based mechanism as spurious explanation.

aggrieved people are routinely denied an opportunity to redress perceived injustices, and even murdered on the mere suspicion of political disloyalty, is unlikely to be viewed as requiring a few minor reforms" (Goodwin 1997, p. 19). It goes without saying that regimes of this type are exposed to grave risks of civil war onset.

Alternative Explanations

The previous sections have attempted to render plausible the role of grievances in conflict processes. Yet, in the absence of direct tests of aggrieved people's attitudes and emotions, the proposed causal pathway that we have so far sketched can be criticized on several grounds.

The most obvious angle of attack builds directly on the ubiquity-of-grievances argument that we introduced in Chapter 2: one could undermine the macro link that connects group-level inequality with conflict by showing that there are other ways to get from inequality to conflict than via grievances (see Figure 3.4). This has indeed been the strategy of the quantitative country-level studies that argue that grievances lose their explanatory power as soon as self-interested and opportunistic factors are accounted for.

Methodologically this approach introduces proxies for both sets of factors and then proceeds by showing that those indicators that are (ostensibly) associated with grievances, notably indices of ethnic diversity and income dispersion, become insignificant once the other factors are introduced into the model (again, see Fearon and Laitin 2003; Collier and Hoeffler 2004). Indeed, if it can be shown that the effect of either political or economic inequality disappears once opportunity-based explanations are controlled for, then our grievance account could well be spurious. In the empirical chapters, especially

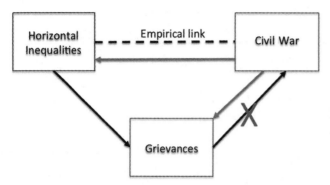

FIGURE 3.5. Grievances bypassed through reverse causation.

in Chapter 7, we will introduce controls of this type in order to show that the effect of inequality remains robust.

It is not difficult to think of possible alternative stories that bypass grievances in this way. Consider the case where poverty in specific regions drives outcomes along the lines of Collier and Hoeffler's (2004) argument concerning opportunity costs. Regional underdevelopment could constitute fertile ground for rebel recruiters who are motivated by greed and power, rather than by group-based grievances. Likewise, Fearon and Laitin's (2003) approach suggests that peripheral location could drive conflict onset due to the state's weakness far away from its center of power. But at the same time, remoteness could also disadvantage economic activity in the relevant area, with horizontal inequality as a consequence. If geographic position causes both onset and inequality, it could well be that the postulated grievance link connecting the two factors is spurious. Fortunately, we are able to control for factors of this type in the empirical analysis in the remainder of the book (see also the Online Appendix).

Assuming that the empirical link holds, however, our explanation could still be invalid. It could be that endogeneity undermines our grievance-based account through reverse causation (see Figure 3.5). It stands to reason that previous violent challenges to the state's power could incline governments to exclude, or even discriminate, the groups in question, or that economic inequality could grow as a direct consequence of previous combat. Furthermore, it cannot be ruled out that acts of violence, especially those targeting civilians indiscriminately, will generate grievances irrespective of horizontal inequalities. This creates a link from civil war to grievances, thus rendering the latter causally ineffective as an explanation of violent conflict.

Finally, even if the macrocausal link points in the right direction, our grievance-based account may fail because of a competing mechanism that connects inequalities with violence, however, without taking the road via grievances. It is notoriously difficult to rule out such an observationally equivalent mechanism, but fortunately, it is also very difficult to think of a plausible candidate.[15] However, while we will address the issue of spurious causation and endogeneity explicitly throughout the book, we feel that it is not our duty to come up with observationally equivalent mechanisms that are unrelated to grievances. We leave this specific task to our critics and are looking forward to challenging these accounts once they materialize. For now, it seems reasonable to focus on the claim that grievances can be dismissed just because standard indicators associated with such explanations are statistically insignificant.

---

[15] For example, one could imagine that large inequality implies that a group is clearly weaker than the state. Yet, the group's weakness would also tilt the power balance in favor of the incumbent government, thus making conflict less likely. In fact, this story leads to exactly the opposite expectation.

PART II

EMPIRICAL ANALYSIS OF CIVIL WAR ONSET

The second part of the book investigates the empirical link between horizontal inequality and civil war onset. Chapters 4 and 5 analyze the effect of political and economic inequalities on ethnonationalist conflict based on samples of ethnic groups drawn from the EPR data set. Chapter 6 extends this analysis to transnational relations, focusing on transborder ethnic kin. Building on the previous findings, Chapter 7 revisits the country level, which allows us to compare factors responsible for both ethnic and nonethnic civil wars.

4

Political Exclusion and Civil War

Do civil wars result from political exclusion? This chapter evaluates empirically the mechanisms that trigger internal conflict as a function of political horizontal inequality, as manifested through the exclusion of ethnic groups from central executive state power.[1] Rather than viewing ethnicity as a politically disconnected, demographic characteristic reflecting linguistic and cultural diversity, as is often done in the contemporary civil war literature, we contextualize ethnicity macro-historically as a political organization form embedded in nationalism.

In Chapter 3, we discussed how nationalist politics leads to the generation of political horizontal inequality. In the present chapter, we shift the attention from the origins of inequalities to their consequences for internal conflict. Nationalism defines the macro setting within which much, possibly even most, large-scale political violence unfolds in the modern world. Drawing on Gilpin's (1981) terminology, this type of transformation can be classified as "nationalist systems change." Viewed as a special case of the broader category of systems change that features fundamental transformations of the main actor types defining politics, this type of macro-historical process prompted nations to play the main role on the world stage along with states, roughly from the time of the French Revolution (Cederman, Warren, and Sornette 2011; see also Hall 1999). The importance of the nation can be found in the way that this entity legitimizes the state. As opposed to the "descending" principle of territorial sovereignty that justifies governance in personal, dynastic, and possibly even divine terms, the French Revolution introduced an "ascending" logic that defines the people, conceived of as the nation, as the locus of political legitimacy (Calhoun 1997).

[1] This first part of this chapter builds on Cederman, Wimmer, and Min (2010), which introduced the first group-level results on political exclusion using the original version of the EPR data set.

This transformation of political legitimacy has profound repercussions for interactions among social actors, including those that are associated with political violence. As first realized by Clausewitz (1984), the most obvious consequences for warfare pertain to the sheer scale of combat that became possible thanks to the *levée en masse* (i.e., popular conscription). By tapping into the demographic resources of the entire state rather than relying on mercenaries or professional troops organized in standing armies, Napoleon and his successors eroded the distinction between warriors and the citizenry (Hintze 1975; Howard 1976; Cederman, Warren, and Sornette 2011).

Yet, nationalist systems change does not only affect geopolitics through changes of the internal workings of states. In addition, and at least as importantly, this type of transformation influences profoundly the very shape and boundaries of the units in question. Wherever the nation happens to coincide with the state, the boundary issue will cause little difficulty. However, where national and state boundaries do not coincide, nationalist systems change will trigger tensions that increase the likelihood of both internal and external conflicts. According to Gellner's classical formula, "nationalism is primarily a political principle, which holds that the political and national unit should be congruent" (Gellner 1983, p. 1).

In some areas, such as preunification Germany and Italy, there were too many states per nation. Competition over who was going to lead the unified nation in many cases led to warfare (Miller 2007). More often, and more importantly to our study, polities can be characterized by a state-to-nation deficit (Gellner 1983, p. 2). This was the case in premodern and colonial multiethnic empires but still applies to most decolonized states (Connor 1972). To the extent that an ethnically homogenous ruling elite refuses to share power and wealth with other ethnic groups, grievances are likely to emerge as dominated populations become conscious of their predicament through improved education and communications.

Since this book is devoted primarily to internal conflict, we focus on the first type of situation, which features a state inhabited by two or more ethnic groups. An adapted version of Tilly's (1978) classical polity model serves as an appropriate starting point (see Figure 4.1). The original model features an actor configuration that centers on the government, to which a number of political groups compete for access. In this and the following two chapters, we assume that the groups in question are defined in ethnic terms. Some of the groups, which we will refer to as *included* or *incumbent* groups, enjoy privileged access to power by virtue of being represented through its elite members within the government's executive organs, typically through ministerial representation within the cabinet. Beyond this set of ethnic groups, there are also ethnic groups that are systematically excluded from power, which we will here refer to as *excluded* or *marginalized* ethnic groups.[2] In the figure, we depict three

---

[2] Cederman and Girardin (2007) use the terms Ethnic Group In Power (EGIP) and Marginalized Ethnic Groups (MEG) for this distinction.

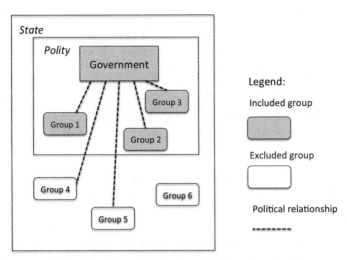

FIGURE 4.1. The polity model with included and excluded groups.

groups as having privileged access to central power, namely Groups 1–3. By contrast, Groups 4 and 5 are excluded from power and Group 6 is irrelevant, in the sense that it plays no explicit role in national politics.

By definition, excluded ethnic groups are exposed to a situation of alien rule, since their state is ruled by "foreign" individuals who are members of other ethnic groups. As we have seen, this type of political inequality constitutes a direct violation of the principle of nationalism and self-determination. Under such circumstances, representatives of the aggrieved groups typically feel inclined to advance claims securing full, or at least partial, sovereignty. Full sovereignty can be established by dislodging the incumbent government and replacing it with one that is under the control of the challenger group. However, power sharing would also ameliorate the situation by allocating a fair share of cabinet seats to the group. Alternatively, the leaders of the marginalized group may seek independence through secession. Again, compromises are also possible along this territorial dimension, for example through various types of regional autonomy arrangements that delegate decision-making authorities in important areas, such as financial or cultural matters.

To the extent that the incumbent elite belonging to the ethnic group in power opposes the challengers' demands, possibly even through repression, the challengers are especially likely to respond with violent means. Such armed resistance may finally escalate to a full-fledged ethnonationalist civil war pitting the included incumbent group against its excluded challenger group. Civil wars confront incumbent governments with political and military organizations that challenge the governments' claim to sovereign rule. This situation corresponds to standard definitions of civil war as a conflict that pits some nonstate actor against the state (Sambanis 2004b; Kalyvas 2007) but excludes communal conflicts between nonstate actors or pogroms in which the state plays less of an active role (though see Horowitz 2002; Wilkinson 2009) as well as one-sided conflicts where the state violently represses a group lacking cohesive organization (Eck and Hultman 2007). In conflicts that are fought in the name of excluded and discriminated groups, rebel movements are composed of mobilized and militarized organizations that challenge the government. In the case of challenges launched in the name of groups that are already represented within government, other actors such as a faction within the army or newly created political organizations and militias might instigate a violent confrontation.

Generating Hypotheses

We now proceed to the derivation of operational hypotheses that link nationalist grievances to the outbreak of civil war.[3] Again, there is no better place to start than with Gellner's (1983) seminal book on *Nations and Nationalism*. According to Gellner, tensions result from the violation of the main nationalist principle pertaining to the congruence of political and cultural boundaries: "Nationalist *sentiment* is the feeling of anger aroused by the violation of the principle, or the feeling of satisfaction aroused by its fulfillment" (p. 1). Given the widespread state-to-nation deficit that results from the "musical chairs" logic referred to in the previous chapter, many ethnic groups will find themselves without adequate representation within their respective countries' executives. Such nationality problems are further exacerbated by intermingling of ethnic groups' settlement areas:

It follows that a territorial political unit can only become ethnically homogenous, in such cases, if it either kills, or expels, or assimilates all non-nationals. Their unwillingness to suffer such fates may make the peaceful implementation of the nationalist principle difficult (Gellner 1983, p. 2, see also p. 40).

Although Gellner's sweeping macrohistorical theory constitutes an excellent point of departure for the structural framing of the link between grievances and violence, it is not, and was never meant to be, directly applicable to individual cases. In order to do precisely this, we need to identify the pivotal institutional variable that most directly influences the probability of conflict. Clearly, access to state power is the crucial resource that ethnonationalist groups compete over. Rather than being a neutral arena for competing group interests, the state itself has to be seen as a prize. Thus,

the state has become the decisive political vehicle and political arena for ethnic groups – dominant and subordinate – in modern conditions of rapid change in which it redistributes even higher proportions of its citizens' and subjects' general income and assets. To protect and articulate their social, cultural, and economic interests, grievances, claims, anxieties, and aspirations, ethnic groups must enter the political arena – that is, they much add the quality of becoming conflict groups to their previous qualities of

---

[3] See also Cederman et al. (2010), who derive similar hypotheses.

being status groups, interest groups, cultural groups, and the like (Rothchild 1981, p. 232).

Already introduced in Chapters 2 and 3, this institutional logic stipulates that where the incumbent regime insists on blocking access for challenging groups despite repeated explicit demands for an opening of the polity, the risk of armed conflict becomes acute. Systematic and persistent refusal to open the polity to the whole population leaves the excluded groups with few feasible alternatives other than resorting to a direct, and possibly violent, challenge to the incumbents' rule. Applying the same argument specifically to ethnic groups, Brass (1991, p. 238) identifies the conditions under which violence becomes particularly likely:

Where ... the government or the leading political party draws its support exclusively or overwhelmingly from a dominant ethnic group and propagates a chauvinist or racist ideology, then the society in question is headed for civil war and secessionism.

Rather than being primarily a matter of the group's own actions, the central state's institutional and informal policies determine the power status of ethnic groups living within its borders. Of course, the latter are sometimes able to influence the central government's decision by applying pressure and extracting concessions, but wherever the state's vested power elite refuses to back down and even escalates the tension by resorting to violent repression, civil war becomes a distinct possibility.

In view of this straightforward reasoning, we derive the following general hypothesis:

> H4.1. Ethnic groups that suffer from limited access to state power are more likely to experience conflict than those that enjoy full access.

Most obviously, we should expect excluded groups to be more likely to experience conflict than incumbents who already enjoy governmental representation. As observed in Chapter 4, such expectations are in line with the findings of Gurr's research. Based on analysis of the MAR data set, he finds that group disadvantages, including political ones, tend to generate conflict: "Resentments about restricted access to political positions and a collective history of lost autonomy drive separatist demands and rebellion more generally" (Gurr 1993b, p. 188).

Furthermore, we postulate that the risk of conflict decreases gradually according to the precise degree of power access. This means that there are also considerable differences in terms of conflict propensity within the included and excluded categories respectively. In particular, groups that are not only merely marginalized, but also exposed to state-led discrimination, have been found to be even more inclined to resort to armed resistance (Gurr 1993a; 1993b). Recent evidence confirms these results. For example, the predictive model of political instability assembled by Goldstone et al. (2010) indicates that state-led discrimination increases the probability of conflict.

So far, we have considered the effect of power status on conflict propensity in static terms. Viewed from a dynamic standpoint, however, the impact may be felt even more acutely, especially where a group's status is downgraded. As argued in Chapter 3, the shock of demotion is likely to trigger strong emotional reactions that spill over into violence in order to "reverse a reversal" (Petersen 2002). The sense of loss will be very obvious to those groups that have enjoyed a privileged position. As pointed out by Rothchild (1981, p. 217), "favored ethnic groups come to take a proprietary view of their traditional overrepresentation." For these reasons, we articulate a second hypothesis pertaining to power access:

H4.2. Groups that have experienced recent loss of state power are especially likely to engage in internal conflict.

It should be noted that under specific circumstances power upgrades may also cause conflict, at least to the extent that the incumbent offers insufficient and reluctant concessions. According to Tocqueville's ([1856] 1956) classical account of the French Revolution, this phenomenon, which can be referred to as "too little, too late," typically features vacillation between inclusive and exclusive stances. It is a common response by authoritarian and unrepresentative regimes to challengers' pressure for increased regime openness (see Taylor 1948; Goodwin 1997).

Beyond such status shifts, we would expect the size of the group in question to matter directly for the perception of grievances. Other things being equal, the larger the excluded group, the bigger the perceived injustice. Grievances are prone to result "if the rulers of the political unit belong to a nation other than that of the majority of the ruled, this, for nationalists, constitutes a quite outstandingly intolerable breech of political propriety" (Gellner 1983, p. 1). More generally,

A sense of injustice is likely to form when a majority perceives its position as "below" a minority (when the language of the minority is the language of state and education, when minorities hold disproportionate numbers of political positions, and so on) (Petersen 2002, pp. 51–52).

This effect operates within both democracies and nondemocracies. Democratic systems are known to suppress representation of minorities that are viewed as threatening and uncooperative. Referring to the individual rights of democratic representation, such states may also refuse to grant ethnic groups any concessions whether in terms of power sharing or group autonomy. A prominent example is Turkey, where the supreme court has banned Kurdish political parties alleged to challenge the "indivisible unity of the state, the country and the nation."[4] However, even autocratic political systems depend on at least some support from the broader population. The risk of revolution increases in cases where the state elite is viewed to be drawn from an especially narrow basis, as was the case in South Africa under Apartheid and remains the case of the Assad family's Alawite minority regime in Syria at the time of writing. Suffering from an acute deficit of political legitimacy, such regimes are particularly dependent on threats and actual execution of violence against their own citizens to uphold their precarious claim to power. It goes without saying that the risk of civil war is higher in these political systems than in those that rely on a broader and more secure basis of population support.

In principle, democratic polities cease to be democracies as soon as a majority of the population is excluded, but ethnonationalist politicians sometimes attempt to claim democratic status by simply excluding selected parts of the populations from citizenship. Thus, the "demos" can be redefined in more narrow terms as an "ethnos" (Mann 2005). The European colonial empires clung to this double standard as their metropolitan cores democratized. Ultimately, however, the pressure for representation made such minority rule within the colonies unbearable and sometimes violent decolonization followed.

We sum up the demographic aspects of the grievance mechanism in the following way:

H4.3. Large excluded ethnic groups are more likely to experience conflict than are smaller excluded groups.

It should be noted that group size does not merely capture the extent of grievances held in a population. This dimension can also be expected to correlate with a group's resources and likely ability to challenge the state. Most obviously, large numbers translate into the availability of more fighters and more generally, material support from more individuals (Cederman, Buhaug, and Rød 2009; Cederman, Wimmer, and Min 2010). Yet, the argument advanced here is that sheer size, irrespective of grievances, plays no important role in this relationship.[5] Indeed, H4.3 applies to excluded groups only, since they are the ones more subject to grievances according to H4.1. Stated differently, opportunities for conflict alone have no independent role absent clear motivation. As we will see below, it is possible to separate this grievance-related effect of group size from the capacity dimension. If, however, group size increases

[4] See, e.g., Robert Tait, "Turkey bans main Kurdish party over alleged terror links," *The Guardian*, Saturday 12 December 2009, online at http://www.guardian.co.uk/world/2009/dec/12/turkey-bans-main-kurdish-party.
[5] Thus, as opposed to previous related studies, our test interacts the effect of relative group size with that of group-level exclusion. Moreover, in order to capture the comparative logic, we employ a relational indicator that compares the group's size to that of the incumbent groups. In contrast, Cederman et al. (2010) rely on a nonrelational measure of group size.

conflict propensity for incumbent groups as well, the pure resource perspective seems more plausible.

Finally, grievances are deeply contextual, especially with respect to prior histories of conflict. Long-standing conflict processes that involve repeated outbreaks of violence reflect the fact that the incompatibility fought over has not been resolved. Such situations are likely to foster an increasingly deep sense of resentment among the conflict parties, especially among those who have lost family members, close friends, or property in previous conflict episodes. Indeed, following Barbalet (1998, ch. 6), we expect vengefulness to trigger a stronger action tendency than mere resentment.

Thus, conflicts become self-reinforcing if previous losses fuel new violence in addition to the effect exerted by the unresolved inequality at root of the conflict. Clearly protracted conflict histories of this type involve suspicion and fear, as argued by theorists of the security dilemma (Posen 1993), but the emotional reactions typically surpass a general loss of trust:

Reiterated feelings of hostility can crystallize into intense and rigid sentiments of genuine hatred so strong as to incite violence even in the absence of specific provocation. Desires for revenge are extremely powerful components of long-continued violent conflicts (Williams 2003, p. 139).

Tendentious oral history as well as ideologically biased writing and teaching of history can further perpetuate the hatred and stimulate calls for revenge decade after decade (Kalyvas 2006). Of course, this effect should not be confused with essentialist accounts referring to "ancient hatred." These cycles of ethnonationalist violence are distinctly modern (Mann 2005), but this does not prevent them from being long-lasting and extremely difficult to escape from. In fact, the literature on ethnic conflict has been so rash in its desire to debunk primordialist journalistic accounts that it typically downplays the importance of historical sequences of violence (Petersen 2002).

The empirical literature supports the general logic of our reasoning. In interstate relations, there is evidence that "enduring rivalries" between pairs of states can lead to a high likelihood of new outbreaks of violence (Diehl and Goertz 2000). More recently, similar patterns have been detected in internal conflict (DeRouen and Bercovitch 2008). However, these studies are pitched at the country level and do not consider ethnonationalist conflict more specifically, beyond flagging incompatibilities arising over specific disputed territories. Thanks to our group-level data, we are able to formulate and empirically evaluate a more specific hypothesis:

H4.4. Ethnic groups that have experienced conflict in the past are more likely to experience conflict onset than those that have not.

Since all of our hypotheses have been developed for relations involving groups, we need to evaluate them at this analytical level as well. It is therefore necessary to move beyond the abstract theoretical schemes that we introduced in Chapter 3. Rather than aggregating our analysis up to the level of entire countries (though see Chapter 7), or disaggregating it all the way down to individuals, we follow the lead of researchers who have relied on group-level data sets such as the Minorities at Risk (Gurr 1993a; 2000b).

Our strategy is to find operational measures of horizontal political inequalities affecting specific ethnic groups and to measure conflict outbreaks associated with the corresponding entities. This approach allows us to shorten the inferential leap from country-level inequality measures to political violence. Indeed, group-level analysis has the advantage of being much more precise in its attribution of independent and dependent variables than country-level studies. It is clear that many civil wars only affect specific parts of states, such as Kashmir in India and Chechnya in Russia, rather than engulfing their entire territories (Buhaug and Lujala 2005; Cederman and Gleditsch 2009). Proceeding with country-level measures, then, risks blurring important causal connections that can be assessed only if we have access to information about substate units and are in a position to tally this information for both sides of the causal connection.

At the same time, the intermediate-level disaggregation takes us closer to the level of individuals, who are the units capable of harboring grievances. As we have seen in Chapter 2, however, treating groups as units is fraught with difficulties and certainly does not protect our analysis from ecological fallacies deriving from group-level reification. Yet, for empirical tractability reasons, our approach refrains from validating our theory at the level of individuals and subgroup organizations, and we leave this for future research.

Data

It is now clear that our empirical strategy hinges critically on the availability of suitable data on ethnic groups and their institutional access to power in a wide and unbiased sample, as well as on conflict indicators associated with the same ethnic groups. In fact, there are several possible data sets that offer information about ethnic groups. The *Atlas Narodov Mira* (ANM, Atlas of the Peoples of the World) was the first major data source of this type (Bruk and Apenchenko 1964). Assembled by Soviet anthropologists in the early 1960s, the atlas covers ethno-linguistic groups around the entire world, but says little about religious cleavages and nothing about the groups' political status. The narrow conception of ethnicity, together with its apolitical approach and the fact that the original material is now quite dated, makes it less suitable for our purposes.[6] Fearon's (2003) more recent list of ethnic groups attempts to offer a selection of politically relevant groups, but the criteria for inclusion are not

---

[6] The *ANM* provides useful information about ethnic groups' settlement areas, which has served as a useful basis in the construction of new geographic information systems, such as the Geographic Representation of Ethnic Groups (GREG) data set (Weidmann, Rød, and Cederman 2010) and the GeoEPR data set (see Chapter 5 and Wucherpfennig et al. 2012).

entirely transparent, and like the *ANM*, it fails to provide explicit measures of political and institutional access.

As argued in Chapter 2, the most important listing of ethnic groups remains the Minorities at Risk (MAR) project. The work on this pioneering resource started in the 1980s and was first presented by Gurr (1993a). Since then MAR has undergone a number of updates and has quickly become the most popular source of information on ethnic groups in the empirical social-science literature. Most quantitative studies of ethnic conflict rely on the MAR data (see, e.g., Saideman 2001; Regan and Norton 2005; Olzak 2006; Walter 2006). By focusing on the notion of minorities "at risk," the MAR breaks new ground as regards political relevance, but unfortunately at the price of threatening selection bias. While the sample includes some "advantaged" minorities, it remains incomplete since Gurr and his colleagues do not include dominant majority groups, some of which may be at risk of being challenged by disadvantaged minorities, and the data also do not include politically relevant minority groups that are not considered "at risk."

Data on Ethnic Groups' Access to Central State Power

In preparing the empirical foundations of this book, it became clear that existing data sets would not be able to carry the weight of our empirical analysis. Therefore we launched a tailor-made data project that allows us to test our hypotheses directly. In an effort to improve on previous attempts to capture ethnic groups' power status (Cederman and Girardin 2007; Buhaug, Cederman, and Rød 2008; Cederman, Buhaug, and Rød 2009), Cederman's research group at ETH Zürich teamed up with Andreas Wimmer and Brian Min, then at University of California at Los Angeles, in a major data collection project that relied on an online expert survey with more than 100 participants. The fruit of this collaboration was an entirely new data set called Ethnic Power Relations (EPR). The original version of the data set identifies all politically relevant ethnic groups and their access to state power, where political relevance is defined by including groups that are active in national politics and/or directly discriminated by the government (Cederman et al. 2010). In this book, we use a new version, EPR-ETH, assembled by the International Conflict Research group at ETH Zürich.[7] Whereas the original data contain information about politically relevant ethnic groups around the world from 1946 through 2005, the new version improves the coding in many cases and extends the coverage up to 2009.

---

[7] The new data are publically available through our data portal GROW[up], see http://growup.ethz. ch. Descriptions of the data can be found at http://www.icr.ethz.ch/data/growup/epr-eth. We would like to thank all the experts who helped us with the coding, including Susanne Böhn, Nils-Christian Bormann, Johan Brosché, Michael Bürge, Naomi Furnisch Yamada, Armando Geller, Omar Kassab, Thomas Klepsys, Ether Leemann, Dirk Leuffen, Jasan Miklian, Gudrun Østby, Navitri Putri Guillaume, Seraina Rüegger, James Scarritt, Michael Schmitz, Guido Schwellnus, Corinne Trescher, Jessica Trisko, Manuel Vogt, Judith Vorrath, and Toru Yamada. See http://www.icr.ethz.ch/data/other/epr_old/experts for a list of experts who contributed to the coding of the original EPR data set.

The structure of the data in the new version remains essentially the same as in the original version. In agreement with constructivist principles, the ethnic identities are allowed to vary over time, such that the political relevance or the main level of political identification may move from one level to another. For each group and time period, the demographic weight and access to power are provided.[8] The latter dimension is operationalized on the basis of the influence over the country's executive, including cabinet seats or control of the army in military regimes.[9]

The data set divides power status into three main categories depending on whether the group in question (1) controls power alone, (2) shares power, or (3) is excluded from power. Goups that fall into the two first categories are classified as included and those that belong to the last category are excluded. The EPR classification offers subcategories for each of the three main status categories:

Undivided Power
In case a single ethnic group controls the executive, there are two types of rule, namely:

- *Monopoly*: In this case, the members of the group enjoy total monopoly on executive power at the exclusion of other ethnic groups. The power monopoly of the Americo-Liberians in Liberia until 1981 illustrates this situation.
- *Dominance*: Falling short of full-fledged monopoly, this situation allows for some limited but politically irrelevant participation of "token" members of other groups. Tariq Aziz, Iraq's foreign minister until the fall of Saddam Hussein, is Christian rather than Sunni Muslim, but by no means represented his own ethnic group in any politically meaningful way.

Power-Sharing Regimes
The second class of power configurations entails power-sharing arrangements, whether of a formal or informal nature. Included groups that share power play either a senior or junior role measured by their absolute influence over the cabinet.

- *Senior partner*: If the representatives of the ethnic group in question have at least as much executive influence as other powerful partners in the power-sharing arrangement, then the group is classified as a senior partner.

---

[8] The EPR data set captures absolute influence irrespective of demographic weight.

[9] Partly due to data limitations, EPR does not measure legislative political power. While also relevant as an indicator of political influence (see, e.g., Birnir 2007; Brancati 2009), control over the executive is arguably the most crucial aspect of influence since minorities can be systematically outvoted in majority systems.

In Switzerland, for example, the Swiss Germans are usually allocated the greatest number of cabinet posts by virtue of their demographic status as a clear majority of the country's population.

- *Junior partner*: If the group's representation lies clearly below that of the most powerful members of the power-sharing arrangement, then it is relegated to the status of junior partner. In Switzerland, both the Swiss French and Swiss Italians usually (but in the latter case not always) enjoy representation within the executive, although clearly below the level of the Swiss Germans. Thus, we code them both as junior partners.

Exclusion from Central Power

The third main class of power configurations features groups that have no regular representation within the executive and can therefore be labeled as being excluded. There are four types of categories:

- *Powerless*: The group's representatives hold no executive power, whether at the central or regional level, but they are not systematically and openly discriminated against. For example, the Israeli Palestinians are represented within the Knesset, but have had their representation within the Israeli cabinet blocked through informal measures (Shelef 2010).
- *Discriminated*: The members of the group in question are subjected to explicit and targeted discrimination that effectively blocks their access to executive power. Discrimination can be implemented through denial of political rights, including citizenship, but may also be carried out through a systematic ban of parties that represent the ethnic group. The Kurds have been systematically discriminated by the Turkish regime at least since 1946. Similarly, the governments of Estonia and Latvia discriminate against their Russian populations by denying them citizenship, or at least severely restricting their opportunities for becoming citizens through language proficiency requirements.
- *Regional autonomy*: In this case, the group's elite members are excluded from central power but have been granted access to regional executive power through a scheme of territorial autonomy. By "regional" is meant a substate unit below the level of the state as a whole, such as provinces and federal administrative units, though not local counties. For example, within the former Yugoslavia, the Vojvodina Hungarians enjoyed regional autonomy of this type.
- *Separatist autonomy*: This condition applies if the group's representatives declared de facto independence from, and against the will of, the central government. Here the group has chosen to exclude itself rather than having been excluded. Examples include the Bosnian Serbs walking out of the central government of Bosnia Herzegovina or the Abkhazians having declared independence from Georgia when the country became independent in 1991.

Data on Ethnic Groups' Conflict Participation

Having described our data on ethnic groups and their power access, we now turn to the information sources that reveal their role in conflict. In this and the next two chapters, we rely on a dependent variable that is based on a group-level coding of the Uppsala Conflict Data Program's and the Peace Research Institute Oslo's UCDP/PRIO Armed Conflict Data Set (Gleditsch et al. 2002), with supplementary information from the Non-State Actors data set (Cunningham, Gleditsch, and Salehyan 2009). The ACD2EPR data set assures that each conflict onset is mapped to the corresponding EPR group, provided that the rebel organization expresses an aim to support the ethnic group and members of the group in question participate in combat. We note that there can be more than one organization claiming to represent an ethnic group, and we will return to the mapping between EPR groups and rebel organizations in Chapter 8.

Variables

In the current chapter, we use a dichotomous dependent variable that indicates whether a group experienced an outbreak of conflict with the incumbent government. The onset variable is coded one for a group year during which a conflict started and zero otherwise. We drop observations with ongoing conflict. Since ethnic groups that already enjoy monopoly or dominance by definition cannot rebel against themselves, we also discard these groups from our group-level analysis.

We proceed by describing the independent variables at the group level. Our main independent variables pertain to the power access status of the group in question.

- In many models, we use a dichotomous measure that captures EPR's distinction between *excluded* and *included* groups as defined above.
- In other cases we extend the power access variables to all status categories of EPR by using dummy variables for each of these categories: *junior*, *powerless*, *discrimination*, *regional*, and *separatist autonomy* (using senior membership in power sharing as the reference category, while dropping all cases pertaining to *monopoly* and *dominancet* status since groups cannot challenge themselves).
- Finally, we consider a dummy variable labeled *downgraded*, indicating if the group suffered a decline in EPR status during the last two years.

Demographic group size is measured through EPR-ETH's population size estimates. Denoting the group's population as G and the population of the incumbent as I,[10] we operationalize the relative group size as follows:

---

[10] Note that the incumbent group can consist of several groups. In this case, I is computed as the sum of these groups' population.

- Relative group size $g \in [0,1)$ in the primary dyad is defined as $G / (G + I)$ if the group is excluded and as G/I if the group is included (since the rebelling group left the incumbent coalition and would otherwise be counted twice).

We also include a measure reporting on previous conflict history:

- The count variable *number of previous conflicts* indicates the number of conflicts the group has experienced since 1946 or the independence of the country.

We introduce a number of variables to control for country-level properties:

- Logged *GDP per capita* of the country as a whole, lagged (Penn World Table 7.0, see Heston, Summers, and Aten 2011).
- Logged *population size* of the country, lagged (Penn World Table 7.0, see Heston et al. 2011).
- Dummy variable *ongoing conflict* based on the ACD2EPR conflict data indicating if there was an ongoing conflict involving any other group in the country during the preceding year.
- Number of years since the previous conflict, entered as a nonlinear function, based on natural cubic splines with three knots (see Beck, Katz, and Tucker 1998).
- Finally, since we contrast ethnic exclusion as distinct from general differences in degree of democracy and autocracy, we consider a measure of the extent to which countries are democratic (Scalar Index of Polities, see Gates et al. 2006).[11]

Results

Having described the data and the main variables, we are now ready to evaluate our hypotheses on the effect of political horizontal inequality. This section starts by presenting descriptive statistics followed by multivariate regression analysis that allows us to control for potentially confounding factors.

Our data set contains 29,740 group years all pertaining to politically relevant ethnic groups in independent states from 1946 through 2009, excluding all years associated with ongoing conflict. Of all these observations, only 207 group years featured conflict onset. This suggests that the outbreak of conflict is very much a low-probability event. As a first assessment of H4.1,

---

[11] The Scalar Index of Polities (SIP) democracy measure combines information on the regulation of executive recruitment and executive constraints from the Polity data (Jaggers and Gurr 1995) with data on the extent of political participation from Vanhanen (2000). The conventional Polity index has been criticized for relying on coding of "factionalized competition," which could reflect political violence (see Vreeland 2008). Using the SIP measure allows us to avoid the problems of factionalized competition in the conventional Polity data as well to take into account the participation dimension, which is largely ignored in the institutional focus of the Polity data (see, e.g., Paxton 2000; Vanhanen 2000).

TABLE 4.1. *Comparing Excluded and Included Groups' Conflict Propensities*

	Group Years	Onsets
Group included	8,951	29 (0.32%)
Group excluded	20,582	178 (0.86%)
Total	29,533	207 (0.70%)

Table 4.1 compares excluded and included groups as regards their conflict proneness.[12] Whereas the former category experienced as many as 178 outbreaks, the latter merely contains 29 such cases. These numbers translate into starkly different relative frequencies: the marginalized groups attained a conflict onset frequency of 0.86% per year, while the rate for incumbent ones groups is merely a third of this frequency, 0.32%. In this simple cross tabulation, the difference between the two power status classes is clearly significant ($p > 0.001$). This is a first, albeit crude, indication that power access does reduce the frequency of conflict, as suggested by H4.1.

We proceed by breaking up the composite cases of included and excluded groups into their respective EPR power status categories. Table 4.2 reports on the results of this exercise. Again, the descriptive statistics correspond to our expectations. The most privileged groups are those that experience the least conflict, and not surprisingly we see no conflict onsets involving dominant groups. Senior partners in power sharing arrangements have as low a conflict rate as 0.23%, compared to junior partners whose rate is much higher (0.37%). The excluded groups, however, exhibit more variation: as would be expected, those groups that enjoy at least regional autonomy experience the least conflict, namely in only 0.47% of the years, followed by powerless groups (0.64%). When we turn to discriminated groups, the likelihood of onset increases to 1.24%. Finally, the special case of separatist autonomy, that is, of self-excluded groups, corresponds to an extremely high rate of 5.23%.

Descriptive statistics are useful to provide a first assessment of whether power access influences conflict behavior. Yet, it is difficult to test the other hypotheses in this way, and we cannot rule out that other, confounding factors might make the grievance effects spurious. Therefore, we introduce a series of multivariate regression models that allow us to compare the influence of several independent variables simultaneously. In all these models, we use the same sample as in the descriptive analysis, namely all group years from 1946 through 2009 except politically dominant groups, and those that are not politically relevant or characterized by ongoing conflict. Subject to data availability, this leaves us with a sample of 28,302 observations. The analysis is conducted by

---

[12] Again, it should be noted that groups enjoying monopoly or dominance have been dropped from the included category since our conflict variable only records challenges to state power.

TABLE 4.2. *Ethnic Groups' Conflict Propensity by Power-Access Category*

	Group Years	Onsets
Included groups:		
Monopoly	1,846	0
Dominance	2,105	0
Senior Partner	3,074	7 (0.23%)
Junior Partner	5,877	22 (0.37%)
Excluded groups:		
Regional Autonomy	5,320	25 (0.47%)
Powerless	9,735	63 (0.64%)
Discriminated	5,038	63 (1.24%)
Separatist Autonomy	489	27 (5.23%)
Total	33,484	207 (0.61%)

means of logit regression models with robust, country-clustered standard errors and corrections for temporal dependence according to Beck et al. (1998).

Our main results are displayed in Table 4.3. All three models reported measure the effect of a series of group-level properties in addition to country-level controls. We start by considering Model 4.1, which introduces a dichotomous classification of power access (see Table 4.1 above). In agreement with H4.1, the *excluded* dummy variable has a strong positive effect that is highly significant as well. There is also convincing evidence in favor of H4.2, since the *downgraded* indicator is also substantively and statistically significant. Moreover, we likewise detect a positive effect of relative group size in support of H4.3. Finally, turning to our final group-level measure allows us to corroborate H4.4, which links rebellion to the number of previous conflicts. Moreover, we find that the influence of two out of our three country-level control variables can be safely distinguished from zero. Ongoing conflict elsewhere in the country significantly increases the probability of conflict. Unsurprisingly, ethnic groups in wealthy countries are less inclined to be involved in violent conflict with the government. The only control variable that seems to have no effect is the overall population size of the country, which is one of the most robust correlates of civil war risk at the country level (Hegre and Sambanis 2006).

Proceeding to Model 4.2 enables us to disaggregate the dichotomous categorization of included and excluded groups. Using senior partners in power-sharing arrangements as the base category, the series of categorical variables successively decreases the access to executive power, as was done with descriptive statistics in Table 4.2. As we move down this scale, we notice that the coefficients increase and become increasingly significant for each step. More specifically, we find that *junior* power-sharing partners are more conflict prone than senior ones, although not significantly so. As we shift the attention to

TABLE 4.3. *Political Horizontal Inequality and Group-Level Onset of Civil War, 1946–2009*

	Model 4.1	Model 4.2	Model 4.3	Model 4.4
Group-level variables:				
Group Excluded	1.0958**		0.7086*	1.2182**
	(0.2020)		(0.3042)	(0.2446)
Junior Status		0.8392		
		(0.5210)		
Autonomy Status		1.1844*		
		(0.5758)		
Powerless Status		1.4248**		
		(0.5294)		
Discriminated Status		2.0008**		
		(0.5048)		
Separatist Status		3.2109**		
		(0.6592)		
Downgraded	1.4816**	1.5762**	1.4879**	1.4305**
	(0.2988)	(0.2935)	(0.3004)	(0.3404)
Rel. Group Size	1.1020**	1.3885**		1.3067**
	(0.3406)	(0.3145)		(0.3941)
Rel. Group Size (Excl.)			1.3578**	
			(0.3978)	
Rel. Group Size (Incl.)			0.0860	
			(0.8046)	
Number of Previous Conflicts	0.6732**	0.5571**	0.6763**	0.7219**
	(0.0742)	(0.0972)	(0.0716)	(0.0897)
Country-level variables:				
Ongoing Conflict, lag	0.6116*	0.3876	0.6126*	0.6664*
	(0.2903)	(0.2882)	(0.2886)	(0.2997)
GDP/capita, lag, log	−0.1982*	−0.1672*	−0.1885*	−0.2303*
	(0.0809)	(0.0727)	(0.0822)	(0.0927)
Population, lag, log	0.0076	0.0827	0.0156	0.0050
	(0.0929)	(0.0895)	(0.0885)	(0.0875)
Democracy, lag				0.6033
				(0.4404)
Constant	−4.1221**	−5.7704**	−3.9416**	−4.5297**
	(1.0654)	(1.0971)	(1.0573)	(1.0498)
Observations	28,302	28,302	28,302	26,306

Robust standard errors in parentheses; estimates for peace-year correction not shown.

** $p < 0.01$, * $p < 0.05$.

the excluded categories, the coefficients increase even further, culminating with *discriminated* status. Again, we treat *separatist autonomy* as a special case with extremely high levels of conflict, due to their extraordinary challenge to the central authorities, and in many cases involving prior mobilization. The other group-level indicators replicate the behavior of Model 4.1, thus confirming all four hypotheses (although H4.3 only approximately). Moreover, there are no major differences as regards the country-level controls.

We are now ready to study Model 4.3, which provides a more nuanced assessment of the size effect as stipulated by H4.3. While the two previous models captured these effects for all ethnic groups, the current model distinguishes between excluded and included groups. This distinction enables a more precise evaluation of the grievance dimension. Instead of measuring group size across the board, we divide this variable into two components by interacting it with the dummy variables corresponding to excluded and included groups, respectively. The results indicate that relative group size increases conflict propensity if the group in question is excluded. In contrast, the relative size of incumbent appears leave conflict propensity mostly unchanged.

We have argued that exclusion is distinct from general differences in degree of democracy and autocracy, and that ethnic exclusion is more relevant for the motivations to resort to conflict than the presence or absence of democratic institution in terms of individual representation. Although ethnic exclusion and democracy are clearly conceptually distinct, and ethnic exclusion can occur under relatively competitive democratic institutions, it is also the case that ethnic exclusion is likely to be more widespread in nondemocracies. To ensure that our results regarding exclusion do not arise as an artifact from not considering political democracy we test the relationship between political democracy and conflict directly in Model 4.4. Consistent with previous research using the polity data, we find no statistically significant effect of political democracy on the outbreak of ethnic civil war at the group level (see Wimmer, Cederman, and Min 2009). However, the coefficients for excluded and downgraded groups remain large and statistically significant, confirming our argument that ethnic exclusion is more relevant for the outbreak of conflict than lack of democracy per se. Additional robustness tests using a curvilinear relations specification of the relationship between democracy and civil war similarly find no consistent effect of democracy on civil war, while the effects of ethnic exclusion and downgrading remain highly statistically significant and consistent with Models 4.1 and 4.4.

While promising, the regression results presented in Table 4.3 indicate effects on the log-odds of conflict that are somewhat difficult to interpret, especially when it comes to the interactive terms. Therefore, we introduce several graphs that report on the implied outcomes in terms of conflict probabilities. Based on the estimation of Model 4.1, Figure 4.2 compares the predicted probability of conflict onset for included and excluded groups while holding all other independent variables at their means. The comparison yields a clear picture: excluded

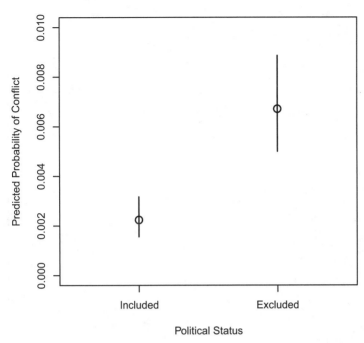

FIGURE 4.2. Comparing the effect of power access status on civil war onset.

groups are much more likely to rebel than included ones. Their conflict probability exceeds 6.8%, which is about three times as high a conflict propensity as for the ethnic groups in power. The respective confidence intervals (which correspond to two-sided standard errors with $p > 0.05$) are well separated, thus indicating that the difference between the two basic status categories is statistically quite robust.

We illustrate the results of Model 4.2 with an expanded graph (see Figure 4.3). This illustration reports the predicted conflict propensity for each separate EPR power status category. The figure confirms, and renders more intuitive, what we have already found in Table 4.3. Indeed, the conflict likelihood increases gradually with decreasing power access, moving from left to right in the graph. As would be expected, the most inclusive category, which pertains to *senior* partners in power-sharing arrangements, is the one that is the most pacific (predicted annual onset probability = 0.13%), followed by *junior* partners, which experience a probability of onset more than twice as high (predicted probability = 0.31%). When we turn to the excluded groups, we can see that the likelihood of conflict increases still further. Groups enjoying *regional autonomy* have a predicted probability of 0.44%, *powerless* ones a probability of 0.55%, and *discriminated* ones a probability of 0.97%. In agreement with the coefficient estimates reported for Model 4.2, we find that *separatist autonomous*

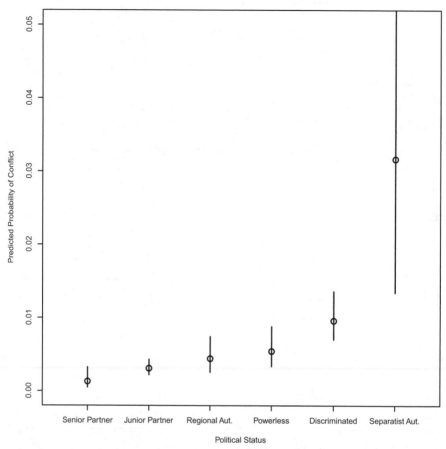

FIGURE 4.3. Comparing the effect on civil war onset for EPR categories.

groups are extremely conflict prone (predicted probability = 3.24%), however, with large error bands due to few observations.

   Having found very strong support for the general claim that power access is negatively related to conflict risk, as stated by Hypothesis H4.1, we now turn to the consequences of downgrading or reversals in power status. According to H4.2, groups that lose power should experience a much higher risk of conflict than other groups. Based on Model 4.1, Figure 4.4 provides a straightforward comparison of the predicted probabilities for those groups that suffer a loss of power status to those that do not. The graph reveals that downgrading leads to a massive increase in conflict risk, from 0.46% to 2.0%, or an almost fourfold increase.

   Our graphical investigation of the key hypotheses proceeds with an evaluation of H4.3, which postulates a size-dependent increase of conflict probability for excluded groups. Using 0.05 error bands, Figure 4.5 plots the predicted

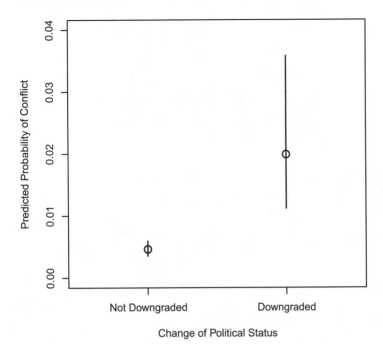

FIGURE 4.4. The effect of status reversals on the probability of civil war onset.

probability of conflict as a function of relative group size for excluded and included groups (see the upper and lower curves with dark and light gray error bands, respectively). Whereas the size of the incumbent groups makes little difference for the probability of onset, the effect is strongly increasing for the excluded ones. Furthermore, except for very small relative sizes, the error bands are clearly distinct for the two categories, thus indicating that the two types of groups are very different in terms of conflict risk. As postulated by H4.3, demographic size should have a much higher conflict-inducing effect for excluded groups that voice grievances more readily than included ones. The separation in terms of size dependence is a strong indication that demographic variables operate together with grievances rather than being mere proxies for resource endowments.

Finally, we consider the role of conflict history as stipulated by H4.4. Based on results drawn from Model 4.1, Figure 4.6 displays the predicted probability of conflict onset for increasing numbers of previous conflict. The graph suggests that the more groups are exposed to conflict, the more likely they become to experience renewed conflict onsets. For the maximum number of prior onsets, the probability of conflict rises above 0.2 per annum, although the small number of cases that falls into this category broadens the error bands. All in all, H4.4 receives very strong support based on this graphical depiction.

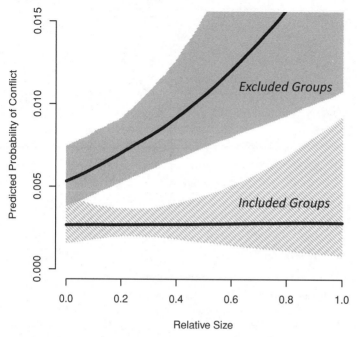

FIGURE 4.5. Conflict propensity of included and excluded groups as a function of their relative size.

Validating the Causal Arguments

Although suggestive, the statistical evidence presented in this chapter does not prove that the mechanisms that we have highlighted actually generate the observed relationship. In this section, we present a brief analysis of some of the specific conflict onsets that are consistent with our results, focusing on the four main hypotheses in this chapter. Our intention here is to provide examples that can help establish whether our postulated mechanisms actually operate as expected; presenting full-fledged case studies with original material for each conflict is beyond the scope of what we can cover in this book. However, we will also consider the main peaceful anomalies where we would have expected conflict and assess what lessons can be learned from these. Finally, this section discusses the robustness of our findings, especially as regards the threat of endogeneity.

We first turn to our most basic claim as formulated in H4.1, which links inhibited power access to a heightened risk of war. Table 4.1 shows that by far the largest number onsets can be found among the excluded groups. Apart from the special case of separatist autonomy, to which we will return, our theory expects discrimination to generate especially explosive grievances. Of these numerous cases (there are as many as 62 onsets), some clearly involve repressive

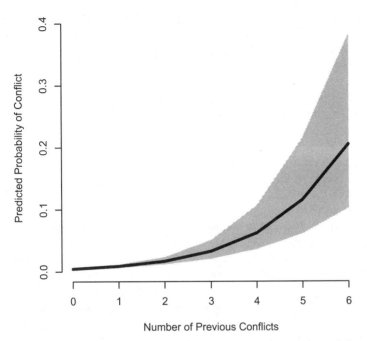

FIGURE 4.6. Conflict propensity as a function of the number of the group's previous conflict onsets.

states adhering to explicitly ethnonationalist ideology and discriminated groups reacting violently to such treatment.

We start our exploration of discriminated groups by studying the conflicts associated with the Turkish Kurds. Modern Turkey under the leadership of Mustafa Kemal Atatürk, emerging out of the ruins of the Ottoman Empire after the end of World War I, has adhered to an especially ambitious program of nation building. In an effort to modernize and centralize state power, the Turkish nationalists distanced themselves from the religious identities of the *ancien régime*. However, the commitment to secular patriotism did by no means imply ethnic inclusion, and ironically actually weakened the religious bonds that had previously held some ethnic groups together, most notably the Turks and the Kurds (Kirisci and Winrow 1997, p. 97). Categorically refusing to recognize the country's ethnic diversity, the Turkish national ideology consistently blocked the minorities' political representation and resorted to discriminatory and repressive measures to thwart any challenge to Turkish identity (Gunes 2012).

Kurdish nationalism developed in direct reaction to the Turkish nation-building project. The Kurds rebelled as early as in the 1920s and 1930s (Kirisci and Winrow 1997, p. 100). Although the Turkish state appeared to grow somewhat more tolerant in the early 1970s, especially under Prime Minister

Bülent Ecevit, the government reneged on its initial promises and did not implement any significant reforms. Consequently, the Kurdish nationalist opposition radicalized and came under the sway of the Kurdistan Workers' Party (PKK). Alarmed by the expressions of Kurdish separatism, the military devoted massive resources to control the minority in the 1980s. In 1982 a new constitution was adopted, which reinforced the commitment to Kemalist principles. In 1983, a special law was introduced to ban the use of the Kurdish language in any context (Kirisci and Winrow 1997, p. 111). In response, the PKK launched its insurgency in 1984, which is the year of onset in our data set. In sum, the Kurds in Turkey constitute a classic case of political discrimination causing internal conflict through a grievance mechanism.

In keeping with its historical role as the original incubator of ethnic nationalism, Eastern Europe offers other prominent examples of discrimination triggering conflict. The former Yugoslavia stands out in the post–Cold War period. Our data record two conflict onsets involving discriminated groups, namely the Serb minority in Croatia in 1991 and the Albanians in Serbia (Kosovo) in 1998. In both cases, the respective governments advanced aggressively ethnonationalist projects that explicitly targeted ethnic minorities. Both Croatia under Tuđman and Serbia under Milošević engaged in aggressive nation-building programs that reversed the multiethnic system of federalism of the former Yugoslavia (Brubaker 1996). Because of their geopolitical importance and intensity, the discriminating policies and resulting grievances have been extensively covered in the literature. In his careful study of emotions and ethnic conflict, Petersen (2002) shows how the Tuđman government used anti-Serb symbols, such as the red and white checkered flag associated with the infamous Ustaša regime during World War II and explicitly downgraded the constitutional status of the Croatian Serbian minority, thus expelling Serbs from "almost all day-to-day positions of dominance" in Croatia (p. 228). These ambitious and uncompromising projects triggered armed resistance through an onset of internal conflict in 1991, primarily in the Krajina region of Croatia.

The discrimination of the Albanian minority in the former Yugoslavia has deep roots. It was mitigated through federal reforms granting Kosovo autonomy in 1966. However, in 1989 the Milošević regime abolished the autonomous status of the Albanian-majority province, a move that escalated the already considerable tensions in Serb-Kosovar relations and accelerated the centrifugal tendencies within the federation. This move, combined with other discriminatory practices by the Serb-dominated government in Belgrade, triggered the most immediate violent reaction in Slovenia, Croatia, and Bosnia-Herzegovina, but the tensions rose inexorably in Kosovo in the course of the 1990s as a direct consequence of the Milošević regime's oppressive policies toward the Albanian minority that amounted to "virtual military occupation" (Gagnon 2004, p. 123; see also discussion in Chapter 5). Although the initial organized resistance by the Kosovar community focused on non-violent resistance and developing separate institutions under Rugova's Democratic League of Kosovo, a violent insurgency broke out in 1998 with the emergence of the Kosovo Liberation Army (UÇK), which subsequently triggered Belgrade-led ethnic cleansing and NATO's intervention in 1999.

The Israeli-Palestinian conflict constitutes another textbook example of ethnonationalist discrimination fueling conflict. At the root a classical nationality problem where two peoples claim the same territory, the confrontation started well before the independence of Israel in 1948. Reacting to increasing anti-Semitism in Western Europe, the Zionist pioneers soon opted for Palestine as their homeland. Given that they mostly stemmed from Eastern Europe, it is not surprising that the ideological project was directly inspired by ethnic nationalism originating from that part of the world (Shindler 2002; Shlaim 2009). The British withdrawal from the Palestinian Mandate left a power vacuum that the Israeli Jews used to launch a systematic and effective campaign of ethnic cleansing that drove the vast majority of Palestinians into exile (Pappe 2004; Shlaim 2009). In contrast, Palestinian resistance proved erratic and badly organized, as was the armed intervention by neighboring Arab states that followed the Israeli declaration of independence in May 1948. The onset associated with the Palestinians in 1948 can reasonably be seen as a direct reaction to overt and brutal discrimination as manifested by the Israeli campaign.[13] As a reflection of their intense grievances, the Palestinians refer to the events of 1948 as "Nakbah," the catastrophe. According to Pappe (2004, p. 141), this event has been "kindling the fire that would unite the Palestinians in a national movement. Its self-image would be that of an indigenous population led by a guerilla movement wishing without success to turn the clock back." Palestinians who chose not to flee were subjected to military rule that extended the state's explicitly discriminatory policies to the beginning of the occupation of the West Bank and Gaza in 1967 (Pappe 2004).

This geopolitical upheaval perpetuated explicit discrimination of the Arabs but shifted the target of discriminatory policies from the Israeli Arabs to the Palestinian refugee populations in the occupied territories. While the Jewish state's relations with the former group has been tense but relatively peaceful, relations with the latter group are still characterized by enduring conflict. The most recent case of severe escalation is referred to as the al-Aqsa intifada, a Palestinian uprising that reacted to the deliberately provocative visit to the Temple Mount by prime minister Ariel Sharon in September 2000 (Shlaim 2009). Here we see a clear-cut confirmation of the conflict-fueling effect of discriminatory policies: the conflict onset involving the Palestinians in 2000 reflects the Palestinians' intense resentment, cemented into hatred and a deep sense of hopelessness and humiliation. These grievances resulted from several decades of Israel's oppressive and ethnically biased policies concerning political influence, and more generally all aspects of everyday life.

---

[13] However, there may be some concerns about endogeneity when it comes to the sequence of discrimination and the onset of civil war in connection with Israeli independence.

Our postulated casual pathway passing through grievances receives further support from other cases where discrimination triggers conflict outbreaks. The ethnocratic policies of the state-controlling Burmese help account for a number of long-standing separatist conflicts in Myanmar involving groups such as the Karenni, Kachins, and Shan (Brown 1994). These groups have resisted state-led oppression and assimilatory centralism and retreated into inaccessible terrain, fighting the Burmese state with insurgency tactics (Scott 2009). Likewise, ethnic domination by the Amhara in Ethiopia, first through the imperial regime of Haile Selassie and subsequently the Marxist junta under Mengistu, triggered a series of conflict onsets. These challenges to central power took the form of anticolonial campaigns in response to the government's persistent unwillingness to make concessions in terms of power sharing or regional autonomy (see Scarritt 1993; Young 1996). Whereas the Eritreans managed to secede from Ethiopia in 1991, other groups have been involved in enduring conflict, such as the Somalis in Ogaden.

Other conflict cases are less characterized by ideological claims and counterclaims along ethnonationalist lines, but rather by de facto ethnic domination through overwhelming military force. In Nigeria, Africa's first great post-independence war – the Biafra war that caused over a million casualties overall – was the immediate consequence of a military coup by Northern officers mainly from the Hausa-Fulani ethnic group and the subsequent pogroms against Igbos in the northern region. Despite a federalist state structure, the uneasy cohabitation of Nigeria's three major ethnic groups – the Hausa-Fulani, Yoruba, and Igbo groups – had deteriorated into an intense ethno-political competition over power in the central government. Eventually, a military coup by mostly Igbo officers in January 1966 – intended to reunite the country behind a pan-Nigerian ideology – brought Nigeria's First Republic to an end (Lloyd 1970, pp. 10–11; Ige 1995, pp. 290–6, 303, 309–11). Under the circumstances, the coup rapidly became perceived as an Igbo strike against northern dominance and ignited deep fears in the north of becoming politically excluded (Lloyd 1970, p. 11; Morrison, Mitchell, and Paden 1972, p. 316; Ige, 1995, pp. 319–20). This led to a much more clearly ethnically motivated countercoup by mostly northern officers only six months later, followed by massive anti-Igbo violence in the north. The secession of the self-declared Republic of Biafra – the Igbo-dominated eastern region of Nigeria – in May 1967 was portrayed by the secessionist leaders as a last resort to ensure Igbo survival in the face of a northern-dominated central government. Hence, the ensuing civil war constituted the bloody culmination of this ethno-political power struggle and demonstrates the dangerous consequences of political exclusion in the highly competitive political systems of Sub-Saharan Africa (Diamond 1988).

Many subsequent conflicts in Sub-Saharan Africa were fought mainly among elites, with only modest popular support. Examples include the more recent insurrection of the Ijaws in Nigeria (Zinn 2005), the insurgency against the oppressive "Arabism" of the Sudanese government (Prunier 1995), and the northern rebellions in Côte d'Ivoire in 2002 and 2011 (Vogt 2007; Bouquet 2011; McGovern 2011), as well as other challenges to central rule of the Tuareg, Arabs in Mali 1994 (Humphreys and ag Mohamed 2005), and the Langi/Acholi in Uganda in 1986 (Lindemann 2011). Even Charles Taylor's invasion in Liberia in 1989 drew mostly on support from the Gio and Mano ethnic groups – precisely those groups that had suffered the most under Doe's Krahn-dominated dictatorship (Outram, 1999; Bøås 2001; Ballah & Abrokwaa 2003). All these examples clearly underline the causal mechanisms behind our statistical results, demonstrating how political exclusion or discrimination along ethnic lines may lead to ethnic civil conflicts.

Yet, the most extreme cases of "internal colonialism" are the violent attempts to overturn oppressive and explicitly racist minority rule over large majorities, as illustrated by the African National Congress' struggle against the Apartheid regime in South Africa (which turned violent from 1981); the armed struggle in 1967 against Ian Smith's white supremacists in Rhodesia; the repeated Shiite armed resistance to Saddam Hussein's Ba'athist rule in Iraq in 1982, 1987, and 1991; as well as the violent toppling of the Americo-Liberians in 1980.

Although spanning a wide spectrum from ideologically sophisticated ethnonationalism to brute ethnic domination, these conflict cases all feature at least some measure of reactive grievances protesting the unfair treatment of discriminated groups. The EPR category of "powerlessness" encompasses mostly smaller, marginalized groups. Their limited demographic size explains why they tend to attract less attention from the government than discriminated groups. All the same, grievances are prone to form among members of peripheral groups, especially where the state is seen as exploiting "their" resources. A fitting example is the Acehnese revolt against Jakarta's projection of power and perceived exploitation of the natural gas fields that were discovered in the 1970s. As Aspinall (2007) observes, general grievances along these lines were widespread in Aceh from the late 1970s:

The perception that Aceh's resources were being drained to benefit others remained central to Acehnese discontent over succeeding years. After the fall of Suharto, even a casual visitor to Aceh would be regaled with stories about how "Java," "Jakarta," or "the center" sucked the territory's natural wealth away from it (p. 955).

According to Aspinall (2007), ethnic mobilization was broadened when the Free Aceh Movement (Gerakan Aceh Merdeka, or GAM) successfully managed to transform these general resentments into an effective collective action frame, ultimately leading to a conflict onset in 1990. The occurrence of natural resource riches superficially appears to vindicate the greed-driven account of Collier and Hoeffler (2004) and other political economists. However, the fact that resources captured by the center generate collective action through grievances and appeals to normative principles of fairness is consistent with our theoretical framework and clearly inconsistent with Collier and Hoeffler's account.

It is not difficult to find other examples of small peripheral groups that engage in armed resistance as a response to the state's encroachment on their perceived homeland, especially in cases where the settlement area contains oil fields or other natural resources. Like the Acehnese, the Papuans have revolted against a perceived pattern of exploitation. In the cases of West Papua, the conflict has concerned, among other things, the center's hunger for tropical timber (Sukma 2005, p. 15). Beyond Indonesia, we find a similar pattern of conflict in China's colonization of Tibet (Ye 2007), the Sudanese government's marginalization of the South (Ali et al. 2005), and the Cabindan Mayombe in Angola (Malaquias 2000). These cases generally coincide with Weiner's (1978) stylized conflict type involving the "sons of the soil," who react to the imposition of "alien" rule through immigration campaigns from the center to the periphery, as illustrated by insurgencies in India triggered by the Kashmiri Muslims, the Bodo, the Mizo, and indigenous Tripuri.

The powerless minorities discussed so far are relatively small compared to the state-controlling groups. Yet, the EPR-ETH data set indicates that some African conflicts concern larger, more centrally located groups, whose elites compete for control over the state with representatives of other groups of comparable size. Attempting to overcome ethnic exclusion, elite representatives engage in struggles to secure their access to executive power, as illustrated by the Bakongo who fought the Angolan government through the rebel organization National Liberation Front of Angola (Frente Nacional da Libertação de Angola, FNLA) from 1994 (Malaquias 2000), the Ewe in Togo, who challenged central power in 1988 (Decalo 1996), or the Lari/Bakongo's rebellion in Congo in 1998 and 2002 (Clark 2008). Grievances were clearly present in these cases, even if not necessarily as widespread and deeply rooted in the respective groups' populations as in the more ideological cases referred to above.

The EPR category of regional autonomy entails the mildest form of exclusion since the government has granted ethnic groups considerable autonomous powers. However, nationalist leaders representing such minorities may find the concessions insufficient since they exclude meaningful influence over the state's executive power. Moreover, some representatives may radicalize and claim a higher measure of autonomy all the way to full independence. Typically such radicalized elites splinter away from more moderate politicians who are willing to collaborate with the central government. Such splintering and radicalization often leads to recurrent outbreaks of secessionist conflict, as shown by insurrections by small groups such as the aforementioned Aceh, as well as the Naga, Tripuri, and Manipur in Northeast India (Bhaumik 2007) and the Moro in the Philippines (Coronel Ferrer 2005).

Where the terrain is especially inaccessible, the groups in question may even manage to escape the reach of the state though de facto secession (Scott 2009). As we have postulated, such cases of separatist autonomy will almost certainly end in violent conflict because even weak states are loath to abandon the aspiration of territorial sovereignty, especially given the possible precedent this might set with respect to other minorities (Walter 2006; 2009b; though see Forsberg 2013). This stands in stark contrast to the previous category of regional autonomy, which implies a relatively low risk of conflict compared to other types of ethnic exclusion. The main difference, of course, is that in the case of separatist autonomy, groups themselves decide to shift power to the regional level, rather than autonomy being granted by the government. Interestingly, conflict onsets involving separatist autonomy only seem to occur in Eurasia. Prominent instances include the Abkhazians and the South Ossetians in Georgia (Cornell 2002), the Chechens in Russia (Zürcher 2007), several ethnic groups in Myanmar (Brown 1994; Callahan 2005), and the Kurds in Iraq (Yildiz 2004).

So far, we have considered conflicts that erupt in response to different degrees of ethnic exclusion, from stark cases of discrimination to partly cooperative situations involving far-reaching group autonomy. Although there is considerable variation in the explicitness and intensity of ethnonationalist grievances, the qualitative evidence offers ample support for the causal chain sketched in Chapter 3. According to H4.1, we would expect groups that enjoy access to executive power to experience less conflict, but the hypothesis is, of course, not deterministic.

In fact, we record several onsets involving included ethnic groups. Clearly, power-sharing arrangements can help manage peaceful relations between groups but may also generate violent conflict. When is such a development likely? Our data tell us that, even though the conflict frequency is considerably lower in inclusive ethnic arrangements, several groups that participated in ethnic governing coalitions as junior partners took up arms against the rest of the government (see also Wimmer, Cederman, and Min 2009). The most obvious reason why such cooperation collapses is that radical members of groups that play a secondary role in power sharing are unhappy with the power distribution, especially if clearly underrepresented in relation to their demographic weight. After years of Tutsi minority rule and military oppression in Burundi, the regime allowed for some opening and brought Hutu members into the government in the late 1980s. However, Hutu radicals had little trust in these concessions and considered them "too little, too late" (Lemarchand 1994, p. 132). In 1991, fighters belonging to the radical resistance group Palipehutu took up arms against the government. These events were followed by a larger explosion of violence in 1993 when radical Tutsi officers murdered the democratically elected Hutu president Melchior Ndadaye and several other Tutsi officials (Lemarchand 2004, p. 63).

Other relatively large groups in junior positions that have reacted violently include the Oroma in Ethiopia, the Chadian Sara in 1992, Bosnian Croats in 1993, the Macedonian Albanians in 2001, and the Afar in Djibouti in 1998. However, even where the group in question is small, splintering may lead to extremist groups pushing for secession, as has been the case with the Assamese and Punjabi-Sikh campaigns against Delhi's rule (Mitra 1995).

For obvious reasons, such feelings of underrepresentation are unlikely to apply to groups playing senior roles in governmental coalitions. Besides groups in dominant or monopoly positions, senior partners are least likely to engage in conflict at any rate. When violence does arise, however, the source of conflict is usually a general lack of trust in government. In particular, the fear of being downgraded by other senior partners, particularly those who dominate the armed forces, can prompt representatives of senior groups to opt for early secession rather than risking a status reversal. Despite their formal equal rights within the Yugoslav Federation, the Slovenes and Croats anxiously followed, and eventually experienced first-hand, Milošević's anti-federal, centralizing campaign aimed at boosting Serb influence at the expense of other nationalities. Following the revocation of Kosovo's autonomy in 1988, "Milošević and his allies sought to impose their conservative line on the country as a whole by attempting to undermine the autonomy of the other federal units" (Gagnon 2004, p. 80). Needless to say, these developments generated fear that ultimately undermined the support of moderates in the other republics and tipped the balance in favor of secession in Slovenia and Croatia (Gagnon 2004, p. 81).[14]

Having investigated the support for H4.1 at some length, we now turn to H4.2, which says that downgraded groups should be especially susceptible to civil violence. Our data set contains 20 cases of downgrading followed by conflict. Although this is a relatively small number (and downgrading itself is a rare event), our statistical analysis shows that downgrading entails a much higher risk of conflict (see Figure 4.4 and Table 4.3).

The events leading up to the aforementioned secessionist war of the Igbo against the North in 1967 correspond closely to the conflict-fueling logic of downgrading. In fact, the path to war featured two status shifts. There was initially a shift to perceived Igbo dominance following a coup staged by Igbo army officers in 1966. After losing power to the Northern Hausa-Fulani groups through a countercoup in 1966, however, the Igbo were subjected to intense discrimination that also included massacres, which convinced the group's elite to launch an ultimately ill-fated and violent secessionist bid, which resulted in the Biafran War. Although political economists find it tempting to account for this war in terms of natural resource dependence, most importantly evidenced by the occurrence of oil within Igbo territory, the main logic according to our interpretation stresses a power struggle among ethnic groups, as explicated above. Zinn (2005) likewise stresses the role of coups in changing the political status of different groups as central for conflict.[15]

---

[14] Moreover, there is evidence that this type of fear of future status loss and possible exclusion also extends to junior partners in power-sharing arrangements (see the Online Appendix).

[15] Zinn (2005) shows convincingly that the attempt to capture ethnic causes of war through blunt ethno-demographic measures, such as Collier and Hoeffler's (2004) "domination," which is a dummy variable indicating if the largest ethnic groups make up 45 to 90 percent of the total

Another example of downgrading triggering conflict is the insurgent attack launched by the Lari-Bakongo against the incumbent government of the Republic of Congo in 1998. This was a response to the dominance by the previously excluded Mbochis' having ousted the other groups in June 1997 (Clark 2008). As in Nigeria, the sudden change of fortunes of competing ethnic groups was the main driver of violence. Similar patterns can be observed in other African countries such as Cameroon and Chad.

Another much publicized reaction to a dramatic status reversal occurred in Iraq after the fall of Saddam Hussein. The Sunni loss of power through the fall of the dictator in 2003 inspired armed resistance targeting the Shia-Kurdish governing coalition, as well as invading forces led by the United States, from the following year. Although the United States has tried to encourage cooperation between the different ethnic groups, the December 2011 arrest order for Iraqi vice president Hashemi, a prominent Sunni Arab politician, was seen by many as a move to reassert Shia dominance under Prime Minister Maliki. Further moves in this direction have a high potential for reigniting conflict.

In sum, even a superficial exploration of the conflict onsets following downgrading indicates that the reaction to such traumatic events generates especially intense grievances that increase the risk of conflict outbreak. A sense of unfairly lost entitlement and the lust for revenge fuel such conflict processes, which sometimes even lead to sequences of power shifts through coups and countercoups.

Our statistical analysis of group size confirmed that populous, excluded groups are overrepresented in the conflict statistics, as postulated by H4.3. While the hypothesis was tested with a continuous group size variable encompassing the entire size spectrum, we here focus on the instances of very large excluded groups engaged in conflict as highlighted by our analysis. Onsets where the excluded group is larger than the ethnic group(s) in power are of particular interest since such settings should bring forth intense grievances in response to the "scandal" of rampant underrepresentation.

Such a focus leads us to revisit some of the cases that involve brutal discrimination that were discussed at the beginning of this section. So much has been said and published about the Apartheid regime that we hardly need to produce detailed evidence of how the demographic lopsidedness contributed to its lack of legitimacy (for a summary of the conflict, see Rubenzer 2007). In addition to the Apartheid elite's blatant racism, the small population share of the Afrikaners compared to the excluded and discriminated masses turned the regime into an icon of colonial-style oppression. The Liberian and Rhodesian [Zimbabwean] conflicts ending minority rule also fall into this category. Beyond that,

---

population. Calling for a more explicitly power-sensitive measure of political dominance, in line with the EPR measures of political status, she observes that "[m]inority groups could also control the system, as occurred after the January 1966 coup, or there could be institutionalized power sharing, akin to Nigeria's coalition government of the early 1960s."

the Middle East is, and has been, home to three other dramatic cases of repressive ethnocratic minority regimes, namely Saddam Hussein's Sunni-dominated rule, the Sunni leadership in Bahrain, as well as the Assad family's Alawite domination of Syria. While the former triggered a series of Shiite revolts in 1982, 1987, and 1991 that were all brutally suppressed by the Iraqi military, Syria only shows up in our conflict data in connection with the Sunni-led challenge to power in 1979, and Bahrain not at all. At the moment of writing, however, a civil war is currently raging that pits Assad's murderous regime against the other ethnic groups. Furthermore, Bahrain also experienced a violent revolt against the Sunni power monopoly in 2011, which is beyond the current coverage of the EPR-ETH data. However, these conflicts constitute clear out-of-sample predictions of high conflict risk based on our theory, and our estimation sample does not include any information from the period of the "Arab Spring" in 2011.

We now turn to possible anomalies. Hypothesis H4.3 would be undermined by the presence of large, excluded groups that have remained peaceful. To explore this issue, we consider those large and excluded groups that never saw conflict at any point during our sample period from 1946 through 2009. We found about two dozen cases of excluded groups that are larger than the included groups. Encouragingly, it was possible to account for these potential anomalies relatively easily in most cases. In one case, namely Bahrain, a Shiite rebellion erupted in 2011 targeting Sunni minority rule (see above). In many other instances, we see clear evidence of political violence, such as coups and electoral violence, below the 25 battle deaths threshold used by the Uppsala Conflict Data Program, UCDP (e.g., the coup in Guinea-Bissau in 1980, the Indo-Guyanese in Guyana, and the East Indians in Trinidad and Tobago). One important case of an apparent non-conflict, the Palestinian Arabs in Jordan, turns out to include violent conflict, as evidenced by the Black September conflict in 1970 when the government cracked down on Palestinian refugees and the Palestinians fought back.[16] Another category comprises ethnic groups that did not make it into our strict coding of onset because there was no rebel organization advancing aims in their name despite there being significant recruitment along ethnic lines. Examples include the Mbochi in the Republic of Congo, the Teso in Uganda and the Hill Brahmins and Madhesi in Nepal, and the Sharchops in Bhutan.

Still, some puzzling "non-barking dogs" remain. The relatively wealthy Hausa in Niger were excluded during long periods. However, they dominated the economic life of the country during the authoritarian regimes in place from 1960 to 1990 in which the Djerma-Songhai group very much controlled political power (Ibrahim 1994; Lund 2001). Transborder trade with their kinship in Nigeria helped the Hausa counterbalance the negative consequences of their

---

[16] This event is not included in the UCDP/PRIO Armed Conflict Data Set as it does not fit their criteria for incompatibilities, as the Palestinians neither demanded territory nor control over the government (see Salehyan and Gleditsch 2006, pp. 344–5).

political exclusion. This may explain why ethnic conflicts could be avoided in Niger during that long period (Vogt 2007, pp. 38–9). In the Sudan, finally, some of the northern Arab groups have remained both excluded and peaceful. This could possibly be attributed to their unwillingness to get embroiled in the larger north-south conflict that the country has suffered for decades.

Our fourth and final hypothesis, H4.4, stipulates that previous conflict instances make new outbreaks more probable. A look at the data reveals that the Iranian Kurds have as many as six onsets, followed by the Somali in Ethiopia with five, and the Iraqi Kurds, the Naga in India, and Karenni in Myanmar with four onsets. Extending the scope to three onsets, implying two previous conflicts, adds more conflict groups to the list, including several in Myanmar and India, as well as the Papuans and the East Timorese in Indonesia. These cases certainly exhibited especially harsh discrimination imposed by uncompromising governments. Although there can be no doubt about the reality of grievances in these cases, discrimination can be found in other conflicts as well, as we have seen at the beginning of this section. In addition to persistent discrimination, and our expectation that revenge is a major driver of recurrent strife, conflict recurrence appears to stem from state weakness and group remoteness. Having to cope with several separatist challenges at the same time, as well as political turmoil at the center and interstate disputes with neighboring countries, some states such as Iran, India, Myanmar, and Ethiopia have been unable to sustain a constant pressure on their minorities. As a result, resistance flares up whenever the central government is ready for a new round of repression or succumbs to a period of weakness that can be exploited by peripheral rebel groups.

We end this section on the validity of our mechanisms by returning to a major threat to causal inference, which we introduced in Chapter 3. As stressed by Blattman and Miguel (2010), problems of endogeneity continue to haunt quantitative studies of civil war. It is clear that our main explanatory variable, ethnic groups' power access, is not randomly assigned and could therefore be at least partially dependent on our outcome variable, conflict onset (Fearon 2011; Fearon and Laitin 2011). As pointed out by Fearon (2011), such a bias could emerge because of two reasons. First, it is possible that our expert coders have overstated the extent to which groups are excluded or discriminated in cases that involve armed conflict, while underestimating the same coding for relatively peaceful groups. However, while this is certainly possible, the coding of EPR-ETH was carefully monitored for this eventuality. Ultimately, the burden of proof is on the critics to show that this is the case, and the data set can be corrected should detailed criticism specifying erroneous or biased coding be brought to our attention, which has not happened so far.[17]

---

[17] For example, Fearon (2011, p. 19) criticizes the EPR data set explicitly: "Countries where there has been no ethnic conflict and where ethnic relations have been calm are for that reason judged to have a low value of 'exclusion.'" Yet, he fails to provide evidence of specific cases where the coding can be said to be biased in this manner.

Yet, the second objection has to be taken much more seriously. Indeed, in what Fearon dubs "policy regressions," we have to be worried that what is treated as an independent variable is actually a governmental policy chosen in anticipation of future outcomes that relate directly to the dependent variable (Fearon 2011). This type of bias could lead to either underestimation or overestimation of the effect. If opportunistic governments tune the level of exclusion to "what they can get away with," thus aiming at primarily less threatening groups, the causal effect of the policy variable will be underestimated. As such, this would therefore hardly pose any threat to our findings. Such a pragmatic approach is invoked by representatives of dominant ethnic groups who prefer to keep as much of the state's resources as possible, while at the same time being willing to make concessions in the name of interethnic peace. This sensitivity to power relations could be motivated by ethnic nepotism and more ideologically motivated strategies of ethnic nationalism.

The opposite applies to situations where the government tries to preempt anticipated conflict by excluding threatening groups for security reasons. Such precautionary measures could be implemented in order to prevent ethnic competitors from staging coups from within the government. Applying this argument to Sub-Saharan Africa, Roessler (2011, p. 313) suggests that "ethnic exclusion serves as an expedient mechanism to eradicate perceived enemies." Incumbent leaders may even prefer waging low-intensity wars in peripheral parts of the country rather than running the risk of being backstabbed by ethnic competitors within the governing coalition. As opposed to the previous scenario, this logic would undermine our statistical conclusions because this case of reverse causation biases the estimated effect of exclusion on conflict upward, thus undermining causal inference.

Because neither of these two possibilities is inherently implausible, it is notoriously difficult to establish which, if any, of them applies. For sure, one should not exaggerate the extent to which the decision to exclude groups reflects a quickly changing governmental policy. Quite on the contrary, as demonstrated by the cases of South African Apartheid and Israeli ethnonationalist exclusion of the Palestinians, many instances of political exclusion and discrimination stem from long-standing decisions that are primarily ideological and only indirectly security related. Where the level of political access does change, however, the effect is very much compatible with our grievance-based account. Indeed, the strong conflict-fueling effect associated with the downgrading variable strengthens our belief that our findings are not due to endogeneity, especially in cases where power reversals can be attributed to external shocks, as experienced by Sunnis and Shiites in Iraq after the fall of Saddam Hussein, in the wake of the United States–led invasion in 2003.

This said, it may actually be possible to arrive at a more conclusive answer as regards the two possible directions of reverse causation. Despite the difficulties of finding an exogenous measure of ethnic groups' power access that is not related to conflict, there are historical situations that can be exploited to construct an instrumental variable that fulfills this function. Focusing on internal conflict in post-colonial states, Wucherpfennig, Hunziker, and Cederman (2012) come to the conclusion that the distorting impact of endogeneity has been overstated. By exploiting systematic differences between the strategies of the French and British colonial empires toward ethnic groups, this study instruments for exclusion of each group at the moment of independence. As opposed to the French colonies where ethnic groups' power access mostly follows a straightforward center-periphery logic privileging groups at the coast, the British were much more likely to apply a strategy of "selective indirect rule" that allowed peripheral groups to have a much higher influence than in the French cases. Based on the results from an analysis using this instrument for exclusion, we conclude that our current, uncorrected analysis if anything tends to underestimate the effect of exclusion on conflict onset.

Conclusion

This chapter represents the first step in our empirical evaluation of the postulated link between inequality and civil war onset. As opposed to highly aggregate studies at the country level and research focusing on micro-dynamics, it does so by investigating causal mechanisms at the group level. Rather than investigating grievances directly, we have employed an indirect method that establishes whether ethno-political exclusion of ethnic groups is more likely to trigger conflict than less-exclusive regimes. The EPR-ETH data set allows us to capture groups' access of power around the world and during specific time periods.

Our statistical analysis shows that the less power access a group has, the more likely it is to fight the government (H4.1). This effect becomes even stronger should the group recently have experienced a power reversal (H4.2). As shown in the previous section, a large number of cases confirm the link between impaired power access and conflict-proneness, ranging from groups reacting to discrimination and exclusion in narrowly ethnonationalist regimes to less ideologically driven conflicts.

We also found strong evidence of a demographic size effect, whereby populous excluded groups are overrepresented in the conflict statistics (H4.3). This is an important result, because it suggests that it is not primarily group size itself, viewed as a proxy for the group's resources, but the political framing of the demographic relationship that matters. This strengthens our evidence that conflict is to a large extent driven by grievances, because the perceived injustice should increase with the size of the excluded population, rather than with group size in general.

Finally, the findings confirm that groups that have already been involved in previous conflict are more likely to see new outbreaks of violence (H4.4). However, in this case, it is less obvious that the grievance logic acts as the main engine of conflict. Rather, a second look at the cases of recurrent conflict points in the direction of limited territorial state reach.

In the previous section, we also considered the reasons why causal inference may be less robust, most importantly the threat of endogeneity. Although such concerns cannot be entirely eliminated, we believe that our analysis rests on firm ground given that some of the possible biases actually strengthen our results and short-term changes in our independent variable through downgrading fuel conflict. We refer the reader to the Online Appendix for further details on this issue and other matters relating to the robustness of the results.

These findings are of considerable theoretical importance, because they cast doubt on those studies that deny or downplay the centrality of ethnic grievances in conflict processes. We argue that the main reason why the grievance-skeptics have failed to find evidence of such mechanisms relates to their tendency to use blunt demographic proxies that have very little to do with political aspects of ethnicity. By shifting the theoretical stress from ethnicity to ethnic nationalism, and from merely cognitive to motivational mechanisms, we propose a theoretical framework that puts ethnicity in its proper political context. Yet, our rendering of horizontal inequality does justice to only one dimension, even if perhaps the most important one. In the next chapter, we broaden the conceptual scope of our empirical evaluation of grievance-related conflict mechanisms by considering economic inequalities between ethnic groups.

5

Economic Inequality and Civil War

Horizontal inequality concerns more than political power. Following Stewart (2008a), we have conceptualized it as a multidimensional concept in Chapter 3. Indeed, most studies of inequality evaluate the consequences of differences in wealth and income rather than in terms of political influence. As a complement to the previous chapter, we therefore continue our investigation of group-level effects by considering the impact of economic horizontal inequality.[1]

Again, we are up against what is commonly perceived as a nonresult. As was shown in Chapter 2, the contemporary quantitative literature on civil war finds no evidence for a link between economic inequality and internal conflict. Based on indicators measuring individual wealth distributions, these studies find no statistically distinguishable relationship to internal conflict (e.g., Fearon and Laitin 2003; Collier and Hoeffler 2004). Yet, inequality continues to occupy a prominent place in the qualitative literature on civil wars and has repeatedly been linked to conflict processes (Wood 2003; Sambanis 2005, p. 323; Boix 2008; Stewart 2008a). Earlier research relying on the Minorities at Risk data link found that economically discriminated groups were more likely to mobilize or protest (see, e.g., Gurr 1993a; Goldstone et al. 2010). However, this line of research has tended to look at measures of political instability broader than civil war. Their claims about groups have been largely ignored by much of the conventional civil war literature, which has focused on countries rather than groups. Moreover, in the last few years, some quantitative studies of civil war have started to appear arguing that the current literature's failure to connect distributional asymmetries to conflict behavior may actually be due to inappropriate conceptualization and imperfect measurements, rather than

---

[1] This chapter draws heavily on the approach developed in Cederman, Weidmann, and Gleditsch (2011). We are grateful to Nils B. Weidmann for major conceptual and methodological contributions.

reflecting a fundamental absence of any causal effect (Østby 2008b; see also Cramer 2006; Stewart 2008a).

Following up the main theoretical focus on horizontal inequality, this chapter joins these recent contributions in shifting the explanatory focus from individualist to group-level accounts of inequality and conflict. Because formidable problems of data availability associated with the uneven coverage and comparability of surveys have stood in the way of assessing such differences, most scholars have had to contend themselves with selective case studies or statistical samples restricted to particular world regions.

In order to overcome these difficulties, we combine our newly geo-coded data on politically relevant ethnic groups' settlement areas with Nordhaus' (2006) spatial wealth measures, both with global coverage. Based on this novel strategy, we present a worldwide comparison of economic horizontal inequality and ethnonationalist civil wars. Building directly on the previous chapter, we show that both backward, and to some extent also advanced, ethnic groups are more likely to experience such conflict than those groups whose wealth lies closer to the national average. Moreover, in agreement with Stewart's broad conception of horizontal inequalities, we find that economic inequalities trigger conflict primarily for excluded groups.

Previous Literature on Economic Inequality and Conflict

In Chapter 2, we offered a general survey of the literature on inequality and conflict. We showed that the classical literature dating back to the 1960s and 1970s took a keen interest in the effects of economic inequality. This is hardly surprising, since the ideological battle between East and West during the Cold War revolved around class-based, rather than ethnic, politics. Much of this debate centered on the Third World, where insurgent activities, partly in connection with decolonization, drew inspiration from Marxist writings and attracted considerable Soviet support.

Marx's theory obviously covered much more than political violence. Indeed, this aspect does not play an important role in the overall theoretical edifice other than as a part of his notion of socialist revolution. Within this context, rebellion is viewed as a class-based reaction to sustained capitalist exploitation. As ever larger numbers of workers are exploited, the theory predicts that capital owners' attempt to oppress the masses will give rise to collective grievances that finally trigger a revolt of the working class. In this sense, "the expropriators are expropriated" (Boswell and Dixon 1993).

Although the original formulation of these ideas in Marx and Engels' writings concerned industrial societies, their more recent intellectual followers extended this intellectual heritage to encompass peasant revolts in the Third World. After all, Russia, the most important country to come under the influence of these ideas. was predominantly rural at the moment of the triggering revolution. As liberation ideologies spread in the Third World after

World War II, the Western academic literature responded to the challenge of analyzing peasant rebellions from a neo-Marxist angle. For example, Paige (1975) theorized such revolts as responses to zero-sum situations that pit land-lords against rural workers. In his classical study of the *Moral Economy of the Peasant*, Scott (1976) applied anthropological methods to uncover how a breakdown in traditional patron-client relations triggers revolutionary conditions. In a more recent study, Booth (1991) argues that persistent inequality and exploitation of peasants by rich landowners in Central America triggered revolutionary challenges to incumbent regimes in the 1970s and 1980s. Focusing on conflict during this period, Booth (1991, p. 34) claims that

economic development trends worsened the region's historically extreme maldistribution of wealth and income, intensifying grievances among negatively affected class groups.... Such problems led the aggrieved to demand change and sparked growing opposition to incumbent regimes by political parties, labor unions, religious community organizers, and revolutionary groups. Violent repression of opposition demands for reform...not only failed to suppress mobilization for change but actually helped forge revolutionary coalitions that fought for control of the state.

In this account, we can identify a distinctive causal chain starting with persistent inequality leading to grievances among the peasant population, and fueling demands for political change and redistribution. Denied such reforms, and possibly even encountering state-led repression, the aggrieved are more likely to see little choice but to rebel.

An even more recent contribution to this literature has been offered by Boix (2008), who refines the standard argument about inequality and conflict by considering the impact of factor mobility. According to his logic, conflict is likely only in those cases where inequality relates to immobile resources, since wealthy elites are unable to move their wealth abroad should political change threaten their assets. Relying on structural measures of landownership rather than comparisons of income levels directly, Boix reports strong support for a link between wealth differentials and conflict behavior. Likewise, influential formal politico-economic models that take classes or social interests as actors, such as Acemoglu and Robinson (2005), postulate a strong relationship between income distributions, policy preferences, and incentives for violent revolution.

However, these studies stand out as exceptions to the anti-grievance trend that we documented in Chapter 2. Generally, students of opportunity structures and resource mobilization have been critical of positing motivations as explanations of conflict onset, a criticism that also pertains to inequality:

The basic assumption of these theories is that the sources of discontent that lead to violent political conflict are inherent in all societies and that the occurrence of political violence is a function of political opportunities and constraints of the immediate political environment, rather than variations in levels of economic inequality or the intensity of economic discontent (Schock 1996, p. 104).

As we have also found, most prominent studies of civil war have come to similar conclusions. Whether inspired by Marxist or liberal principles, most scholarship on inequality and violence adopts a class-based or individualist perspective, respectively. Yet, another stream of research emerged that stresses skewed wealth distributions that may stem from, or interact with, ethnic cleavages. Broadly compatible with Tilly's categorical inequalities and Stewart's horizontal inequalities, this strand of thinking highlights inequalities between identity groups that are demarcated in other ways than through wealth. In particular, ethnicity serves as the most important criterion of boundary formation. Whereas both Marxist and Liberal scholars expected ethnic differences to fade away through "modernization," students of ethnicity were more convinced of the staying power of ethnic relations (Schock 1996; Cederman 1997, ch. 7).

Early contributions to this research stream were inspired by Marxist ideas of exploitation and accorded economic processes a central role. As we have seen in Chapter 2, Hechter (1975) proposed a theory of internal colonialism that explains how ethnic cores come to dominate the territorial peripheries, such as Wales and Scotland. In this perspective, political dominance leads to a cultural division of labor that allocates low-status jobs to members of the subordinate ethnic groups (Hechter 1978). As later argued by Tilly (1999), political entrepreneurs can use ethnic boundaries for distributional purposes in order to exploit and hoard wealth for the ingroup. High levels of economic discrimination tend to produce reactive identity formation and stronger solidarity within the exploited groups, which in turn tends to spill over into political mobilization and possibly violent revolts.

From a less-materialist perspective that privileges socio-psychological mechanisms such as group apprehension, Horowitz (1985) proposes an explanation of secessionism among "backward" and "advanced groups." As does Hechter's theory of internal colonialism, Horowitz expects less advanced groups to be the most likely to rebel. Having little to lose, these groups are highly motivated by economic grievances and thus less sensitive to the potentially high costs associated with separatist campaigns. However, advanced groups may also opt for exiting the state to the extent that they are unhappy with the revenue-expenditure balance. We will return to the topic of how inequalities in both directions can trigger violence. All in all, Horowitz's findings derive from his erudition and detailed knowledge of a large number of cases, but his propositions are never subjected to systematic evaluation.

Relying on his Minorities at Risk (MAR) data set, Gurr (1993a; 2000b) exposes similar reasoning to quantitative tests. Earlier versions of the MAR data set offer expert assessments of the level of "economic discrimination" but no systematic economic data. Based on these measurements, Gurr comes to the conclusion that economic disadvantages, as well as political ones, fuel the risk of conflict: "Economic disadvantages, especially those associated with discrimination and poverty, are consistently correlated with economic and social grievances and with demands for greater political rights" (1993b, p. 188).

Other recent research attempts use new data sources to evaluate the wealth of ethnic groups.[2] Recognizing the difficulties of measuring horizontal inequalities based on explicit economic data, research emanating from Stewart's research group has so far primarily relied on individual country case studies or a comparison of a few countries rather than large N comparisons (see, e.g., the Stewart 2008b edited volume). The picture that emerges from this research suggests that both disadvantaged and advanced groups are more often involved in internal conflict than groups closer to the country average (Stewart 2008a). Yet, some quantitative studies have attempted to generalize to a larger set of countries. Relying on household surveys conducted in 39 developing countries, Østby (2008a) finds evidence that social horizontal inequality is associated with civil war, although the economic dimension appears to be weaker (see also Østby 2008b). In a follow-up study based on geo-coded conflict and survey data from Sub-Saharan Africa, Østby, Nordås, and Rød (2009) reach firmer conclusions, showing that both economic and social group-level differences appear to drive conflict behavior.

Deriving Hypotheses on Economic Horizontal Inequalities and Civil War

We now turn to our own account of economic inequality and conflict. What are the observable implications of our analytical framework? Building directly on the derivation of causal mechanisms that we introduced in Chapter 3, we develop straightforward hypotheses. The first, and most obvious, expectation is a positive effect of economic horizontal inequalities on civil war onset even when we control for political horizontal inequality. If the causal chain operates as we have postulated, there should be a statistically discernible signal indicating that ethnic groups with per capita income far from the country average have a higher risk of experiencing conflict.

Before stating our hypotheses, however, we need to differentiate between the conflict proneness of advanced and backward groups. As Horowitz (1985) explains, arguments can be advanced for both types of economic horizontal inequalities leading to a higher risk of conflict. Poorer groups, especially those residing in backward and peripheral regions, often desire to break away from the core of their countries regardless of the cost because they perceive themselves to be systematically disadvantaged compared to their wealthier compatriots in terms of economic development and distribution of public goods. Yet, perceptions of disadvantage also characterize members of some relatively wealthy groups, especially if they feel that state-level redistribution denies them

---

[2] In a pioneering statistical test, Barrows (1976) detected an influence of group-level differences on conflict in Sub-Saharan Africa.

the fruits of their success: "Advantaged regions usually generate more income and contribute more revenue to the treasury of the undivided state than they receive. They believe that they are subsidizing poorer regions" (Horowitz 1985, pp. 249–50). Since these groups have more to lose, and are sometimes demographically represented outside their original settlement area, they are typically more cost sensitive as regards secession. However, such cases do occur, as illustrated by the Basques in Spain and the Slovenes in the former Yugoslavia (cf. Gourevitch 1979).

Nevertheless, there is no reason to assume that the effect of group inequality is perfectly symmetric around relative equality. Remaining agnostic as to the relative impact of horizontal inequalities in either direction, we therefore submit these arguments to separate tests:

> H5.1. Relatively poor ethnic groups are more likely to experience civil war than those that are closer to the country average.
>
> H5.2. Relatively wealthy ethnic groups are more likely to experience civil war than those that are closer to the country average.

As we have seen, an uneven wealth distribution is not the only possible type of structural asymmetry. Drawing on Stewart's multidimensional conceptualization of horizontal inequalities, we hypothesize that both economic and political horizontal inequalities contribute jointly to the outbreak of civil war. Even when controlling for political horizontal inequalities, such as groups' exclusion from political power, income inequalities among ethnic groups should increase the risk of civil war. Indeed, Cederman, Weidmann, and Gleditsch (2011) find exactly such an independent impact of the two dimensions. It goes without saying that groups disadvantaged in both ways would be more exposed to the risk of onset than those that suffer from horizontal inequality in one dimension only.

Some scholars argue that there may even be an interaction effect rather than a merely additive relationship between these two types of horizontal inequality. Echoing Hechter's notion of cultural division of labor, this theoretical reasoning also mirrors Stewart's (2008a, p. 18) hypothesis that "political mobilization is especially likely when there are consistent horizontal inequalities, that is both political and economic horizontal inequalities run in the same direction." Based on statistical evidence from Sub-Saharan Africa, Østby (2008a) finds support for a strong interaction effect between interregional asset inequality and political exclusion. Case studies of Côte d'Ivoire (Langer 2005) and Nepal (Murshed and Gates 2005) confirm this finding (see also Stewart, Brown, and Langer 2008, pp. 289–90; cf. Hegre, Østby, and Raleigh 2009).

Although the consistency argument is intuitively appealing, we derive an asymmetric dependency between the two dimensions. More specifically, we postulate that economic horizontal inequality is conditional on political inequality. Rather than contributing symmetrically to the risk of conflict, political exclusion takes causal precedence because the framing of inequalities in terms of blame attribution should be much easier to justify if the group in question is exposed to alien rule than in power-sharing arrangements. Whether economic inferiority stems from political marginalization or other processes, the presence of power asymmetries makes politicization much more likely.

The first case corresponds to governments' actual favoritism of incumbent groups at the extent of those outside the polity. As we have argued in Chapter 4, politically dominant groups are inclined to favor their own kin not only in terms of political opportunities, but also more broadly, as regards the distribution of both private and public goods. In extreme cases, the central government may neglect the infrastructural needs of entire provinces, as illustrated by Khartoum's lack of investments in Sudan's South before the recent secession (Ali et al. 2005). Moreover, discrimination in terms of business opportunities may follow directly from ethnic nepotism, or indirectly from inferior educational investments in the excluded groups' populations thus reducing their chances to perform economically. Under such circumstances, rebel leaders are able to frame economic inequality along group lines as a result of political decisions made by incumbent groups rather than as a matter of differential resource endowments or skill levels. Of course, there are some examples, such as Saudi Arabia (Byman and Green 1999) and Russia in the 1990s (Treisman 1999), where the center has been able to buy off peripheral groups, but this strategy has its limitations, most obviously because of its costs. Persistent inequality without political influence will give rise to a sense of frustration with the existing political system that could trigger violent protest.

The second case pertains to situations where blocked power access is not the main cause of underdevelopment, but discriminatory governmental policies nevertheless can be blamed for the economic gap. For example, it is possible that the peripheral geographic position disadvantages an ethnic group, or that prior colonial or imperial regimes may have set development back so strongly that the group in question enjoyed a much lower living standard even before the current exclusionary government's rise to power. Whether it is true or not, governmental elites are usually blamed with the economic fate of entire countries since they constitute convenient lightning rods for discontent. As argued by social-psychologists, blame shifting and scape goating may be a convenient strategy for the protection of a group's self-esteem (Hechter 1978; Horowitz 1985; see also Herrera 2005).

The contingent effect of economic horizontal inequalities should apply to disadvantaged groups, thus inviting us to modify H5.1. We would not expect such a dependency in case of economically superior groups. These groups are already likely to have at least some shared power access, and even if they do not, being granted more power is unlikely to solve the problem since their grievances stem from having to share their wealth with other groups. In such cases, the urge to exit the polity will be strong indeed, as illustrated by the

Slovenian and Croatian declarations of independence from Yugoslavia. Little would have placated these groups short of almost total budgetary autonomy, and it is even less probable that the less wealthy but politically powerful Serbs would have granted them such concessions.

Taking into account the limited scope of the interaction effect, our final hypothesis on economic horizontal inequality summarizes these theoretical expectations:

> H5.3. Economic inequality makes less wealthy, excluded groups more likely to experience civil war.

Global Data on Horizontal Inequalities and Other Dimensions

Our theoretical expectations must now be confronted with empirical evidence. As we have seen, data availability constitutes a major stumbling block in studies of inequality and conflict. So far, virtually all existing statistical studies of horizontal inequalities have used survey data on economic welfare by households, as collected by the Demographic and Health Surveys (DHS) project.[3] Although these data offer a relatively direct measure of wellbeing and are therefore useful as grievance indicators, the information source and survey approach are associated with a number of practical limitations. The DHS project is limited to a selection of primarily developing countries, relatively few countries that experience conflict are covered, and surveys in conflict-affected countries tend to cover only those areas not directly affected by violence. Moreover, information on ethnic affiliation or the geographic location of households is only available in some of the surveys.[4] Although the surveys are constructed so as to be nationally representative, the number of responses for an ethnic group or location may often be very low, and there is no guarantee that the samples will be representative. Finally, survey data are subject to a host of potential response biases, both conscious and unconscious. For example, aggregate responses from surveys may well be systematically biased against finding evidence of inequality if poorer individuals overstate their assets and richer individuals consistently understate theirs. In sum, survey data may be helpful for many purposes, but the DHS data do not provide a plausible alternative for evaluating the role of horizontal inequalities on a global basis, although they can serve as a useful complement (see below).

Given these difficulties, it makes sense to consider spatial data sets as an alternative to survey-based methods. The only broadly available cross-national

---

[3] For these data, see http://www.measuredhs.com/.
[4] See, e.g., Baldwin and Huber (2010), who draw on survey data from 46 countries to evaluate the impact of ethnic diversity on public goods provision. As noted above, Østby (2008a; 2008b; Østby et al. 2009) also uses survey data in her studies of horizontal inequalities and conflict in Sub-Saharan Africa.

data source on variation in wealth within countries is the G-Econ data set, developed by Nordhaus (2006; see also Nordhaus and Chen 2009).[5] The G-Econ data set tries to assemble the best available data on local economic activity within countries for geographical grid cells, and convert these to comparable purchasing power parity figures to allow for meaningful comparisons. The resolution of the spatially explicit data set is one-degree square grid cells. The data are constructed from a variety of sources, including regional gross product data for the lowest available political subdivision, estimates of regional income by industry, and estimates of rural population and agricultural income. The specific methodologies differ by country and data availability. The database has global coverage, but the temporal scope is limited to a single year, namely 1990.[6] We therefore restrict our analysis to the post–Cold War period.[7]

Despite its relatively broad coverage, there are a number of disadvantages to the Nordhaus data for testing propositions on horizontal inequalities. Many of the classical cases of substantially wealthier-than-average ethnic groups such as the Chinese in East Asian Countries or Indians in East Africa that some researchers such as Chua (2003) have argued are particularly likely to become involved in ethnic conflicts are dispersed. Since these groups lack a spatially concentrated homeland or region, spatial data cannot be used to estimate relative wealth differences among groups. Any measure of the value of economic production is strictly speaking a "flow" measure and hence an imperfect proxy for the "stock" of wealth, although this criticism obviously applies with equal force to national-level productivity measures. Since the quality varies considerably across countries, the data are likely to understate the extent of inequality in countries with poor data coverage. Indeed, in some countries the official data may be of such poor quality that the variance is suppressed and the advantages over survey reports may be questionable. We will return to these issues at the end of this chapter.

Based on the G-Econ data, Buhaug et al. (2011) present the first global analysis of the relationship between spatial inequalities and the location of civil conflict outbreaks. However, their research design focuses on local measures of inequality across geographic grid cells and the specific location where conflict first breaks out and does not capture group-level participation or wealth differences, which may extend far beyond the original onset location. Another useful approach estimates the wealth of regional subunits of states (Sambanis

---

[5] Another promising avenue is to use light emissions as a proxy for economic activity, see, e.g., Elvidge et al. (2009). Chen and Nordhaus (2011) report that this data source primarily is useful for poor countries with low light emissions and where official statistics are especially poor.

[6] G-Econ 2.2 provides separate estimates for gross cell products in 1995 and 2000. However, these estimates simply adjust the 1990 estimates by updated population figures for 1995 and 2000. As such, the 1995 and 2000 figures contain no independent economic data over the 1990 values.

[7] Since it is well known that relative inequalities, as opposed to absolute measures of wealth, are characterized by considerable stability and inertia over time, relative inequalities in 1990 seem plausible proxies for prior group inequality ratios (Tilly 1999; Stewart et al. 2008).

and Milanovic 2011; Deiwiks, Cederman, and Gleditsch 2012), but these do not always overlap with ethnic group settlement patterns, sometimes intentionally breaking up ethnic groups or making groups minorities in larger regions. A more direct assessment of horizontal inequalities requires geo-coded data on ethnic groups, and, in view of H5.2, also information about their access to executive power.

In order to obtain spatial estimates of economic performance for EPR groups based on the Nordhaus grid, we need information on their settlement areas or region. Since this overlay operation requires data on the precise extent of these regions rather than a simple textual description, existing data sets such as Minorities at Risk are insufficient. We therefore rely on the GeoEPR data set, a comprehensive geo-coded version of the EPR groups (Wucherpfennig et al. 2012). The most recent version of GeoEPR builds directly on the newly updated nonspatial EPR-ETH database that offers improved coding with coverage from 1946 through 2009. In short, GeoEPR provides two types of information about ethnic groups. First, for each group in EPR, the data set categorizes the type of settlement pattern, distinguishing between regional, urban, and migrant groups (plus mixed categories). For all groups with a regional base, GeoEPR represents the settlement area of the group as a polygon (or a set of polygons, if there are more than one distinct settlement cluster for a group in a country). In contrast to earlier geocoding attempts, GeoEPR also tracks major changes in the settlement pattern of a group over time, including those resulting from ethnic cleansing.

Deriving Operational Measures

The G-Econ data allow for deriving ethnic group-specific measures of wealth by overlaying polygons indicating group settlement areas with the cells in the Nordhaus data. Dividing the total sum of the economic production in the settlement area by the group's population size from the spatial data enables us to derive group-specific measures of per-capita economic production, which can be compared to the nationwide per capita product.

A visual illustration helps explain the estimation of group GDP per capita from the Nordhaus data. Figure 5.1 shows the G-Econ estimates as grey cells, where darker shadings indicate wealthier cells. The map shows the spatial variation in wealth across the Yugoslav federation in 1990, based on the CShapes data set for the historical boundaries (Weidmann, Kuse, and Gleditsch 2010). Relatively wealthy pockets appear primarily in the northwest of the country, in the constituent republics of Slovenia and Croatia. Compared to the other parts of the country, Serbia shows up as a generally poor region.

Together with the settlement areas of GeoEPR, the G-Econ data can now be used to estimate group wealth spatially. Figure 5.1 also shows the settlement regions for the Slovenes and the Albanians. Using similar techniques as those pioneered in Buhaug et al. (2008) and Cederman, Buhaug, and Rød (2009), we

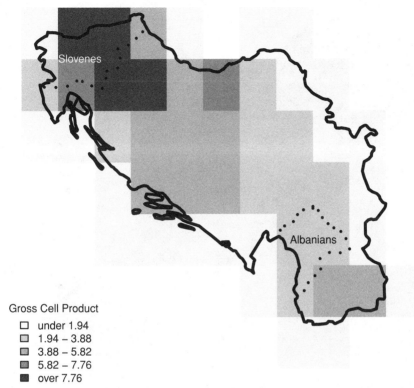

Gross Cell Product

☐ under 1.94
☐ 1.94 – 3.88
▨ 3.88 – 5.82
▨ 5.82 – 7.76
■ over 7.76

FIGURE 5.1. G-Econ cells for Yugoslavia overlaid with GeoEPR group polygons for Slovenes and Albanians.

derive an indicator of group wealth by summing up the (population-weighted) proportions of the Nordhaus cells covered by a group.[8] For example, as a result of this procedure, the Slovenes get a high score, since their settlement region is located in the rich parts of Yugoslavia. Measuring horizontal inequality as the ratio of the group's GDP per capita estimate divided by the average value for the entire country, Figure 5.2 shows the result of this computation for Yugoslavia, depicting wealthier groups in darker shades and poorer ones in

---

[8] This spatial aggregation process retrieves all the G-Econ cells that are covered by a group polygon and computes the total wealth estimate as the sum of the cell values. However, in a number of cases cells do not align perfectly with group polygons, and there is only a partial overlap between a cell and a group polygon. For these cases, only the overlapping area's wealth should enter the group wealth computation. We estimate the wealth of a partial G-Econ cell by distributing its total value as given in the data set to much finer cells of 2.5 arc-minutes (approx. 5 × 5 km, or 1/576 of the area of a G-Econ cell). This distribution is population weighted, that is, it assumes that wealth is proportional to the number of people in each of the smaller cells. This weighting was done using the Gridded Population of World (GPW) data set (version 3, available at http://sedac.ciesin.columbia.edu/gpw/).

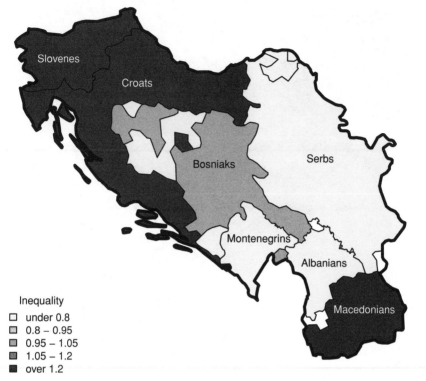

Inequality
- ☐ under 0.8
- ☐ 0.8 – 0.95
- ☐ 0.95 – 1.05
- ▨ 1.05 – 1.2
- ■ over 1.2

FIGURE 5.2. Result of spatial wealth estimation for groups in Yugoslavia.

lighter shades. Slovenes and Croats receive high scores, but the opposite is true for the Albanians in Kosovo, which are among the poorest groups in the country.

As a further illustration, Figure 5.3 shows the same information for the Sudan. Unsurprisingly, the southern and western groups, the latter including the Fur, emerge as the most impoverished in that state. Extending the comparison to Myanmar, we also illustrate the limitations of our spatial approach (see Figure 5.4). Despite considerable wealth discrepancies between peripheral and central areas, the Nordhaus data exhibit very limited variation due to underlying data quality issues. To the extent that similar measurement problems afflict other country cases that experienced conflict, we can expect the effect of inequality to be underestimated by our study.

As explained by Mancini, Stewart, and Brown (2008), there are many different ways to operationalize horizontal inequalities, most of which apply to entire countries. In this chapter, we use a straightforward group-level measure of income inequality. Letting y_g denote the GDP per capita of the ethnic group, and y_c the average GDP per capita of all groups in the country, we measure

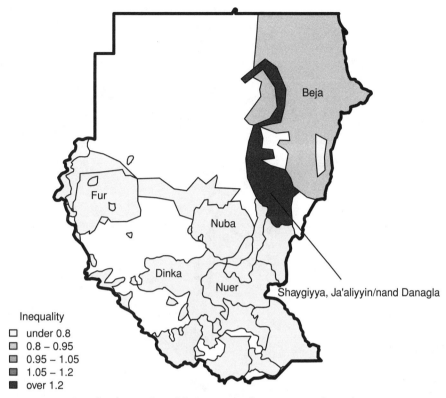

FIGURE 5.3. Result of spatial wealth estimation for groups in the Sudan.

inequality asymmetrically with two variables that correspond to groups that are poorer and wealthier than the country average, respectively:

$$low\_ratio = y_c/y_g \quad \text{if } y_g < y_c,$$
$$1 \quad\quad \text{otherwise;}$$

$$high\_ratio = y_g/y_c \quad \text{if } y_g > y_c,$$
$$1 \quad\quad \text{otherwise.}$$

This operationalization guarantees that deviations from the country mean are always positive numbers above one.[9] For example, a group that is twice as wealthy as the average has *low_ratio* = 1 and *high_ratio* = 2, and a group that is three times poorer has *low_ratio* = 3 and *high_ratio* = 1.

[9] Note also that this specification differs from Cederman, Weidmann, and Gleditsch (2011), who use zero rather than one as the default value for their asymmetric equality measures. The current formula has the advantage of ruling out discontinuities between zero and one.

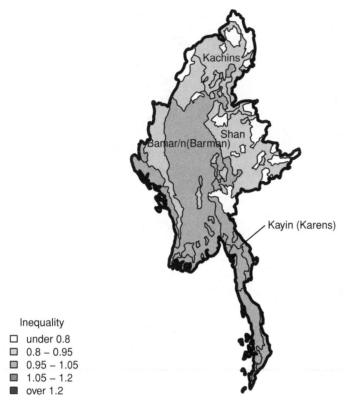

FIGURE 5.4. Result of spatial wealth estimation for groups in Myanmar.

As regards all other variables, we refer the reader to the previous chapter. Indeed, the current analysis relies on the same specification of the dependent and independent variables, as well as the temporal controls.

Results

We are now ready to present the results. Given the limited temporal availability of the inequality data (which refer to 1990), we restrict the sample to group years after the Cold War, from 1991 through 2009. All groups represented in GeoEPR are included.[10] This leaves us with a total of 5,377 group years with only 59 conflict onsets, which constitute a subset of the dependent variable used in Chapter 4. Also in agreement with the previous analysis, we compensate for country-level dependencies by estimating clustered standard errors. Because

---

[10] We drop all dispersed groups, which normally cover the entire territory of a country, except in those cases where dispersed dominant groups interact with minorities that cover only a part of the country's territory, as is the case with the Turks and Kurds in Turkey.

of measurement difficulties, we reduce the sample by discarding all groups that have a population of less than 500,000. Our spatial method becomes unreliable for small population sizes primarily due to the low resolution of the G-Econ data and the limited precision of the population estimates for tiny groups.[11]

Table 5.1 presents the main results. Our starting point is Model 5.1, which replicates Model 4.1 for the restricted sample as described above. The replication confirms that both power access (H4.1) and downgrading (H4.2) continue to have a strong impact on the dependent variable. The other two hypotheses, H4.3 and H4.4, receive weaker support for reasons related to the limited sample. The effect of relative group size does not reach significance due to the censoring of small groups. Likewise, the influence of previous conflicts is blunted by the temporal sample restriction to the post–Cold War cases. Finally, the control variables have the same signs as in Model 4.1, but the variable measuring ongoing conflict fails to reach significance in the current analysis.

We are now ready to test the first two of our new hypotheses (see Model 5.2). Still controlling for political exclusion, we introduce the two ratio variables *low_ratio* and *high_ratio*. Whereas very little changes with regard to political horizontal inequality, this extension of the analysis uncovers an association between relative poverty and conflict, thus confirming H5.1. Figure 5.5 provides a graphical illustration of this finding. The probability of conflict onset in a given year increases steadily as a function of *low_ratio*. Compared to parity, which corresponds to a relatively low probability of conflict of 0.004, groups that are three times poorer than the country average more than double their conflict propensity to roughly 0.01. The error bands that mark the 5th percentile are wide for high deviations from the country average due to data scarcity, but the increase of the curve is very clear.

However, the conflict propensity of groups that are wealthier than the country average is even higher than for less wealthy groups, but the estimated effect is only statistically distinguishable from zero at the level of $p = 0.07$. These results suggest that groups that are wealthier than the country average may have a higher likelihood of being involved in conflict, but there is only limited support in the data for a clear trend, which may be due to both large variation in conflict propensity and a limited number of groups notably wealthier than the country average. Moreover, as previously mentioned, our results are unable to consider horizontal inequalities involving ethnic groups that are not spatially concentrated or discrete. All in all, we believe our results are consistent with a tendency for wealthier groups to be more prone to see conflict, but we do not have strong evidence for the robustness of H5.2.

---

[11] This sample restriction drops a number of tiny groups, especially in China and Russia, for which no reliable spatial estimate can be computed (see the Online Appendix).

TABLE 5.1. *Economic Horizontal Inequality and Group-Level Onset of Civil War, 1991–2009*

	Model 5.1	Model 5.2	Model 5.3
Group-level variables:			
Group Excluded	1.2411**	1.2730**	1.1371**
	(0.3671)	(0.3746)	(0.3557)
Low Ratio		0.4736**	
		(0.1120)	
High Ratio		0.6329	
		(0.3440)	
Excluded × Low Ratio			0.5233**
			(0.0944)
Excluded × High Ratio			0.5160
			(0.2749)
Included × Low Ratio			−1.1450
			(1.0853)
Included × High Ratio			0.8760
			(0.8642)
Downgraded	1.9858**	1.9469**	1.9275**
	(0.4497)	(0.4562)	(0.4559)
Rel. Group Size	−0.2000	−0.0277	−0.1441
	(0.6348)	(0.6721)	(0.6467)
Number of Previous Conflicts	0.1784	0.2251	0.2306
	(0.1581)	(0.1795)	(0.1758)
Country-level variables:			
Ongoing Conflict, lag	0.3596	0.3701	0.3526
	(0.4078)	(0.4081)	(0.4071)
GDP/capita, lag, log	−0.2334*	−0.3239*	−0.3224*
	(0.1144)	(0.1310)	(0.1331)
Population, lag, log	0.0532	−0.0039	−0.0133
	(0.1466)	(0.1803)	(0.1815)
Constant	−2.7347	−2.9462	−2.4067
	(1.5729)	(1.6779)	(2.0276)
Observations	5,377	5,377	5,377

Robust standard errors in parentheses; estimates for peace-year correction not shown.
** $p < 0.01$, * $p < 0.05$.

The other variables behave similarly to the previous model. Again, we depict graphically our findings. Figure 5.6 reveals that the predicted probability of conflict increases considerably with increasing relative group wealth. Yet, as we have discussed above, the error bands are extremely broad and almost encompass zero.

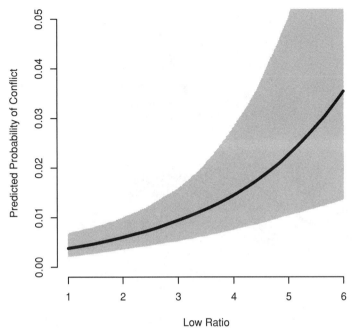

FIGURE 5.5. Conflict probability for groups less wealthy than the country average.

Having considered H5.1 and H5.2, we now test H5.3, which postulates that the causal impact of economic horizontal inequality hinges on power access. Retaining the specification of the previous model, Model 5.3 introduces interaction terms that separate the consequences of economic inequality according to whether the group in question is included or excluded. According to our hypothesis, the less wealthy groups should be consistently overrepresented in the conflict statistics. We find strong evidence that excluded and less wealthy groups are more prone to conflict, and this is the only interaction term that clearly reaches significance at conventional levels. However, we note that the coefficient estimate for the interaction term between excluded and high ratio is of similar magnitude as the interaction term with less wealthy groups and reaches significance at 0.05 in a one-tailed test. This suggests that there is some tendency for wealthier excluded groups to be more likely to be involved in conflict, even if the result may be less consistent than for relatively poorer groups. We stress again that there are few cases of excluded wealthier groups. It may even be the case that the greater resources for using force against the state that wealthier excluded groups can muster could make such groups more likely to receive accommodation and become included. For included groups we find that both of the interaction terms are very far from significant, and the odds

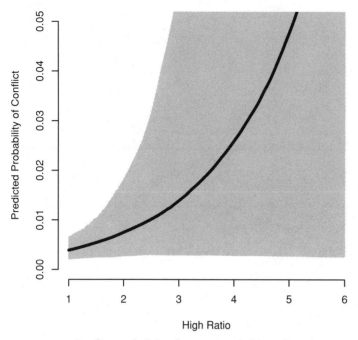

FIGURE 5.6. Conflict probability for groups wealthier than the country average.

of conflict for included groups at any level of wealth are always lower than those for excluded groups. For the control variables we again detect no major changes compared to Model 4.2.

As stated in Chapter 4, interaction terms can be tricky to interpret based on tabular results alone. Therefore we offer a graphical illustration of the conditional logic implied by H5.3 (see Figure 5.7). The chart plots excluded and included groups' predicted probability of conflict against their relative poverty compared to the country average. The upper curve, which belongs to the marginalized groups, reflects a strongly positive effect that is clearly separated from the conflict propensity of incumbent groups for the range of inequality ratios up to about three. Beyond that level, the error bands become so wide that the effects can no longer be clearly distinguished.

In order to bring out the difference between included and excluded groups more clearly, we present in Figure 5.8 the first-order difference of conflict probability for excluded groups, using the included ones as the base of comparison. Based on this analysis, we conclude that excluded groups are affected much more strongly by inequality than included ones. In fact, the differential effect is significant for the range moving from parity to ratios of relative underdevelopment amounting to a factor of almost 4.

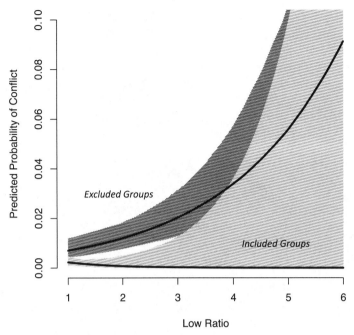

FIGURE 5.7. Comparing the effect of relative poverty on the conflict probability of included and excluded ethnic groups.

Validating the Causal Arguments

Parallel to the validation analysis in the previous chapter, this section offers a brief discussion of selected conflict onsets that support our statistical results. Again, we will evaluate each hypothesis in turn. There are a number of cases consistent with hypothesis H5.1, which states that relatively poor groups are more likely to rebel. Most spectacular are the two Chechen wars that broke out in 1994 and 1999.

There can be no doubt about Chechnya's abject poverty in comparison with other parts of Russia. In fact, the Republic of Chechen-Ingushetia constituted by far the poorest part of the country (Hale and Taagepera 2002). However, in line with our theoretical expectations expressed in Chapter 3, it was not Chechnya's underdevelopment that directly triggered conflict. Rather, it took a nationalist mobilization campaign orchestrated by ethnonationalist entrepreneurs to bring about the rebellion (Herrera 2005; Giuliano 2011). To be sure, the nationalists had plenty of historical grievances to work with. In fact, large parts of the Chechen population had been deported to other parts of the Soviet Union by Stalin's regime after World War II under the pretext that they had collaborated with the Nazi invaders. Although the Chechens were allowed

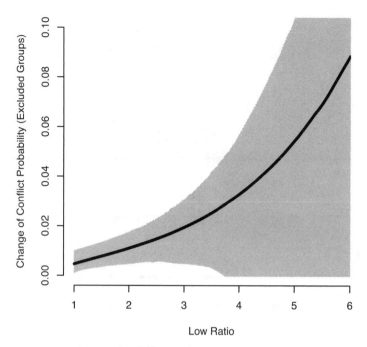

FIGURE 5.8. First-order difference between excluded and included groups.

to return to the Caucasus in the late 1950s, Stalinist repression had severely disrupted the local economy and caused considerable hardship that worsened the economic position of an already-underdeveloped region (Derluguian 2005). Thus, there was a strong sense of nationalist grievance that lingered until the 1990s, despite Soviet transfers and development projects.

Among the ethnic groups in the Russian Federation, the Chechens are not alone in exhibiting nationalist mobilization driven by economic horizontal inequality. Arguing that this pattern was also present in Tatarstan, Tuva, Bashkorostan, and Yakutia, Giuliano (2011, p. 208) uses discourse analysis to trace the grievance mechanism that triggered separatism:

Nationalist leaders framed issues about ethnic economic inequality in order to establish boundaries between titular and nontitular persons. They claimed that titulars were unfairly limited in their own republics because they lagged behind Russians in terms of urbanization, education, and professional achievement. The current system, the nationalist claimed, unjustly privileged Russians and denied full participation to titulars in the local economy. Using this framing, nationalist leaders defined titulars as victims, placed blame on a discriminatory state, and claimed that obtaining state sovereignty would restore justice to the nation.

This pattern illustrates neatly the postulated mechanism that transforms inequality into grievances via group identification, intergroup comparison, evaluation of injustice, and framing and blaming (see Chapter 3). Ethnic distinctiveness due to lacking state penetration and previous suffering had already helped set the stage for the Chechen nationalism. According to Derluguian (2005, p. 244), the economic activities of the Soviet state, especially in the oil industry, created a situation that clearly favored the local Russian population:

Many Chechens found themselves driven into a semi-proletarian existence on the outskirts of Grozny and in the sprawling villages. In contrast to the industrial cities, in such locations the state provisions of employment, housing, and welfare benefits remained minimal – which only served to perpetuate among the Chechens a widespread distrust of the state after the deportation.

It was these "sub-proletarians" who enthusiastically supported Dzokhar Dudayev's bid for sovereignty in the early 1990s. A successful air force general, Dudayev was inspired by Baltic nationalism when he returned to Chechnya to lead the resistance against Moscow (Gall and de Waal 1998). Unfortunately for the Chechen nationalist project, quasi-independence from Russia failed to deliver the economic windfall through oil revenue that Dudayev had hoped for, and soon a new, even more destructive confrontation with Moscow followed. In sum, the Chechen wars were to a large extent caused by economic grievances, even though both sides of the conflict were guilty of widespread criminality and thuggery (Zürcher 2007). Thus, rather than being incompatible alternative motivations, greed comfortably coexisted with grievance in this case.

Although ultimately successful in their secessionist endeavor, the Kosovo Albanians' campaign resembles the Chechen case in more than one sense. Also the most backward region in a communist ethnofederal state, Kosovo early on developed a strong sense of economic grievance vis-à-vis Belgrade that exploded in student unrest in Pristina in 1981 shortly after Tito's death (Koktsidis and Ten Dam 2008; see also Woodward 1995). As with the Chechen case, the discriminating policies of the central state directly contributed to escalating the conflict. As we discussed in Chapter 4, Serb centralization efforts led to the revocation of Kosovo's autonomy in 1989, followed by increasingly repressive measures targeting the Kosovars throughout the 1990s. Ballentine and Nitzschke's (2005, pp. 8–9) summary account of the causes of the conflict is clearly consistent with our grievance interpretation:

Driven by long-standing nationalism and the ever-multiplying political and socioeconomic grievances of Kosovo Albanians, the crisis was sparked by destabilizing processes resulting from the disintegration of the Socialist Federal Republic of Yugoslavia. Socioeconomic underdevelopment, massive unemployment, and widening inter-ethnic inequalities brought about by the policies of systematic discrimination and exclusion carried out by the Milošević regime led to the establishment of the shadow "Kosovo Republic," a parallel government under the leadership of Ibrahim Rugova.

The Palestinians' resistance to Israeli ethnonationalist repression represents another prominent case of economic inequality causing conflict. In Chapter 4, we discussed the political aspects of horizontal inequality in this conflict at some length. Apart from having their access to state power systematically blocked, the Palestinians have been persistently disadvantaged in the economic realm. Starting with the hardship imposed by the dismal conditions in refugee camps, this discrimination extends to unlawful and overtly ethnically motivated land expropriations in favor of settlers as well as disruptive limits on internal and external movements and economic activity under occupation (Pappe 2004). In fact, Israeli settlers and entrepreneurs have come to exploit cheap Palestinian labor to such an extent that Khalidi (2008, p. 13) refers to the "Arab-Israeli economy as a marginalized, impoverished, and largely subservient *region* of a *national* (Jewish/Zionist) economy." In addition to the intense and long-standing political oppression of the Palestinians by the Israeli state, these omnipresent frustrations in everyday life have done much to fuel Palestinian grievances.

Similar tales of economic inequality triggering conflict can be told about other ethnic groups around the world. The indigenous peoples of Mexico were exposed to what González Casanova (1965) characterized as "internal colonialism."[12] Their grievances were partly a consequence of political exclusion by the Mexican state, but poverty combined with perceived threatening land reforms in the early 1990s as well as various forms of land grabs by agro-industrialists paved the way for the Chiapas rebellion of 1994 (Alschuler 1998-9).

The predicaments of peripheral peoples within Thailand and the Philippines also constitute clear cases of similar internal colonialism. Warning against a one-sided focus on religion in recent analyses of conflict in Southeast Asia, Liow (2006, p. 7) stresses the centrality of ethnonationalist grievances of Muslim minorities in these two countries and concludes that

a major reason that global events gain currency in local discourses and narratives is the existence of very real and longstanding grievances among the Malay-Muslims in southern Thailand and the Bangsamoro Muslims in southern Philippines stemming from palpable socio-political and economic marginalization and in some instances outright victimization by repressive central authorities.

In another study of group-level conflict in Southeast Asia, Brown (2008, p. 281) finds that "a combination of regional and ethnic horizontal inequalities and demographic marginalization on 'ethnic peripheries' of modern nation states create the potential for violent separatism."

The complicated nature of the Darfur conflict makes it difficult to disentangle the role of economic grievances. However, like the southern provinces, Darfur

---

[12] The notion of internal colonialism and its economic dimensions was further developed by Hechter (1975), who applied it to peripheral nationalism in the United Kingdom.

has suffered from an almost total neglect on the part of Khartoum with regards the provision of public goods, a neglect that started already during the colonial period (Prunier 2005). Thus, the horizontal inequality in favor of the Arabs of the Nile valley is not just political but also explicitly economic. Thus it is not surprising that the Fur hold both political and economic grievances (Ylönen 2005).

As indicated by the quantitative analysis in this chapter, we have been unable to find robust evidence for H5.2, which states that relatively wealthy groups are associated with conflict. For sure, there exist some cases of wealthy groups that have expressed wealth-related grievances with their respective capitals, such as the Slovenes and Croats of Yugoslavia (Woodward 1995) and the Basques of Spain (Gourevitch 1979), indicating that this mechanism has generated conflict in specific cases. However, the dearth of cases fails to yield statistically significant results with regards to violent conflict.

At one level, this may reflect that there simply exist relatively few cases of wealthier groups that are politically peripheral. The weakness of H5.2 is hardly surprising in the light of Horowitz's (1985) original theory of group-level inequality and conflict. It also lends credence to Giuliano's (2011) criticism of the "wealth hypothesis" according to which secessionism tends to emerge in wealthy regions as a reflection of the material rewards that would accrue to secessionist elites in case of independence. Several students of the former Soviet Union have advanced variations on this argument, including Treisman (1999) and Hale (2008). Yet, putting most of her explanatory weight on the framing of grievances, Giuliano prematurely rejects structural inequalities along the lines of Hechter's cultural division of labor and our own theoretical perspective based on horizontal inequality. Although Giuliano argues that these authors have come to the wrong conclusion by ignoring secessionism in several poor, peripheral republics beyond Chechnya, we find strong evidence that backward groups are more likely to rebel, and some support for the claim that wealthy groups are more likely to challenge the government if one limits the sample to Eastern Europe and the former Soviet Union (see the Online Appendix). Finally, we stress that we have only considered resort to violence, and that many cases of developed separatist groups have relied largely on non-violent means, perhaps in part because they have greater resources to wield political influence.

By contrast, the qualitative evidence is very solid in support of H5.3, which postulates that the inequality effect of H5.1 is conditional on political horizontal inequality. Our case illustrations in this section suggest that economic grievances are typically expressed together with sometimes intense complaints concerning adverse political conditions. Indeed, it is difficult for nationalist activists to boost mobilization in the absence of a political logic targeting the state as the main problem. Relatively poor groups that enjoy privileged access to central power are much less likely to resort to arms since they have peaceful ways to further their economic development, as illustrated by several black groups in South Africa as well as the Sunni Wahhabi minority in Saudi Arabia.

We end this section with a few remarks about the robustness of our findings. It should be recalled that data limitations have forced us to drop all Cold War cases as well as many smaller groups. Because of the small number of conflict outbreaks, our findings are sensitive to specific conflict cases, in particular the two Chechen wars. All the same, we retain these models for consistency with the other chapters, but more careful analysis using rare events estimation (King and Zeng 2001), and focusing on territorial onsets only (Buhaug 2006), yield robust results even if extreme cases are removed from the sample (see the Online Appendix). Encouragingly, our findings get even less sensitive if we complement the spatial data from G-Econ with group-level inequality estimates from surveys around the world.[13]

As mentioned above, we expect the data limitations to be especially severe in poor countries with weak statistical data collection. In general, the G-Econ data set exhibits less variation in such countries, thus making it harder to establish a link between horizontal inequality and conflict onset. For example, the relative poverty of the Tuareg in Mali and Niger has been cited as a source of conflict (see Humphreys and ag Mohamed 2005 and Krings 1995, respectively), but our data do not exhibit any significant inequality in these cases. Nor do they register that the northern groups in Côte d'Ivoire suffer from economic disadvantages, which have been articulated as grievances against the government (Langer 2005). Thus, we have good reasons to believe that we are underestimating the effect of economic horizontal inequality with our spatial approach.

As we saw in the previous chapter, endogeneity always poses a potential threat to causal inference. Fortunately, structural indicators of economic horizontal inequality are much less likely to be endogenous to governmental policies compared to those measuring political exclusion (see our discussion in Chapter 4). The main reason for this is that economic asymmetries among ethnic groups are much more stable over time than governmental policies of inclusion and exclusion (Tilly 1999; Stewart et al. 2008). Although at least partly dependent on the government's provision of public goods, ethnic groups' relative economic performance typically does not exhibit much change over the decades. For example, the Kosovo Albanians were at the bottom of the Yugoslav league table in the 1950s and remained so in the 1970s (Lang 1975).

---

[13] We are indebted to John Huber and his colleagues at Columbia University for providing the survey data (see Baldwin and Huber 2010). Relying on surveys of household income complements our spatial data in useful ways, especially since the G-Econ data record all economic activity including natural resource extraction, which may not benefit the local population as is the case with the Ijaw in Nigeria and the Aceh in Indonesia. Cederman, Weidmann, and Gleditsch (2011) find that excluding income from resource extraction in the G-Econ data does not change the main findings with respect to the effect of inequality on civil conflict.

Conclusion

This chapter has taken a second step in the empirical evaluation of our grievance perspective. The findings strongly suggest that economic horizontal inequality is linked to the outbreak of civil war. Previous studies have struggled to find systematic data at the group level for a large number of countries. This chapter overcomes this problem by relying on a spatial method that measures wealth differentials through overlay of spatial income data and ethnic groups' settlement areas. This approach makes it possible to estimate differences in economic performance across all ethnic groups that can be reasonably pinned down geographically.

In agreement with an earlier study of this kind (see Cederman, Weidmann, and Gleditsch 2011), we have found solid support for the proposition that groups that are poorer than the country average fight more wars than groups closer to the country norm (H5.1). As opposed to the previous study, however, we concede that the evidence for a higher risk of conflict is weaker when it comes to the opposite end of the wealth spectrum when we do not impose a symmetric effect of inequality. Although specific cases, such as Slovenia and Croatia in the former Yugoslavia, indicate that relatively wealthy groups may harbor grievances because of the perceived injustice associated with fiscal redistribution in favor of less-wealthy groups, this effect appears to be less robust for violent conflict and cannot be reliability established with much confidence on a global basis (H5.2).

This chapter also shows that the impact of economic horizontal inequality on conflict risk hinges on the group in question being politically excluded (H5.3), which is an entirely new finding. As with the politically conditional size effect that we investigated in the previous chapter (H4.3), this result indicates that political horizontal inequality plays a pivotal role in the perception and framing of grievances. While economic comparisons make a difference, they appear to be less conflict-inducing in, and possibly compensated by, inclusive political settings. We will return to the policy implications of this finding in Chapter 9, but for now we note that this offers some hope that short-term political reforms may partly help to compensate for long-term economic inequalities.

While suggestive, our findings do suffer from limitations that will have to be addressed in future research. The spatial data offer important advantages in terms of global coverage and uniformity, but are associated with important weaknesses as regards data quality in the least developed countries. Moreover, inequalities among groups whose settlement areas are not distinct cannot be measured. For these reasons, it would be useful to complement our data with information from other data sources, including survey research (Baldwin and Huber 2010) and satellite data (Agnew et al. 2008; Elvidge et al. 2009; though see Chen and Nordhaus 2011).

Furthermore, it should be kept in mind that, even though our analysis is more disaggregated than the customary country-level proxies used in quantitative civil war research, the group-level analysis presented here also hinges on theoretical interpolation in order to connect structural inequalities with collective-level violence. Although our proposed causal mechanisms are potentially capable of closing this explanatory gap, as suggested by our brief case discussion in the previous section, we cannot provide more extensive, direct evidence of their operation in this book. Beyond citing separate case studies in confirmation of these mechanisms, it would be desirable to improve and expand existing data sets such that interactions between incumbent governments and their challengers can be traced in greater detail, while relying on systematic information on repression and mobilization before violence breaks out (see, e.g., Cunningham 2010). Building on the pioneering efforts of Gurr (1993a; 2000b) and his team, who have also collected extensive data on social and cultural horizontal inequalities, such information would help disentangle the process at lower levels of aggregation and help us establish whether the causal imputations remain robust to such scrutiny. Fine-grained temporal measurements could also help develop an explicitly endogenous account of horizontal inequalities, which have been kept exogenous in this book. As we have pointed out, although this assumption may be less precarious with respect to political horizontal inequalities, studying endogenous changes in public goods is interesting and valuable in its own right.

6

Transborder Ethnic Kin and Civil War

In the previous two chapters, we have explained how the likelihood of civil war outbreak depends on internal conditions within states. In this chapter, we relax this limitation.[1] Indeed, beyond the demonstrated importance of domestic grievances and opportunities, civil wars are often influenced by the wider international environment. A series of recent studies has shown that civil wars can be caused not only by factors inside countries, but also by effects operating across state borders (see, e.g., Salehyan and Gleditsch 2006; Gleditsch 2007). Whereas a first wave of quantitative studies demonstrated that such effects make the "closed-polity" assumption untenable, more recently researchers have made efforts to identify and examine particular causal mechanisms driving conflict, including the role of transborder ethnic kin (TEK) in conflict processes. In contrast to earlier contributions to this literature, which tended to stress identity as the key motivating factor, contemporary scholarship typically highlights how the conjunction of ethnicity and power politics increases the risk of conflict, suggesting that "identity politics is often more about politics than about identity" (King and Melvin 1999/2000, p. 109; see also Mousseau 2001; Thyne 2007; Cederman, Girardin, and Gleditsch 2009). We have emphasized the importance of ethnic exclusion in states, but the political role of ethnicity is of course equally relevant for groups spanning national boundaries.

Despite these recent advances in studying transnational ethnic linkages, a central puzzle remains unresolved, namely how ethnic groups that at least in theory could count on support from large TEK groups often have remained surprisingly peaceful. The most prominent "dog that didn't bark," or

[1] This chapter draws directly on Cederman, Gleditsch, Salehyan, and Wucherpfennig (2013). We are grateful to Idean Salehyan and Julian Wucherpfennig for major contributions to the current analysis. Arman Grigorian and Andreas Wimmer offered important conceptual input at an earlier stage of the project.

perhaps better "bear that didn't growl," in this sense are the Russians in the "near abroad." There was widespread anticipation that the Russian diasporas stranded in former Soviet republics after the collapse of the Soviet Union in the early 1990s would resort to violence, but these communities have remained relatively calm. However, the picture looks entirely different if we consider the Albanians in the former Yugoslavia, or the Armenians in Azerbaijan. These groups have been involved in major fighting with active support from TEK groups. Given a similar pattern of domestic marginalization and cross-border ethnic kin, why then do some groups rebel while others do not?

In this chapter we seek to ascertain whether there is any systematic link between the transnational ethno-demographic balance and the probability of conflict. We conjecture that the effect is not linear: as the size and power of the TEK group rises, conflict should be more likely, but very strong kin groups – such as the Russians – can in fact deter conflict. Our argument has been anticipated by others. In an article on "hypotheses on nationalism and war" that appeared shortly after the end of the Cold War, Van Evera (1994) proposed the existence of such a curvilinear effect. Offering a more thorough theoretical derivation, Van Houten (1998) addressed the same puzzle, arguing that large external states controlled by TEK groups could have a pacifying effect on ethnic politics. Yet, the author himself admits that his study should be seen as a plausibility probe rather than a definitive test, since the evidence is limited to selected case studies. Thus, almost two decades after the publication of Van Evera's initial conjecture, evidence of the conflict-reducing TEK effect remains uncertain.

Here we test whether the curvilinear proposition between the size of TEK groups and the risk of conflict applies more generally. Progress in data collection now allows us to evaluate this proposition systematically across a large number of cases. Drawing on a new transnational extension to the Ethnic Power Relations (EPR) data set that we have relied on in the previous two chapters (EPR-ETH), we find strong quantitative support for the hypothesis. Indeed, the propensity of conflict is highest for TEK groups in the intermediate range of relative sizes. As "power parity" theories would expect, external groups that have approximately the same relative size as the incumbent groups tend to see the most conflict. However, compared to groups without transnational kin, the net effect is contingent on the political status of the TEK group: TEK groups that are excluded from power in their home countries increase the probability of political violence. Included TEK groups, in contrast, appear to decrease the risk of violent conflict, especially when groups are large, relative to the ethnic group(s) in power.

The Literature on Transborder Ethnic Kin and Conflict

Much research on civil war has treated countries experiencing civil wars as "closed polities." It is often assumed that the causes of "internal" conflicts must be found inside the boundaries of those states. However, even a cursory glance reveals that many civil wars display strong linkages to actors and events extending beyond the boundaries of individual countries. Military or non-military support for either the government or rebel side can be decisive for the dynamics of conflict. Soviet support helped sustain the Marxist government in Afghanistan as well as the Mujahedin opposition. Support from Rwanda helped Kabila's Alliance of Democratic Forces for the Liberation of Congo transform from a marginal movement in Eastern Zaire to a military force able to overthrow the Mobutu government. These ties extend to ethnic kin groups as well. The civil wars in the former Yugoslavia, for example, included widespread participation by diaspora communities in other states. Moreover, many of the Albanian National Liberation Army fighting units in Macedonian had previously fought with the Kosovo Liberation Army in Kosovo.

The clear transnational linkages in many civil wars have fostered interest in how civil wars may be shaped or affected by external characteristics. A first wave of research looked at intervention in civil wars, examining either whether certain types of civil war were more likely to see outside intervention or how external intervention shape conflict outcomes (e.g., Moore and Davis 1998; Balch-Lindsay and Enterline 2000; Regan 2000), emphasizing factors such as interstate rivalry, concerns over the externalities of conflict, and shared ethnic ties (Woodwell 2004). However, if transnational linkages can be shown to influence the outcome of ongoing civil wars, then transnational linkages and the prospects for external support should also affect the decision to resort to conflict in the first place.

Another wave of studies notes that civil wars cluster geographically and shows that proximity to conflict can increase the risk that a country will experience a civil war (Hegre and Sambanis 2006; Buhaug and Gleditsch 2008; Bosker and de Ree 2010). Although the tendency for conflict to spread from one state to another could stem from externalities entirely unrelated to the actors, such as cheaper weapons, social links, and affinities between communities across national boundaries seem a very likely source of conflict transmission (Buhaug and Gleditsch 2008; Bosker and de Ree 2010). However, as noted by Cederman, Girardin, and Gleditsch (2009) and Salehyan, Gleditsch, and Cunningham (2011), transnational support from ethnic kin can also help facilitate resort to violence, even when the transnational kin are not themselves involved in a conflict in their home state.

There is little consensus in the literature with regard to the effect of TEK on civil war outbreak. In fact, virtually all conceivable causal relationships have been proposed at some point or another, including both positive and negative influences, as well as no connection at all. Some studies argue that TEK groups have offensive motives linked to ethnic nationalism and postulate a positive effect on conflict. In particular, aggressive interventions driven by irredentism could trigger a spiral of escalating tensions on both sides of the border (Weiner 1971). There are many examples of such border-transgressing processes in the breakup of the former Yugoslavia. Although most of this literature relies on qualitative evidence (e.g., Horowitz 1985; Heraclides 1990; Chazan 1991; Jenne 2007), some scholars have conducted quantitative tests, usually based on Minorities at Risk data, that generally suggest a positive impact on conflict exerted by TEK groups (see Moore and Davis 1997; Saideman 2001; Woodwell 2004).

From the vantage point of bargaining theory, Cetinyan (2002) contends that group sizes and transnational kin groups should not influence the probability of conflict onset. This interpretation recognizes that groups' demands vary with their demographic weight, but rejects that this would have any implications for the outbreak of violence. Potential threats from external kin, he argues, should be reflected in domestic bargaining processes as groups with strong TEK ties receive greater concessions from the state. Cetinyan's analysis is creative, but there are at least two reasons to doubt the theoretical and empirical null results he presents. First, the restricted sample of groups in the MAR data, which by construction are limited to threatened minorities, makes them less suitable for general tests of demographic size. Second, Cetinyan's model rules out the possibility that group size could be correlated with uncertainty. By contrast, a number of scholars postulate a curvilinear relationship between the two, since strategic misrepresentation is most important at parity (e.g., Reiter 2003; Walter 2009a). We present a similar argument below.

In an attempt to overcome some of the sample restrictions associated with the MAR data by relying on alternative, group-level data, Cederman, Girardin, and Gleditsch (2009) find that TEK groups increase the probability of internal conflict by shifting the shape of the observed effects of the power balance between the groups associated with the rebels and the incumbent government. While innovative in its use of geographic information systems, their article has a limited scope in several respects. First, the GREG data on ethnic groups depend directly on the Soviet *Atlas Narodov Mira*, which are defined primarily based on language, and may not correspond to the relevant identities. Moreover, the data are from the 1960s and could thus be said to be outdated (even though ethnic settlement patterns are surprisingly stable over time). Second, their analysis is limited to Eurasia, thus leaving cases in Africa and the Western Hemisphere outside the analysis. Third, and most importantly, their model does not factor in the size of the TEK group itself and therefore does not speak to the size puzzle that is the main focus of this chapter.

In an early discussion of "hypotheses on nationalism and war" that we have previously referred to, Van Evera (1994) develops a subtle argument stating that TEK groups will be less likely to intervene if rescue is either impossible or relatively easy. It is, instead, "in-between situations ... that are most dangerous" (p. 20). However, Van Evera's article never moves beyond listing hypotheses accompanied by selected case illustrations.

Relatedly, Van Houten (1998) offers a more sophisticated attempt to explain the relative peacefulness of the Russian near abroad and similar cases. Focusing on kin states, referred to as "reference states," Van Houten extends Fearon's (1998) theory of credible commitments from minority-majority relations to transborder actors. Noting that Fearon's argument overpredicts violence in cases such as the Baltic states, he argues that external relations may pacify domestic settings under specific conditions. Irredentist intensions may exist among strong states, in which case conflict is very likely. However, *ceteris paribus*, increasing strength of the reference state should stabilize minority-majority relations: "the presence of a militarily strong but only moderately irredentist reference state is most likely to overcome the commitment problem and prevent ethnic violence" (p. 112). Thus, strong external kin states are in a much better position to make credible threats to intervene than their weaker counterparts:

On the one hand, if it is known that the reference state is likely to intervene in the new state if the minority is oppressed, then the ruling majority in the new state has an incentive to protect the minority. This threat allows the majority to credibly commit to do this. On the other hand, if the reference state is too aggressive, it may induce a war with the new state (Van Houten 1998, p. 112).

Recognizing the difficulties of testing an argument that hinges on intensions, Van Houten limits the application of his game-theoretic model to a small number of cases in the Eastern Europe: "I make no attempt to actually prove the *correctness* of the model; rather, I try to show its *plausibility*." Thus, building on, and further developing, Van Houten's ideas, we attempt to go beyond the task of establishing plausibility by testing our hypotheses systematically across a large number of cases.

Theorizing the Effect of Transborder Ethnic Kin

Following pioneering conceptual work by Weiner (1971) and Brubaker (1996), we start our theoretical derivation of the TEK effect by identifying the ethno-nationalist triad as the critical constellation of actors within which border-transgressing influences on conflict operate. Building directly on our dyadic polity model in Figure 4.1, an ethno-nationalist triad can be conceptualized as an extended center-periphery configuration by adding the TEK group to the *primary dyad*, which involves the group challenging the power of an incumbent ethnic group (Cederman, Girardin, and Gleditsch 2009). Through the addition of a TEK group on the challenger's side, the incumbent is now faced with an additional, potentially opposed actor in a *secondary dyad*. The presumably supportive relationship between the TEK group and the challenger constitutes the third leg of the triad.

There are two versions of the triadic constellation depending on the power status of the TEK group in its own state. We illustrate these two possibilities in Figures 6.1 and 6.2, respectively. These figures extend Figure 4.1 with a second state, referred to as State B, which is the host of the TEK group. The primary

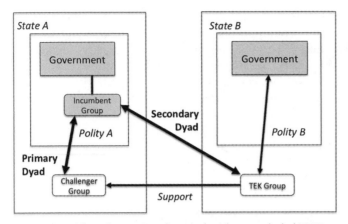

FIGURE 6.1. The ethnonationalist triad with an excluded TEK group.

dyad still connects the government with the challenger group in State A. The crucial addition is the secondary dyad that links the incumbent group in State A with the TEK group in State B.

Let us first consider Figure 6.1. As illustrated by the situation of the Kurds in Turkey (here State A), if the TEK group is excluded in State B (e.g., in Iraq before the fall of Saddam Hussein), we can expect there to be a tension between the TEK group and its government, but also between the governments of States A and B, that is, between Iraq and Turkey. Figure 6.2 depicts a constellation where the TEK group happens to be included in the government. Here we can use Estonia and Russia as examples of States A and B. Within Estonia, the challenger group refers to the Russian minority. Potentially, this

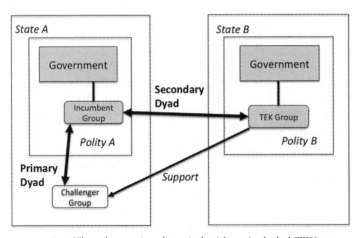

FIGURE 6.2. The ethnonationalist triad with an included TEK group.

group can expect support from its ethnic kin in Russia, where the Russians control the state. Under these circumstances, friction in the secondary dyad could trigger irredentist conflict between States A and B.

Since demographic group size is relatively easy to measure and tends to be exogenous to conflict except under extreme cases of ethnic cleansing, we will continue to rely on this dimension to reflect power in our analysis (see also the justification for group-level analysis in Chapters 2 and 3). For sure, there are instances where the participants of conflict processes constitute tiny fractions of the group's population, such as ruthless warlords and armed bands, but we expect the size of the group as a share of a country's population to be relevant to conflict onset in most cases, in terms of both potential resources and overall support or legitimacy.

Our main task, then, is to extend the study of conflict within the primary dyad to the transnational dimension. To what extent does this conflict process involve the TEK group through the secondary dyad? Assuming that a nationality conflict breaks out between the incumbent group(s) and the challenger, we derive the conditions of conflict as a function of the conditions within the primary and secondary dyads. Our analysis of relative group size in the primary dyad is captured in H4.3, for which we found strong evidence in Chapter 4. Indeed, the larger the challenger group is compared to the population of the incumbent, the more likely violent outcomes become.

We are now ready to consider the secondary dyad's influence on internal conflict. Before discussing the different ways that the TEK group's size can affect the propensity of political violence, we start by considering a categorical effect. Such a formulation would be compatible with a strictly essentialist interpretation of ethnic kin that is unrelated to power relationships. As a reflection of strong ethnic solidarity, all TEK groups should be highly motivated to intervene. According to this approach, such groups are motivated by "reasons of affinity and sentiment rather than ... power or more hard-headed cost-benefit analyses" (Holsti 1996, p. 127; see also Connor 1994). Based on this essentialist logic, we derive the following hypothesis:

H6.1. The probability of conflict increases in the presence of a TEK group.

Nevertheless, we do not expect this hypothesis to be empirically accurate. Although clearly emotionally loaded, ethnic politics is as much about power and politics as it is about ethnic solidarity:

Disputes over the allocation of scarce resources, competing visions of foreign policy directions, domestic political contests, and other prosaic features of political life frequently trump any putative duty that political elites might feel toward individuals who share their language or culture beyond their own frontiers (King and Melvin 1999/2000, p. 109).

Whether orchestrated by state-owning or state-seeking ethnic kin, intervention in transborder conflicts is a risky business that can have massively negative consequences for the TEK group in question (Horowitz 1985). Indeed, it is not surprising that quantitative studies, including Cederman, Girardin, and Gleditsch (2009), have generally failed to find support for the simple hypothesis that the presence of a TEK group by itself influences the risk of conflict.

An alternative account takes power politics more seriously by letting the probability of conflict increase with the relative demographic weight of the TEK group compared to the incumbent. The larger the group, the more confident it will be that its intervention will contribute to the successful challenge of the government in the primary dyad without exposing it to inordinate risks. For example, Jenne (2007) argues that powerful secondary dyads encourage groups in the primary dyad to radicalize and articulate larger demands, which can lead to violence. This logic runs parallel to that of H4.3 in the primary dyad by using relative demographic weight as a rough measure of the dyadic power balance:

H6.2. The probability of conflict increases with the relative size of the TEK group in the secondary dyad.

There are few examples of empirical studies measuring power relations in the secondary dyad and those that do typically find no proportional effect. For example, in their quantitative investigation of irredentism, Saideman and Ayres (2000) do not detect any influence of relative group size, which is also in line with Cetinyan's (2002) findings. Nonetheless, we include this hypothesis and test it, using our new data resource.

There are also important theoretical reasons to discount hypothesis H6.2. The postulated monotonic effect of TEK group size fails to account for the puzzle of the Russian near abroad, because it overlooks the strategic nature of the secondary dyad. As the size of the TEK group increases, more resources will become available to the challenger in the primary dyad, but the incumbent regime should also take this into account when bargaining with the group. We have postulated a linear effect of group size on conflict in the primary dyad, but there are good reasons to believe that such a relationship needs to be amended when it comes to the influence of the secondary dyad. Why should large, powerful TEK groups be able to "protect" their kin, but large groups in the primary dyad be more associated with conflict? Deviating somewhat from Van Houten's (1998) emphasis on commitment problems, we propose two causal mechanisms that generate the same relationship between the size and conflict variables.

First, large challengers in the primary dyad are unlikely to extract bargaining concessions by threatening ruling minorities. Majority groups challenging minority incumbents will remain excluded from state power unless there are exceptional circumstances that make small ruling coalitions unstable. Some small ruling coalitions – such as the White Apartheid government in South Africa – established their dominance through successful coercion and managed to cling to power for decades. Oppressive incumbents are unlikely to compromise with challengers as they fear that concessions will threaten their long-term survival and the benefits of rule. Going down the reform path may lead to the dissolution of the regime at best, and exile, imprisonment, or death at worst. Thus, elites defending minority rule will be inclined to rely heavily on coercion to stifle challenges to their supremacy (Heger and Salehyan 2007).

However, such an uncompromising attitude may be much less viable if overwhelming external groups get involved. While incumbents have greater means to maintain control domestically, transnational actors are inherently more difficult to police and coerce since they can mobilize resources beyond the shadow of repression (Salehyan 2009). Because of the potential threat posed by such interventions, we would expect incumbent regimes to be mindful of ethnic opposition groups' respective "homelands." In other words, large domestic challengers – while potentially threatening – can be successfully controlled by the state's coercive apparatus, but large external challengers are much more difficult to deal with.

This type of caution should increase with the size of TEK groups relative to the incumbent group. Put differently, the latter's willingness to risk violent conflict should be a *decreasing* function of the TEK group's relative size. Yet since the probability of conflict is shaped by both opportunity and willingness, the combination of external resources and external treats produces a curvilinear effect. For small TEK groups, the conflict propensity would be close to zero since these groups would make little difference even if they intervene. Where the TEK groups are relatively large, however, states will be more constrained in their behavior because of the deterrent effect of a possible intervention.[2]

Bargaining theory suggests a second reason to expect more conflict in the mid-range of TEK sizes. Originally applied by Blainey (1973) to interstate relations, this argument hinges critically on uncertainty and strategic incentives to misrepresent one's true strength. According to this reasoning, conflicts are especially likely to break out where the power balance is roughly even (see Reiter 2003). Rough parity makes it difficult for the parties to assess who would prevail in case of combat, and so attempts to misrepresent gain significance (Geller 1993; Lemke and Werner 1996; Wagner 2000). Conflict may then occur as the result of information problems leading to bargaining failure

---

[2] A simple formalization shows why the resulting effect should be curvilinear in terms of the relative size r of the TEK group. Assuming that the effect of the relative weight of the TEK group compared to the incumbent is $r \in [0,1]$, the capacity argument according to H6.2 would be linear in r, and the incumbent's willingness to apply force a decreasing linear function $1-r$. Modeling the combined effect as the product of both these functions, we get $r(1-r) = 1/4 - (r-1/2)^2$, i.e., an inverted U-shaped curve with its maximum value at $r = 0.5$.

(Fearon 1995). This reasoning has generally not been extended to civil wars, which are typically thought to be caused by commitment problems (e.g., Fearon 1995; 1998), but there are clear reasons to believe that uncertainty could be a cause of conflict in such settings. For example, Walter (2009a) points to obvious sources of uncertainty, such as the sources of rebel financing and governmental resolve, to which one might add the extent of popular mobilization on either side.

Yet, the lack of information should be even more pronounced as regards the possible involvement of TEK groups. Transnational interactions tend to be much less transparent than domestic politics. This fundamental information asymmetry is especially severe for the incumbent group, because its intelligence services are likely to encounter much more resistance in their attempts to gather information about the resources and intentions of foreign groups (Salehyan 2009, p. 48). To some degree, the situation resembles the difficulties surrounding extended deterrence in international relations, which is deemed to be especially challenging. The challenge derives above all from the uncertainty and lacking credibility surrounding third parties' propensity to intervene in defense of proxy states (e.g., Huth 1988). Thus, it can be surmised that there will be considerable uncertainties, in terms of both estimating the capabilities of a TEK group and its willingness to intervene, especially if the power balance is close to parity. Furthermore, these uncertainties should dwarf the corresponding ambiguity in domestic politics.

We are thus ready to derive our main hypothesis regarding the functional form of the TEK effect:

H6.3. The probability of conflict follows an inverted U-shape for the relative size of the TEK group in the secondary dyad.

So far, our hypotheses have said nothing about the influence of TEK links on conflict compared to situations without kin. We argue that there is a mediating effect depending on whether the TEK group is included in, or excluded from, executive power in their own state. The most straightforward argument focuses on the superior power of state-controlling TEK (see Figure 6.2). Other things being equal, we would expect TEK groups that control a state to be more powerful. Yet as we have argued above, the relative power balance in the secondary dyad should constrain conflict as TEK groups become more threatening. While we focused on power-as-population above, control of a state and its military apparatus should augment power even further. Thus, while ethnic Russians and ethnic Chinese are numerically large in global terms, they are even stronger than their size alone would suggest as they control powerful states. Marginalized TEK groups, on the other hand, may be willing and able to mobilize resources for their kin in the primary dyad (see Figure 6.1). Yet, there will be considerable uncertainty over the resources and support that they can garner as their capabilities are unknown and resource pools are insecure. TEKs that control states usually operate through official diplomatic channels and have known resource streams and capabilities, which bolster credible threats and reduce bargaining uncertainty.

In addition, we must consider the TEK group's willingness to intervene. Incumbent groups have much more to lose than stateless groups, especially in the case of multiethnic polities that could be seriously destabilized by actions that undermine the sanctity of borders (Horowitz 1985; Cederman, Girardin, and Gleditsch 2009). International norms of territorial integrity applying to states, rather than to nonstate actors, should also restrain incumbent groups from interfering in the internal affairs of neighboring states (Zacher 2001). In contrast, TEK groups without access to state power, such as the Kurds in Turkey, are less bound by such considerations, and generally more likely to have combat experience as a consequence of their marginal position.

In short, TEK groups that control a state can "speak softly and carry a big stick." They are more able to intervene given their control over military forces and these credible threats should be reflected in bargaining in the primary dyad. They may be more reserved in their use of force, given international norms against war, but can still bring the power of the state to bear in diplomatic relations. Marginalized TEK groups, on the other hand, do not face similar constraints. Support for their kin may be uncertain and difficult to mobilize since they do not have the same military capabilities. For these reasons, large included TEK groups tend to deter conflict, while excluded TEK groups can foster bargaining uncertainty and promote conflict. Thus, we state our final hypothesis:

H6.4. The conflict-dampening effect occurs for relatively large TEK groups that are included, and not for those that are excluded.

Data

The empirical assessment of our hypotheses depends on the availability of suitable data on ethnic groups and their transnational connections in a wide and unbiased sample. Thus, we extend the EPR-ETH data introduced in Chapter 4 to encompass TEK links. Since the coding of EPR groups is country-specific, there is no automatic way of identifying such connections. In contrast, the *Atlas Narodov Mira* features one global list of groups, which simplifies its use in the identification of transborder kin (see Cederman, Girardin, and Gleditsch 2009). We therefore decided to code TEK links based on nominal identification by matching group names, including the possibility of synonyms for groups with shared languages. Thus, for example, Swiss Italians are linked to the Italians through the TEK group for all Italians. There is, of course, no guarantee that matching names will yield politically relevant bonds, and indeed in the case of the Swiss Italians automatic identification with "Italian Italians" would be far from obvious. However, this method is less afflicted by bias than attempts to code constructivist interpretations based on partial information (see our online appendix for a full listing of all TEK groups).[3]

The coders were asked to identify all ethnic groups that appear in more than one country and to give them a special TEK code that differs from the country-specific group identifiers. Groups that appear only in one country were not given any TEK code. EPR also features "umbrella groups" composed of several ethnic subgroups. For example, in Mali the umbrella group "blacks" includes ethnic Mande, Peul, Voltaic, and others. In these cases, the composite group can be associated with more than one TEK code, with three as the maximum number of links allowed in the data set.

Before entering the analysis, TEK connections featuring groups from non-contiguous countries were removed from the data set. Long-distance nationalism involving diaspora has also been listed as a possible source of conflict (e.g., Shain and Barth 2003), as has funding of rebel campaigns in the Third World through migrant diasporas in the United States (Collier and Hoeffler 2004). These conflict mechanisms are different from our concern in this chapter, where we focus entirely on *transborder* ethnic kin. Moreover, few countries have the ability to project force across long distances, and such kin group connections are less relevant for threat perceptions.

Variables

The next step is to introduce our main variables. Throughout this chapter, we continue to rely on a dependent variable that is based on a group-level coding of the UCDP/PRIO Armed Conflict Data Set (Gleditsch et al. 2002). As described in Chapter 4, the resulting coding assures that each conflict onset is mapped to the corresponding EPR group provided that the rebel organization expresses an aim to support the ethnic group and members of the group in question participate in combat. Again, the onset variable is coded one for a group-year during which a conflict started and zero otherwise, with ongoing conflict excluded.

We proceed by introducing the independent variables by extending our variable definitions that were introduced in Chapter 4. Denoting the TEK group's population K,[4] and the population of the incumbent I, we operationalize the main independent variables related to TEK as follows:

---

[3] Our team has started coding constructivist exceptions from the name-matching rule, but the coverage of this more refined coding is still only partial and we refrain from using it here. However, using the existing partial corrections makes no substantive difference to the results reported here.

[4] Note that there may be more than one TEK group. In such cases, K is the sum of the population of segments in all neighboring countries.

- Relative TEK size $k \in [0,1)$ in the secondary dyad is defined as $K / (K+I)$.
- Relative size for TEK groups that are state controlling and stateless, k_{INCL} and k_{EXCL} respectively, are computed on the basis of TEK group populations from either group category.
- We also employ a TEK dummy variable, which is coded 1 if the group has at least one TEK group, and 0 otherwise.

The remaining independent and control variables are identical to those used in Chapter 4.

Results

Having described the data and defined our variables, we are now ready to present our main results (see Table 6.1). Using Model 4.2 as the reference model, our sample encompasses all EPR-ETH groups from 1946 through 2009. Again relying on robust country-clustered standard errors, we conduct all analysis with logit models, using the onset of ethnonationalist conflict at the group level as the dependent variable.

As a first step, Model 6.1 introduces a dummy variable indicating whether the group has TEK. Since the effect is indistinguishable from zero, we reject H6.1, consistent with our theoretical expectations. Indeed, the introduction of the TEK dummy variable does little to affect the other coefficients. Confirming the findings of the models in Chapter 4, a group's power access is negatively related to conflict whereas downgraded groups and those with a history of conflict are more likely to experience violence. At the country level, GDP per capita has a negative and significant effect, but the population variable again fails to reach significance.

As a direct assessment of H6.2, Model 6.2 evaluates whether the probability of conflict increases monotonically with the relative size of the TEK group. We retain the TEK dummy, which now serves as an intercept for the linear effect for groups without TEK, where the size is set to zero. Again, the estimate of the size effect in the secondary dyad is far from significant, although it is positive. In agreement with our theoretical anticipation, we reject H6.3 as well.

Our next task is to test the postulated inverted U-shaped curvilinear relationship between TEK size and conflict. Since the indicator for the demographic balance ranges from 0 to 1, both terms should be of roughly equal magnitude and the quadratic term should be negative if the hypothesis is correct. In support of H6.3, the estimates of Model 6.3 reveal that while the monotonic effect of relative group size in the primary dyad remains strong, the relative size of the TEK group influences conflict propensity in an inverted U-shaped fashion. Encouragingly, both the linear and square terms are strongly significant, with the former being positive and the latter negative. Using 90 percent confidence intervals, Figure 6.2 plots the predicted probability of conflict as a function of relative TEK size, indicating that if the other variables are held at their means,

TABLE 6.1. *TEK and Group-Level Onset of Civil War, 1946–2009*

	Model 6.1	Model 6.2	Model 6.3	Model 6.4
Rel. Group Size	1.3807**	1.2713**	1.2622**	1.1783**
	(0.3131)	(0.3347)	(0.3404)	(0.3659)
TEK Group	0.1009	−0.0179	−0.4115	
	(0.1927)	(0.2092)	(0.2440)	
Rel. TEK Size		0.3441	4.2382**	
		(0.3306)	(1.3420)	
Rel. TEK Size, sq.			−4.2058**	
			(1.3620)	
Excluded TEK Group				−0.1967
				(0.2237)
Rel. TEK Size (excl.)				3.3767*
				(1.6882)
Rel. TEK Size, sq. (excl.)				−2.6340
				(1.9853)
Included TEK Group				−0.3549
				(0.2852)
Rel. TEK Size (incl.)				4.5133**
				(1.6719)
Rel. TEK Size, sq. (incl.)				−5.1434**
				(1.6867)
Junior Status	0.8415	0.7939	0.7823	0.7781
	(0.5207)	(0.5295)	(0.5248)	(0.5323)
Autonomy Status	1.2021*	1.1249	1.1647*	1.1097
	(0.5741)	(0.5840)	(0.5811)	(0.5852)
Powerless Status	1.4237**	1.3527*	1.3675*	1.3039*
	(0.5309)	(0.5430)	(0.5396)	(0.5458)
Discriminated Status	1.9905**	1.9315**	1.9273**	1.8952**
	(0.5075)	(0.5194)	(0.5162)	(0.5177)
Separatist Status	3.2137**	3.1275**	3.2512**	3.2108**
	(0.6609)	(0.6818)	(0.6625)	(0.6660)
Downgraded	1.5768**	1.5756**	1.5585**	1.5537**
	(0.2942)	(0.2950)	(0.2922)	(0.2898)
Number Previous Conflicts	0.5481**	0.5469**	0.5173**	0.5070**
	(0.0968)	(0.0959)	(0.0963)	(0.0933)
Ongoing Conflict, lag	0.3903	0.3960	0.4421	0.4634
	(0.2856)	(0.2866)	(0.2864)	(0.2856)
GDP/capita, lag, log	−0.1707*	−0.1674*	−0.1777*	−0.1918*
	(0.0722)	(0.0726)	(0.0728)	(0.0756)
Population, lag, log	0.0866	0.0989	0.1198	0.1386
	(0.0889)	(0.0937)	(0.0957)	(0.0969)
Constant	−5.8275**	−5.9053**	−6.1146**	−6.2274**
	(1.0901)	(1.1246)	(1.1326)	(1.1281)
Observations	28,302	28,298	28,298	28,298

Robust standard errors in parentheses; estimates for peace-year correction not shown.

** $p < 0.01$, * $p < 0.05$.

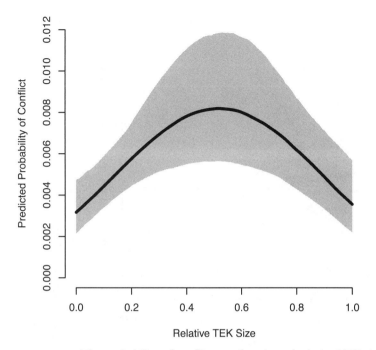

FIGURE 6.3. The probability of conflict as a function of relative TEK size.

conflict propensity increases from around 0.3% to as much as 0.8% per group and year if the relative TEK size is shifted from zero to rough parity. Illustrating the distribution of the observations, the rug plot along the *x*-axis of Figure 6.3 demonstrates considerable variation in the relative size of TEK groups.

Our analysis continues with an evaluation of H6.4, which considers the separate effect of different types of TEK groups compared to the non-TEK baseline. The results of Model 6.4 suggest that both included and excluded TEK groups produce a curvilinear effect on conflict onset. However, it is difficult to compare the net influence of both of these based on the coefficients alone. We therefore refer to Figure 6.4, which displays the respective marginal TEK effects in two separate panels, with the left indicating included TEK groups and the right corresponding to excluded groups. Figure 6.4 thus depicts the first difference in predicted probabilities for given levels of relative TEK size and status, compared to groups without TEK.

It immediately becomes clear that the effect differs significantly between the two types of TEK groups. In support of H6.4, the graphs tell us that for comparable TEK sizes, the conflict propensity is considerably higher for large excluded TEK groups than for included ones. In fact, the conflict-restraining effect can only be observed for state-controlling TEK groups. For very large relative group sizes, the effect appears to be significant since the error bands do not intersect zero in that range. By contrast, the marginal effect of excluded TEKs

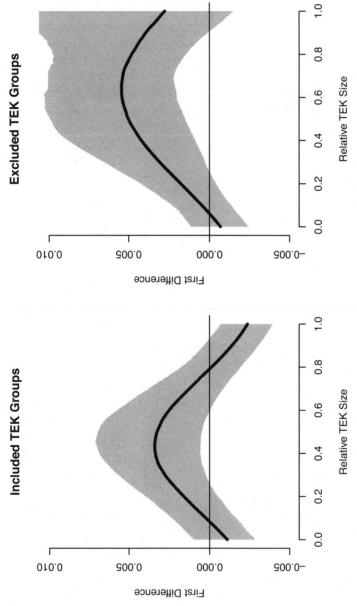

FIGURE 6.4. Conflict probability varying with size of included and excluded TEK groups.

is generally positive and statistically significant for the intermediate size range, but becomes indistinguishable from the corresponding non-TEK situation for extreme values of the size spectrum. However, despite a falling tendency for large groups, the net effect never becomes conflict dampening. Echoing the findings of Saideman and Ayres (2008), we conclude from this that irredentism may be much less important as a general trigger of civil war than often assumed, although we cannot exclude the possibility that other types of violence, such as interstate disputes and wars, could be triggered by included TEK groups. Indeed, our results indicate that the conflict-dampening influence appears to be limited to included TEK groups, which is in line with Van Houten's (1998) account of the relatively peaceful Russian diaspora.

Finally, we explore possible interactions between the relative demographic weights in the primary and secondary dyads. In fact, it is reasonable to expect the effects to be relatively independent. Following the stylized narrative of Weiner's (1971) "Macedonian syndrome," we assume that tensions in the primary dyad usually precede possible activation of the secondary dyad. Thus, decision makers participating in the primary dyad would have to consider a possible shift in the power balance that intervention would entail. This sequential logic should be roughly compatible with additive effects, as we have modeled them above in the regression models. Yet, since we have no strong deductive theory to back up these expectations, it is helpful to evaluate the interaction of the two dyads by estimating both dimensions together by letting the data speak without the constraints of parametric assumptions.

Based on a two-dimensional nonparametric generalized additive model (GAM), Figure 6.5 displays a contour plot of a surface, indicating effects on conflict probability over combinations of relative group size and relative TEK size. As in the previous figures, the x-axis shows the size of the TEK group. Along the y-axis, we plot the relative group size in the primary dyad. The result reflects a high degree of independence between the two dimensions. Moving from the bottom of the plot upward, the predicted probability increases, as indicated by the contours. Moving from left to right over the x-axis, however, implies traveling over a "ridge" with higher conflict propensity, but the values start descending again with very high relative TEK size. Since the ridge is more or less perpendicular to the x-axis, or size of the TEK group, we conclude that the size effects in the primary and secondary dyads by and large are largely orthogonal to one another.

Validating the Causal Arguments

To follow up the quantitative analysis of this chapter, we turn to a few illustrative examples to highlight the causal relationships we discuss above. In Chapter 4, we argued that large excluded ethnic groups are more likely to rebel than relatively small ones. Less intuitive, perhaps, is our claim in this chapter that there is a curvilinear relationship between the size of a group's transnational

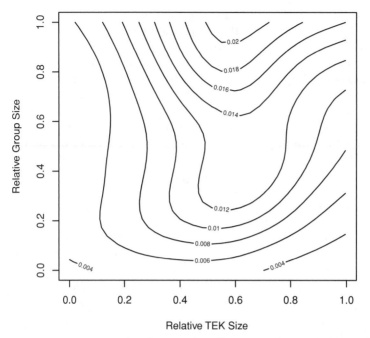

FIGURE 6.5. Contour plot showing the effect on conflict probability of relative group and TEK sizes.

kin and civil war (see H6.3). This qualitative discussion is less suitable to assess whether excluded or included TEK groups are more conflict prone as postulated by H6.4 since it is difficult to assess proportions or relative rates without population data. Therefore, in this section we limit ourselves to examining how kin relations are linked to conflict rather than assessing relative frequencies for different types of relations.

There are quite a number of politically active TEK ties, where stateless ethnic brethren on both sides of the border assist each other. For instance, Kurdish populations in Turkey, Iraq, and Iran have all engaged in separatist activity in their respective countries (McDowall 2005; Marcus 2007; Gunter 2008; Gunes 2012). Kurds represent roughly 20–25% of the population in Turkey, 15–20% in Iraq, and about 10% of the population in Iran. These three countries vary dramatically in terms of their political institutions (Islamic theocracy, authoritarian rule, democracy/semi-democracy) and the dominant ethnic group controlling the state. Yet, all three have historically discriminated against the Kurds and have experienced violence by Kurdish separatist movements.

As we saw in Chapter 4, the Kurdistan Worker's Party (PKK) in Turkey emerged as a socialist-nationalist movement in the 1970s and shifted to violent tactics in the 1980s (Marcus 2007; Gunes 2012). During the period of authoritarian rule in Turkey, the military attempted to crush the organization by force, while denying Kurdish social, political, and cultural rights. More recently, with the Justice and Development Party (AK) in control of a democratic Turkish state, greater Kurdish autonomy has been granted, even as military operations against the PKK continue. In Iraq, two main parties – the Kurdish Democratic Party (KDP) and the Patriotic Union of Kurdistan – opposed harsh authoritarian rule under Saddam Hussein's Sunni-Arab dominated regime. Given rough parity in size between Sunni Arabs in Iraq and the Kurdish population, the Kurds potentially posed an existential threat to Hussein's regime, particularly if allied with the Shia majority. Thus, the Hussein regime used especially draconian tactics, including the 1988 poison gas attack in Halabja, which killed an estimated 5,000 people (McDowall 2005). Finally, the Kurdish Democratic Party of Iran (KDPI) initially challenged the Shah's regime, but later came to oppose the Islamic Republic. While conflicts between the KDPI and the Iranian state have not been as bloody as those in neighboring countries, the group continues to fight for democratic reform and cultural rights.

Even as the particular organizations differ, it is clear that Kurds in all three countries share the nationalist goal of a greater Kurdistan. Such bonds of solidarity are echoed on the KDP of Iraq's webpage:

The KDP believes that the Kurds are one nation. We put forth effort for the strengthening of brotherly relations between our party and the democratic parties and organizations in all parts of Kurdistan. Kurdistan was divided after World War I with no regard to the demands of the Kurdish people for self-determination. The feeling of solidarity and sympathy among people in different parts of Kurdistan is natural and spontaneous, and every uprising that has ever taken place in any part of Kurdistan has always been supported by Kurds in the other parts.[5]

Relations between Kurdish organizations have not always been collegial (Gunter 2008); yet, sympathies and even family ties do extend across national boundaries. Beyond the resources they can garner domestically, it is clear that militant Kurdish groups benefit from resources and physical sanctuaries beyond the borders of their targeted state(s). For instance, although Iraqi Kurdish parties do not publicly condone PKK activities on its side of the border, the organization is firmly entrenched in bases in Northern Iraq. And while there have been calls for cooperation between Turkey and Iraq on security matters, including the PKK question, kinship ties make it very difficult for Iraqi Kurds to turn on their brethren. Moreover, as our theory suggests, while Turkey is able to maintain a relative degree of control over Kurdish activities domestically, the transnational aspects of the conflict are especially hard to monitor and police.

Albanians in Kosovo and Macedonia shared not only ethnic ties, but also material resources and fighters during their independence struggle

---

[5] Kurdish Democratic Party of Iraq website, "General Information about the KDP," http://www.kdp.se/?do=general .

(Phillips 2004; Gleditsch 2007; Pettifer and Vickers 2007). Although Albanian parties had been politically represented in Macedonia since the country's secession from the former Yugoslavia in 1991, many in the large Albanian minority resented the effort to set up a Slav-dominated nation state and demanded greater recognition for their cultural and political rights. The Kosovo war, which ended in the *de facto* termination of Serb control of the Albanian-dominated province, had a radicalizing effect, and many Slavs feared that the large influx of Albanian refugees would destabilize Macedonia. The (Albanian) National Liberation Army (NLA) in Macedonia was set up in 1999 in the aftermath of the Kosovo war. It was headed by a former commander in the Kosovo Liberation Army,[6] and it is widely alleged that many of the NLA combatants had previously participated in the war in Kosovo.[7] The NLA in Macedonia operated out of bases in Kosovo, and virtually all of the fighting in 2001 took place in border areas. The timing and spatial location of the conflict highlights the importance of the transnational linkages. Moreover, transnational factors were also important in the outcome of the conflict, as the refusal of the government of Albania to fully endorse the National Liberation Army may have contributed to prevent further escalation of the 2001 conflict.

The Tuaregs are another important case of a stateless people straddling international borders. Political exclusion and economic marginalization in Mali and Niger provoked grievances and triggered resistance to state power in both countries (Krings 1995; Humphreys and ag Mohamed 2005). There were major refugee flows to Algeria, Mauretania, and Libya as a response to repressive policies that targeted the group in Mali and Niger in the early 1990s. Ethnonationalist mobilization among these refugees has recently come to focus on a secessionist campaign in Mali that increasingly undermined the government's control of the northern part of the country in 2012.[8]

So far, we have surveyed conflicts where excluded kin groups increased the risk of internal conflict. While H6.4 states that TEK connections involving included groups should be less conflict prone than those featuring stateless groups, we still find conflict cases that involve the former. The Rwandan government, led by the Tutsi-dominated Rwandan Patriotic Front, has offered resources and support to its coethnics across the border in the Democratic Republic of the Congo (Prunier 2009). Somalia provided resources and bases to separatist groups in Ethiopia, and even invaded directly in 1977 as it claimed the Ogaden region as its own (Kornprobst 2002). Even though the Serbian regime did not prevent the breakup of Bosnia-Herzegovina against the hopes of the Bosnian Serbs, the link to Belgrade was strong

---

[6] http://www.balkaninsight.com/en/article/ali%20ahmeti.

[7] See http://news.bbc.co.uk/1/hi/world/europe/1231596.stm.

[8] Markus M. Haefliger, "Alt-neuer Wunsch nach Selbstbestimmung," *Neue Zürcher Zeitung*, 2 April 2012, p. 7.

before and during the Bosnian war that started in 1992. Fueling irredentist rhetoric as well as arming and organizing their ethnic kin in both Croatia and Bosnia, the Milošević regime certainly raised the expectations that violence and ethnic cleansing would result in the creation of a greater Serbia (Saideman and Ayres 2008, p. 55). In fact, the identification between the segments of the Serbian group was so strong that Milošević represented the Bosnian Serbs during the Dayton peace negotiations (Holbrooke 1998).

As we have shown, there are many examples where TEKs are likely to have contributed to increasing the risk of conflict. However, we have also argued that TEK ties can decrease the risk of violent conflict if the cross-border segment is so large as to deter incumbent governments from becoming too belligerent. As our primary case, we discuss the Russian diaspora. In the early post-Soviet era, many observers feared that sizable Russian minorities in the "near abroad" would cause significant conflict and irredentist pressures in newly independent regimes (Shlapentokh, Sendich, and Payin 1994). This was especially true in the Baltics, where the combination of a large Russian minority and stridently anti-Russian nationalist elites led to significant fear and anxiety (Laitin 1998).

There have certainly been tensions in post-Soviet states, such as over the status of Crimean Russians and the establishment of an independence movement in Kazakhstan. Yet, none of these latent conflicts have escalated to significant violence. The case of Estonia is particularly instructive. At independence, approximately 30% of the resident population in Estonia consisted of ethnic Russians who arrived during various waves of migration stemming back to the pre-Soviet era. Yet, despite their large social and political influence, nationalist elites moved to deprive Russians of Estonian citizenship and economic benefits (Kolstoe 1995, pp. 120–2). Although the 1995 Nationality Law attempted to resolve the question of citizenship, by 2010 some 100,000 Russians still lack citizenship in Estonia or Russia. In other terms, 7.5% of Estonia's population is officially "stateless."[9]

Latent tensions have at times sparked protests and violent riots. In Tallinn, ethnic Russians protested against the demolition of a Soviet war memorial and clashed with the police in 2007. But while Estonian Russians are a coherent and cohesive group, constitute a sizeable minority, and have a legitimate claim of official discrimination, they have not resorted to large scale organized violence or formed active rebel organizations. Estonia has softened its stance somewhat in recent years, granting greater rights and privileges to Russians. This may in part be due to Estonia's application and ascension to the European Union (Kelley 2004). Yet, this cannot explain similar restraint regarding Russian

---

[9] Clifford Levy, "Soviet Legacy Lingers as Estonia Defines its People," *New York Times*, 15 August 2010.

minorities in Belarus, Ukraine, Moldova, Kazakhstan, and elsewhere who are not part of the EU, nor likely candidates for membership.[10]

Another potential explanation that also applies to the other cases mentioned is Estonia's possible fear of an ascendant Russia, which is increasingly ready to flex its muscle in what it perceives as "its" neighborhood, as evidenced when Russia invaded Georgia in 2008. Estonia is militarily and economically weak compared to its eastern neighbor. Indeed, some conciliatory actions were directly related to Russian threats. For instance, in June 1993, Estonia adopted an Alien Registration Law, which was largely seen as discriminating against ethnic Russians (Kelley 2004). In response, Russia cut off the natural gas supply to Estonia, leading the President to suspend the law just a few days later.[11] In addition, Russian military doctrine, approved by presidential decree in 2000, explicitly states that foreign threats include discrimination against Russians abroad and the suppression of their rights and interests (Zevelev 2001). Zevelev argues (2001, p. 168) that the fact that "the leaders of all newly independent states are well aware of the possible consequences of a crisis involving Russian diasporas" helps preserve stability in the Baltics and elsewhere. As Russian power and influence has grown in the Putin years, countries with notable Russian minorities are likely to be especially cautious of jeopardizing relations.

Similar patterns can be found with respect to the overseas Chinese. Ethnic Chinese are numerically and economically important across Southeast Asia, including in Vietnam, Malaysia, Indonesia, and Myanmar, where they have existed for several centuries. There have been latent anti-Chinese sentiments across Southeast Asia, and occasional riots targeting the group, particularly in Malaysia and Indonesia, where the Chinese are seen as economically powerful. Yet, the Chinese community, while relatively organized, has not sought to establish an armed movement.[12] Beginning in the late 1970s, the Chinese government began to articulate a policy of forging links with the overseas ethnic Chinese communities. Accordingly, foreign governments were asked to "protect the legitimate rights and interests of overseas Chinese and respect their national traditions, customs and habits" (Bolt 2000, p. 54). The backing of such a powerful state may cause host countries to behave more cautiously.

In sum, cases such as Tutsis in the Congo and Kurds across the Middle East demonstrate that ethnic kin groups can and do support their transborder brethren. However, as the Russian case illustrates, kin groups that are especially

---

[10] We find some evidence that actual or prospective membership in the European Union influences the likelihood of irredentist conflict when we included a dummy variable for such countries in our models. However, this modification does not change our main results (see the Online Appendix).

[11] Minorities at Risk, "Chronology for Russians in Estonia." Accessed online at: http://www.cidcm.umd.edu/mar/chronology.asp?groupId=36601.

[12] The Malayan Communist Party, which has engaged in violence, was supported by many members of the Chinese-Malaysian community. However, it cannot be said that the movement's goals were strictly ethnic in nature or that the membership was exclusively Chinese.

powerful – in terms of both their numeric size and their control of a militarily superior state – can obviate the need for rebellion. In such cases, incumbent regimes will be wary of trampling over the rights of the group in question and incurring the wrath of their much more powerful neighbors.

Conclusion

Thanks to improved data and analysis, this chapter has been able to provide considerable empirical support for conjectures that have so far only been postulated theoretically or shown to hold for selected cases. In agreement with earlier studies, we show that as the relative strength of transnational ethnic kin groups increases, the risk of internal conflict also grows, but only up to a certain point. After this point, further increases in the ethnic kin's demographic weight have a dampening impact on conflict propensity. Whereas the former part of the relationship is quite straightforward, the latter part is much less obvious, but nevertheless of great importance. Indeed, it is this conflict-reducing influence of large "homelands" that enables us to resolve our main puzzle relating to the relative peacefulness of the Russian diaspora. It is not surprising that the calming influence is limited to included, rather than excluded, TEK groups, such as the Russians in Russia.

These findings do not imply that transnational politics are always more peaceful than domestic dynamics. In contrast to the conflict-inhibiting influence of large state-controlling TEK groups, we find exactly the opposite effect for intermediate size kin groups. Indeed, the probability of conflict hinges critically on the power status of the TEK group. Stateless communities, such as the Kurds (outside Iraq), exhibit a much higher conflict potential compared to the within-country baseline. Thus, the pernicious effect of political exclusion has a tendency to spill over state borders. Since marginalized communities have little to lose at home, they also are more willing to upset the status quo abroad in the name of ethnic solidarity and commonly felt grievances.

Although our main task has been to test empirically the curvilinear theoretical conjecture and to evaluate TEK groups' net impact on conflict, our empirical analysis has important additional theoretical implications. By introducing the conceptual distinction between primary and secondary dyads, we are able to unpack the "ethnic triad" originally introduced by Weiner (1971), while at the same time going beyond analyses that study the influence of ethnic kin as a dichotomous feature (e.g., Cederman, Girardin, and Gleditsch 2009). Indeed, our results show that the power balance in the primary and secondary dyads affects the risk of civil war in potentially quite different ways. The central curvilinear finding for the secondary, transnational dyad dovetails nicely with international relations theory, especially the strands thereof highlighting the importance of uncertainty and deterrence. As mentioned, several studies using conventional balance-of-power theory have shown that the risk of conflict is the highest at power parity. However, we have not been able to find strong evidence of such an inverted U-shape relationship in the primary, domestic dyad. It seems intuitive that the secondary dyad involves strategic considerations that have more to do with interstate relations than with domestic politics, especially since transnational relations can be expected to feature more uncertainty than domestic dyads. Yet, more research is needed to clarify the causal mechanisms operating in the primary and secondary dyads, as well as possible interdependencies between them.

7

Country-Level Inequalities and Civil War

The previous three chapters have focused on the group level and explored how political exclusion and economic inequalities may generate widespread grievances conducive to ethnonationalist mobilization and armed conflict with the state.[1] In this chapter, we take a step back to the country level and examine how particular configurations of political and economic privileges among groups in a country give rise to differences in the risk of civil war.

Given our focus on disaggregation and the importance of a dyadic approach to civil war, the move back up to the country level might at first seem puzzling. However, comparing the causes of civil war across different levels of analysis is helpful for a number of reasons. Many existing analyses of civil war have been conducted at the country level, which makes it difficult to compare their findings directly with our group-level results. By aggregating the properties of groups and other actors up to the country level, we are able to explicitly explore the relationship between group-level and country-level findings and whether these may differ due to potential scaling effects. Moreover, the number and size of ethnic groups varies greatly between countries. Many existing country profile measures, such as ethno-linguistic fractionalization indices, depend on atheoretical population-weighting procedures that disregard the political status of ethnic groups, and where small groups by construction will carry little weight in the measure. However, as we will show, it is possible to construct more informative country-level measures, reflecting group-level characteristics in a more theoretically informed manner. As such, a country-level analysis allows us to compare the explanatory power of our new proposed measures of horizontal inequalities with existing proxies for societal grievances related to restrictions on political participation and uneven distributions of wealth among individuals.

---

[1] This chapter builds on an article by Buhaug, Cederman, and Gleditsch (forthcoming).

Country-level analysis also allows us to extend the comparisons of the risk of civil war from the group-level analysis. While some countries have multiple ethnic groups, others have no politically relevant ethnic cleavages. The group-level models presented in the previous chapters by construction cannot consider the risk of conflict in countries where ethnic identity has no political relevance. Hence, aggregate analysis of this type allows us to compare the risk-inducing effects of political exclusion and economic marginalization among countries with politically relevant groups to the risk of civil war in countries without politically relevant ethnic groups. The move to the country level also allows us to expand the scope of our analysis by moving beyond strictly ethnic conflict to consider all forms of severe insurgencies and civil wars that pit non-state challengers against the government, regardless of whether nonstate organizations have some kind of ethnic affiliation or not.

Although our unit of analysis is quite different from previous chapters, the theoretical arguments follow a common logic. Building on results from the group-level analyses, we highlight the empirical validation of grievance arguments at the country level. In the following two sections, we derive hypotheses on the effects of horizontal and vertical inequality, respectively, on the risk of civil war.

Aggregating Horizontal Inequalities to the Country Level

Originally framed as a dynamic theory of frustration over time (Davies 1962), the logic of relative deprivation can also be extended to a strictly comparative setting (Gurr 1970). Particular individuals or members of specific social groups may be dissatisfied with their status or resource allocation vis-à-vis other individuals or groups (see Chapter 3). Shifting the theoretical focus from individuals to groups, the three previous chapters investigated how economic and political horizontal inequalities are particularly prone to mobilization and conflict if these overlap with other social cleavages, notably ethnic ones. More precisely, we have showed that civil wars are more common when ethnic groups are excluded from access to executive power, and the risk of conflict increases even more when politically excluded groups are also subject to economic marginalization.

However, many of the existing debates about civil war have been couched in terms of the risk that specific countries will experience civil war, and it is not directly clear from our previous results how horizontal inequality and rebellion at the group level may transfer to the country level or help reveal information about what countries are more likely to see armed challenges to the state. At an immediate level, the units of analysis differ, and one country can give rise to a different number of distinct group observations that are all collapsed to one observation in country-level analyses. More fundamentally, the so-called levels-of-analysis, or scaling, problem tells us that theories and empirical patterns at one level often cannot be applied across levels of aggregation, for example from individuals via groups and organizations to countries. Doing so risks various forms of inference to the wrong level or ecological fallacies (Robinson 1950). For example, many studies have examined theoretical accounts of civil war that focus on inequality and distribution in resource dependent economies or rough terrain at the country level, by identifying different forms of country profiles intended to reflect how common such features are (e.g., Fearon and Laitin 2003; Ross 2012). However, the fact that a country has high inequality or a high share of mountainous terrain does not by itself tell us whether the specific actions of the rebels are consistent with the theory or whether the conflict occurs in the place or manner suggested by the theory. Hence, many such propositions are best assessed at a local level (Buhaug and Lujala 2005).

However, too much disaggregation is not necessarily always better and may miss the proverbial forest for the trees (Cederman and Gleditsch 2009). Many studies of civil war analyze the consequences for the state and argue that features such as natural resource dependence or rough terrain primarily affect the risk of war through its effect on state fragility, and that features of ethnic groups or local characteristics are generally irrelevant once we consider state attributes (e.g., Fearon and Laitin 2003). Contrary to these claims, we argue that the distribution of political and material inequalities and likely grievances among social groups within a state tell us a great deal about its general conflict propensity.

In this chapter, we introduce new empirical indicators that operate according to the principle of the weakest link as a way to overcome the information loss associated with aggregation from substate- to state-level analysis (Hirshleifer 1983; Goertz 2007). Instead of relying on measures that use country-level averages or aggregates, we try to identify measures reflecting the specific actors or subunits most at risk of civil war within a country. Aggregate measures based on averages or summed features will by construction discount small and atypical groups, especially in large countries.[2] For example, there are many ethnic groups in Russia, some of which are considerably poorer than the dominant Russian population. Some of the groups in the Caucasus, such as the Chechens, fall dramatically below the country mean in terms of income per capita (see Chapter 5).[3] However, given their small relative size, these groups will essentially have no influence on national average statistics.

In Chapter 4 we proposed, and demonstrated empirically, that the risk of conflict among ethnic groups decreases gradually by their access to state power. The most conflict-prone groups are excluded groups that explicitly seek

---

[2] This does not mean that the average level of exclusion is not statistically associated with civil-war onset; see Wimmer, Cederman, and Min (2009).

[3] Cederman and Girardin (2007) introduce a country-level measure of the risk of civil war, N^*, based on the product of the dyadic conflict probabilities for each individual ethnic group. The results obtained with that specification are very similar to those emanating from the simpler "weakest link" indicator used in this chapter. See the Online Appendix of this book for sensitivity analysis featuring N^*.

independence from the state, as well as groups subject to active discrimination by the central government. A parallel logic underpins the theoretical argument developed in Chapter 5, according to which economically marginalized groups challenge the state over the distribution of wealth and public goods through violent means. In other words, relative political and economic marginalization generates grievances among groups and increases the likelihood that they will be able to overcome collective action problems and mobilize for armed opposition.

An individual country may contain a large number of dyadic relations between included and excluded groups. In line with the weakest link logic, we postulate that the overall risk of conflict in a country is a function of the degree of political and economic marginalization of the least privileged group. Drawing on arguments about the importance of relative group size for opportunities to wage conflict, we posit that the likelihood of violent conflict in a country should increase with the demographic size of the largest politically excluded or discriminated group relative to the incumbent ethnic group(s) in power. Similarly, expecting a higher risk of conflict the larger the gap, we consider the role of horizontal economic inequality in terms of the difference between the poorest group and the national average.

In a manner analogous to our group-level hypotheses H4.1 and H5.1, the first pair of country-level hypotheses can thus be expressed as follows:

H7.1. Countries where a large group suffers from limited access to power are more likely to experience conflict than countries with less exclusion.

H7.2. Countries where the least wealthy group falls far below the national average are more likely to experience conflict than more equal countries.

Aggregating Horizontal Inequalities to the Country Level

Extending the focus beyond ethnic politics, we now turn to more generalized measures of inequality based on individual differences rather than between groups. Many scholars argue that interpersonal inequalities are central to generating political grievances (e.g., Boix 2008; see also references in Chapter 5). If so, we need to consider what could be the appropriate measures to identify what country profiles have higher risk. Most attempts to evaluate individual-level accounts of how grievances may be related to civil war use ethnic diversity or other ethno-demographic characteristics as proxies for ethno-political grievances. The rationale behind this approach is that more ethnically diverse populations will be characterized by larger heterogeneity in values and preferences as well as corresponding dissatisfaction with any single policy. This is especially likely to be the case in the periphery of countries, assuming that preferences are distributed so that similarity declines at greater distance from the center or capital (e.g., Alesina and Spolaore 2005).

Political economists have long argued that ethnic diversity can lead to instability and unrest. In a classical study, Rabushka and Shepsle (1972) contended that ethnic pluralism is incompatible with democratic stability. A series of more recent studies indicates that ethnically diverse societies face greater political contention arising from diverging preferences and differential skills and habits (for overviews, see Alesina and La Ferrara 2005; Kanbur, Rajaram, and Varsheney 2010). Drawing on socio-biological reasoning about ethnic groups and nepotism, Vanhanen (1999) reaches a similar conclusion about heterogeneity and conflict and finds that significant ethnic divisions tend to produce violent conflict in an extensive cross-national sample. More broadly, Sambanis (2001) and Fearon and Laitin (2003) associate ethnic diversity with a class of arguments outlining the role of ethnic and nationalist grievances in conflict processes, whether primordialist as Vanhanen (1999), or explicitly modernist along the lines of Gellner (1983), Anderson (1991), and other prominent theorists of nationalism.[4]

Yet, ethnic fractionalization, polarization, and related ethno-demographic indices fail to account for political inequality. We argue that the most natural measure of vertical political inequality is simply to consider democracy as an indicator of population-wide access to political power. In contrast to the demographic and societal indices based on individual-level data, a democracy indicator (or some subcomponent, such as participation) explicitly reflects the level of political exclusion in a country. In strictly authoritarian systems, political influence is a zero-sum game in the sense that the privileges of the elite come at the expense of the excluded population. In this sense, our notion of vertical political inequality resembles one of Dahl's (1971, p. 6) two main dimensions of democracy, namely the right to participate. This logic, in turn, is part of a more general argument about the inverse relation between democracy and social grievances. In fact, Fearon and Laitin (2003, p. 79) rely explicitly on regime type as a proxy for political frustrations:

Other things being equal, political democracy should be associated with less discrimination and repression along cultural or other lines, since democracy endows citizens with political power (the vote) they do not have in dictatorships. Even more directly, measures of state observance of civil rights such as freedom of association, expression, and due process should be associated with less repression and thus lower grievances.

---

[4] Others suggest a nonlinear relationship where the risk of conflict is assumed to be the highest for intermediate levels of diversity and lower in both highly diverse and fully homogenous societies, based on the notion that greater diversity beyond some level can encourage cooperation (e.g., Sambanis 2001; Collier and Hoeffler 2004). Some also argue that is not so much diversity that increases the risk of conflict but polarization, or a situation where two roughly equal ethnic groups may compete for influence (Horowitz 1985; Montalvo and Reynal-Querol 2005). Although these arguments are clearly distinct and point to different operational measures, they all emphasize demographic configurations as the origin of insecurity and conflict rather than the role of political power and access.

State policies that discriminate in favor of a particular group's language or religion should be associated with greater minority grievances.

In the light of these arguments, we postulate the following effect of vertical political inequality on the risk of armed conflict:

H7.3. Democratic countries are less likely to experience conflict than nondemocracies.

Even the most egalitarian society is characterized by some level of asymmetry in resource allocation and public goods provision. Such inequalities need not follow other social identities shaped by features such as ethnic affiliation or religious denomination. In culturally homogenous countries (and conceivably heterogeneous societies too), resource distributions may themselves delimit social classes, and grievances resulting from persistent inequalities are likely drivers of discontent and revolutionary activities (e.g., Davies 1962). Arguments inspired by Marxist theory constitute a special case of this approach, for example as peasants may rebel in order to force a transfer of land ownership and other privileges from the landed elite to the masses (see Chapter 5).

Attempting to assess the implications of economic inequality for conflict, prior empirical research has typically relied on summary indicators of individual or household income distributions. The most prominent example of such measures is the Gini coefficient, which reflects the extent to which an observed individual income distribution differs from a completely equal distribution. A Gini value approaching 0 would indicate perfect equality, while values closer to 100 (or 1, if measured as a fraction) reflect greater inequality. The aforementioned arguments about social inequality and grievances suggest a causal chain where persistent inequality leads to grievances in disadvantaged sections of a country's population, in turn fueling demands for political change and redistribution. Denied such reforms, and possibly even encountering state-led repression, the aggrieved may see little choice but to rebel by violent means:

H7.4. Countries with high levels of individual-level inequality are more likely to experience conflict than more equal ones.

We note that our summary of the literature in Chapter 5 shows that most studies find no relationship between violence and general social inequality as reflected by the Gini coefficient (e.g., Fearon and Laitin 2003; Collier and Hoeffler 2004). However, existing studies have failed to jointly consider both horizontal and vertical inequalities, that is, across groups and individuals respectively.

Data and Research Design

Our analyses in this chapter aggregate information from the group-level data used in Chapters 4 and 5 up to the country level. The complete data set contains yearly observations of all independent countries between 1991 and 2009 in the Gleditsch and Ward (1999) list. This amounts to around 2,900 observations, with the specific number of observations depending on model specification and data availability.

The dependent variable, civil war onset, is derived from the ACD2EPR data, in turn based on the Non-State Actors data (Cunningham et al. 2009) and UCDP/PRIO Armed Conflict Data (Gleditsch et al. 2002; Themnér and Wallensteen 2011). In line with the other chapters, we adopt the most inclusive definition of civil war, counting all conflicts with a minimum of 25 battle-related deaths per calendar year. In its simplest form, we use a dichotomous civil war onset indicator that codes initial year of fighting between the main actors as 1 and all years of subsequent conflict as 0. In case of lulls in the fighting or failed peace agreements, we consider renewed fighting to constitute a new civil war onset only if periods of active conflict are separated by at least two calendar years. Aggregated to the country level, the onset variable takes a value of 1 in country years with one or more onsets of intrastate armed conflict. In total, our data contain 99 civil war onsets for the post-1990 period.[5]

As a complement to the simple dichotomous civil war onset indicator, we also specify a categorical onset indicator that separates between different types of civil wars based on the specific incompatibility of a conflict. Our proxies for group-level grievances rely on the categorization of politically relevant ethnic groups, and we expect these to relate primarily to the risk of ethnic conflict, pitting excluded groups against ethnic groups in power. Moreover, previous research has shown that different factors and conditions appear to shape the risk of territorial insurgencies and conflicts over the control of the central government (e.g., Buhaug 2006; Wucherpfennig et al. 2012).

We disaggregate civil war onset along two different dimensions, asking whether the conflict is ethnic and whether the conflict concerns issues of self-determination or claims on the central government. The subset of ethnic conflicts is identified by the ACD2EPR data, linking the UCDP Non-State Actors to the ethnic groups in the EPR-ETH data. Conflicts are coded as ethnic where

---

[5] We do not exclude observations with ongoing conflict from the main models since a country with ongoing conflict in our setup is still at risk of a new conflict onset, as a conflict could arise over a distinct incompatibility. In the UCDP/PRIO data, countries may host several intrastate conflicts simultaneously over different incompatibilities, so it is not the case that countries undergoing civil war cannot be at risk of another conflict. Still, one might argue that observations with an ongoing conflict may be systematically different from countries without any conflict. In sensitivity tests reported in the Online Appendix, we show that the reported results are robust to changes in the treatment of these observations, including dropping ongoing conflicts from the sample altogether.

claims were made on behalf of specific ethnic groups and mobilization and recruitment occur along ethnic lines. The nature of the claims that organizations make – whether related to the central government or a specific territory – determines whether a conflict is classified as governmental or territorial, based on the incompatibility indicator in the UCDP/PRIO Armed Conflict Data Set. This conflict typology in principle encompasses four categories. However, we separate between territorial and governmental conflicts only for the subset of ethnic conflicts, because virtually all nonethnic conflicts concern aspects of the central government.

Finally, we aggregate the conflict data to a country-year format. More specifically, our dependent variable takes on four possible values:

$DV_{cat} = 0$; no onset
$DV_{cat} = 1$; ethnic territorial conflict onset
$DV_{cat} = 2$; ethnic governmental conflict onset
$DV_{cat} = 3$; non-ethnic conflict onset

In the post–Cold War sample, 1991–2009, the dominant form of civil war is ethnic territorial conflict with 42 onsets, followed by 36 nonethnic conflict onsets, and 21 ethnic governmental conflict onsets.

We use a number of indicators to test the proposed links between grievances stemming from intergroup and individual differences in political and economic privileges.

- Horizontal ethno-political inequality (H7.1) is represented by two alternative indicators. The most general variable, *max exclusion*, considers the demographic size of the largest politically excluded group relative to the combined size of the excluded group and the ethnic group(s) in power. This indicator is a country-level version of the relative group size indicator, g, introduced in Chapter 4. In addition, we include an indicator that gives the relative demographic power of the largest ethnic group subject to active discrimination, *max discrimination*. Both indicators are bounded within the interval [0, 1), where higher values denote higher levels of political inequality.
- Horizontal economic inequality (H7.2) is captured by the difference between the national average per capita income level and the per capita income of the poorest ethnic group in the country. More specifically, we define *max low ratio* as the relative income gap between the poorest group and the national average. In other words, this indicator takes the largest value of the *low_ratio* indicator introduced in Chapter 5 for each country year.
- Vertical political inequality (H7.3) is captured by the extent of democracy, based on an updated version of the Scalar Index of Polities (SIP) data set (Gates et al. 2006). The SIP scale combines data on executive recruitment and constraints from the Polity IV data set (Marshall, Jaggers, and Gurr 2011) with data on political participation from the Polyarchy data set

(Vanhanen 2000). In models shown, we use the linear *democracy* term with a one-year time lag. This indicator has a theoretical range from 0 (autocratic ideal type) to 1 (democratic ideal type). In tests not shown, we also include a squared term to allow for a nonlinear democracy-civil war relationship. This specification did not change the other substantive results reported.

• Lastly, vertical income inequality (H7.4) is represented by a Gini coefficient of income dispersion from the World Income Inequality Database (WIID, v. 2.0, see UNU-WIDER 2008). These data cover 140 countries in various years between 1946 and 2005. To minimize missing data problems, we applied linear interpolation between data points and extended the time series by copying the earliest/latest known value to earlier/later years for each country. In our sample, the variable takes on values between 20.4 (Slovakia 1993) and 73.9 (Namibia, multiple years).

In the interest of parsimony and following the model specification of earlier chapters, we consider three control variables plausible related to vertical and horizontal inequality and conflict – *ethnic diversity*, represented by the ELF index (Fearon and Laitin 2003), logged *GDP per capita*, and logged *population size* (Heston et al. 2011). The two latter indicators are lagged by one year.

In addition, we include a set of controls for time dependence in the risk of conflict. To capture the legacy of past conflict, we again use Beck, Katz, and Tucker's (1998) nonparametric approach with a count of time since the previous conflict or first year of observation, measured in years (*peace years*), as well as three natural cubic splines to capture the anticipated non-linear decaying effect of time. Lastly, we control for the (log-transformed) number of *previous conflicts* in each country in the sample period.

Analysis

Before presenting the results from the multivariate regression models, it is useful to briefly compare our grievance indicators and assess to what extent these reflect different features. Figure 7.1 offers a comparison of the most general group-based measure of ethno-political inequality (max exclusion) and the SIP index of democracy. It is clear that the vertical and horizontal inequality indicators tap partly different societal phenomena, even though there is a cluster of observations in the lower right quadrant (consolidated democracies with low levels of horizontal exclusion). Note that although we observe no countries with high democracy score and high exclusion (a logically impossible combination), there are several authoritarian regimes where restrictions on political influence are not accompanied with systematic ethnic exclusion (examples include Cuba, North Korea, and many Middle Eastern countries). Overall, the two indicators for political grievances are moderately negatively correlated ($r = -0.30$).

Along similar lines, Figure 7.2 visualizes the correspondence between the Gini coefficient and our proxy for horizontal economic inequality (max low

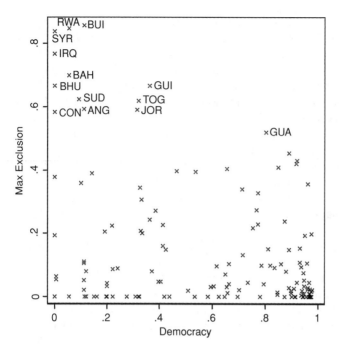

ratio), capturing the relative income gap between the poorest ethnic group and the national average. Countries with low levels of economic disparities between groups display a wide variety in interpersonal wealth differences. Some countries, such as Zimbabwe and Namibia, have high interpersonal inequality but small differences between ethnic groups. Similarly, there is substantial variation in intergroup inequality among countries with similar Gini scores. Russia, for example, is characterized by relatively low-income inequality, which conceals large systematic differences for specific ethnic groups, such as the Chechens and other groups in the Caucasus. It is clear from the figure that interpersonal and intergroup inequalities are hardly related at all ($r = 0.04$).

Figures 7.1 and 7.2 show that our group-based inequality indicators are qualitatively different from standard measures of democracy and income dispersion, and that a number of cases with high interpersonal inequality have low intergroup inequalities and vice versa. We proceed with a brief descriptive assessment of the relationship between societal inequality and civil war onset. Table 7.1 lists the mean values for the various proxies for economic and political grievances by conflict outcome, 1991–2009. Unsurprisingly, we find that the 1,711 country years without civil war onset in this period are less exclusionary and contain fewer interethnic economic differences than the average country at civil war. On average, the no-onset sample is also more

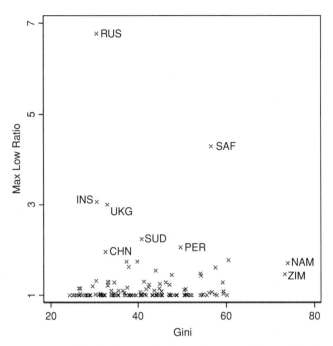

FIGURE 7.2. Vertical versus horizontal economic inequality in 2000.

democratic.[6] Only for the Gini coefficient of vertical income dispersion do we see nearly indistinguishable values for the two subsets, perhaps reflecting the lack of an association suggested in previous research.

However, a more nuanced picture emerges if we disaggregate the dependent variable by conflict type. Countries that have seen one or more new ethnic territorial conflict in the period tend to have substantial intergroup economic differences, as represented by the max low ratio indicator. Yet, intriguingly, they appear to exhibit less interpersonal inequality and are on average almost as democratic as the peaceful sample. This fact reflects how several developed and consolidated democracies have been unable to avoid armed separatist conflict (e.g., India, Israel, and the United Kingdom). Conversely, we find that countries that faced new ethnic challenges to governmental power are characterized by significant ethnopolitical inequality. In fact, the mean exclusion score for these countries is three times higher than for countries without civil war, and the relative difference in terms of active discrimination is larger still.

---

[6] The "no conflict" subsample is hardly homogenous, however, as it includes both most Western democracies and peaceful countries in high-risk environments such as Bangladesh and Kenya, as well as countries with ongoing insurgencies but no *new* civil war onset since 1991 (e.g., Sri Lanka and Uganda). Note that countries that experienced multiple types of conflicts in the period are accounted for under each relevant outcome type. Hence, the total N for the three civil war categories is higher than the N for the aggregate onset category.

TABLE 7.1. *Mean Sample Values by Conflict Outcome, 1991–2009*

Outcome	Max Exclusion	Max Discr.	Max Low Ratio	Democracy	Gini	Obs.
No onset	0.10	0.03	1.13	0.69	40.92	1,711
Civil war onset	0.20	0.07	1.38	0.50	41.05	756
Ethnic territorial	0.11	0.04	1.72	0.59	37.42	293
Ethnic govermental	0.28	0.13	1.16	0.41	42.82	223
Nonethnic	0.18	0.04	1.42	0.49	42.49	466

The subset of countries experiencing nonethnic (and almost exclusively governmental) rebellion falls somewhere in between the ethnic conflict profiles and is characterized by moderate values on the inequality indicators. Overall, Table 7.1 offers tentative support for Hypotheses 7.1, 7.2, and 7.3, although they appear to hold for different subcategories of civil war.

Next, we evaluate the horizontal and vertical inequality indicators in a multivariate setting. We first consider a series of models that test the proposed hypotheses with respect to general civil war risk, using the dichotomous conflict onset variable. Table 7.2 presents four models: two models that include the vertical inequality (VI) proxies and differ only in choice of horizontal political inequality measure (exclusion vs discrimination), and two models that include only the horizontal inequality (HI) indicators.

As shown in Models 7.1 and 7.2, none of the estimates for the interpersonal inequality measures are significantly different from zero at conventional statistical levels. This runs counter to the expectations expressed in Hypotheses 7.3 and 7.4, although it is consistent with earlier failures to find systematic or consistent links between vertical inequalities and civil war risk (e.g., Fearon and Laitin 2003).[7] Perhaps more surprisingly in light of the results reported in Chapter 4, Model 7.1 also fails to produce evidence that a high level of ethnopolitical exclusion makes conflict more likely. Model 7.2 reveals that intergroup political inequality in terms of the smaller set of discriminated groups also seems largely irrelevant. The only proxy for social grievances that behaves in accordance with the hypothesis is horizontal economic inequality; civil wars are overrepresented among countries with large income differentials, other factors held constant. Still, the effect is quite weak at a substantive level. Of the other control variables, the most influential covariates in Models 7.1 and 7.2 are GDP per capita and conflict history, whereas population size and ethnic

---

[7] Note that this nonresult is not due to a failure to specify a nonlinear relationship between democracy and the log odds of civil war onset (e.g., Hegre et al. 2001). In the Online Appendix, we provide results demonstrating that specifications with other functional forms for democracy do not alter the results in any substantive manner.

TABLE 7.2. *Logit Model of Civil War Onset, 1991–2009*

	Model 7.1 Full Model	Model 7.2 Full Model	Model 7.3 HI Model	Model 7.4 HI Model
Democracy	−0.2302	−0.0974		
	(0.5487)	(0.5569)		
Gini	−0.0211	−0.0228		
	(0.0150)	(0.0155)		
Max exclusion	−0.1115		0.0610	
	(0.7258)		(0.5261)	
Max discrimination		1.0537		1.1891
		(0.8463)		(0.6313)
Max low ratio	0.2856**	0.3042**	0.2941**	0.3147**
	(0.0952)	(0.0987)	(0.0961)	(0.1003)
Ethnic diversity	0.7875	0.8271	0.6051	0.6262
	(0.5594)	(0.5566)	(0.4914)	(0.4903)
Population size	0.1365	0.1451	0.2017	0.2154
	(0.1218)	(0.1234)	(0.1087)	(0.1129)
GDP/capita	−0.2581	−0.2742	−0.3209**	−0.3290**
	(0.1727)	(0.1723)	(0.1145)	(0.1141)
Previos conflicts	0.4714	0.4355	0.3867	0.3502
	(0.3379)	(0.3412)	(0.3272)	(0.3292)
Peace years	0.3531**	0.3684**	0.3753**	0.4024**
	(0.1269)	(0.1292)	(0.1142)	(0.1157)
Constant	−2.8187	−2.8974	−3.8044**	−3.9780**
	(1.9517)	(1.9956)	(1.3108)	(1.3815)
Observations	2,467	2,467	2,860	2,860

Robust standard errors in parentheses; estimates for three natural cubic splines not shown.
** $p < 0.01$, * $p < 0.05$.

fractionalization are only weakly correlated with civil war outbreak in the post–Cold War period.

Missing data pose a potentially serious problem in the first two models in Table 7.2 (as well as in earlier attempts to assess the effect of interpersonal inequalities on conflict). Despite interpolation between data points and gentle extrapolation to expand the time series, we still have missing Gini coefficients for many cases. The SIP democracy indicator, too, has missing values for a number of observations in our sample. We have little reason to believe that the excluded observations are missing completely at random. Consequently, in the last two models of Table 7.2, we drop the proxies that do not affect vertical inequality and reinvestigate the impact of horizontal inequality on general conflict risk. Aside from a moderate increase in sample size, this has little impact on the performance of the model. The effect for relative size of the largest excluded group is now positive, as expected, but still statistically insignificant (see Model 7.3). The estimated effect for discrimination becomes somewhat larger (see Model 7.4). Economic marginalization of ethnic groups remains positive and significant throughout, which adds further support to the rationale underlying Hypothesis 7.2. The most visible changes from the full models are found among the control variables. The coefficient for population size increases by about 30% although it still just misses the conventional 95% confidence level. This improvement is primarily due to inclusion of a number of smaller countries that lack data on income dispersion and/or democracy. Also, we now report lowered standard errors and higher confidence in the parameter estimates for GDP per capita. This is not a result of the increased sample size but rather due to exclusion of the collinear democracy index, which has a bivariate correlation with logged per capita income of $r = 0.47$. The ethnolinguistic fractionalization (ELF) index remains insignificant throughout.

As we have seen, there is little evidence of an association between income or political power differentials and a higher risk of civil war in general when they do not overlap with politically relevant ethnic cleavages. In contrast, the general models presented in Table 7.2 indicate that regimes that discriminate sizable ethnic groups are more often challenged by rebel groups, although this effect is considerably weaker for the more sweeping measure of political exclusion. Moreover, we find large economic inequalities across ethnic groups to be consistently and positively linked to civil war.

Yet, it would be premature to draw conclusions about the relationship between grievances and civil war based on these models alone, since we believe particular configurations of material and political status should motivate conflicts of particular kinds (see Table 7.1). In Table 7.3, we evaluate our inequality indicators across the three categories of civil war outlined above. We offer two complementary models, the first one using the extent of political exclusion as proxy for political HI, and the second one focusing specifically on ethnopolitical discrimination.

Again, we find that structural restrictions on political participation constitute a poor predictor of civil war risk; the effect of democracy is insignificant across all outcome types, with the exception of the negative association with ethnic governmental conflict found in Model 7.6, and the marginal impact is generally quite small. The estimate for the Gini coefficient also fails to behave as expected. Indeed, the estimated effect of vertical income inequality is negative and significant for ethnic territorial conflict in both Models 7.5 and 7.6. In line with theories of class-based revolutions, we find a positive coefficient for the individual-level inequality indicator for nonethnic conflict, but this effect is far from statistically reliable. Hypotheses 7.3 and 7.4, postulating a systematic relationship between higher inequalities among individuals and higher conflict risk, both fail to receive support.

By contrast, we find considerably stronger support for political inequality among ethnic groups increasing the risk of ethnic civil war in a country. However, this relationship is more subtle than the simple logit models above

TABLE 7.3. *Multinomial Logit Models of Civil War Onset, 1991–2009*

	Model 7.5			Model 7.6		
	Ethnic Territorial	Ethnic Gov't	Nonethnic	Ethnic Territorial	Ethnic Gov't	Nonethnic
Democracy	−0.2066	−1.0381	−0.1378	0.1116	−1.0110	−0.1137
	(0.6585)	(1.3649)	(0.6591)	(0.7819)	(1.2511)	(0.6709)
Gini	−0.0604*	−0.0205	0.0049	−0.0611*	−0.0172	0.0047
	(0.0243)	(0.0339)	(0.0196)	(0.0283)	(0.0355)	(0.0195)
Max excluion	−6.0190**	2.6146*	−0.1297			
	(1.8503)	(1.1081)	(0.8752)			
Max discrimination				−1.7719	3.4690**	0.1009
				(2.3153)	(1.0932)	(1.7558)
Max low ratio	0.2776**	0.0105	0.2071	0.3067**	0.1573	0.2107
	(0.0896)	(0.6150)	(0.1342)	(0.1086)	(0.4701)	(0.1333)
Ethnic diversity	1.2416	0.1514	0.4263	1.1920	0.5375	0.4128
	(1.2131)	(1.0605)	(0.7204)	(1.4342)	(1.1589)	(0.7093)
Population size	−0.0452	−0.0652	0.2634	0.0388	−0.1299	0.2640
	(0.1932)	(0.3179)	(0.1711)	(0.2082)	(0.3193)	(0.1730)
GDP/capita	−0.1280	−0.3552	−0.2484	−0.1001	−0.4908	−0.2509
	(0.2659)	(0.4150)	(0.2229)	(0.2702)	(0.4263)	(0.2228)
Previous conflicts	1.4108*	0.2162	−0.2729	1.3567	0.1167	−0.2814
	(0.6682)	(0.5530)	(0.3943)	(0.7471)	(0.4548)	(0.3915)
Peace years	0.3533*	0.6991**	0.2078	0.3644*	0.7903**	0.2096
	(0.1748)	(0.2175)	(0.2166)	(0.1694)	(0.2857)	(0.2052)
Constant	−2.2612	−2.0174	−4.8279*	−4.1131	−0.5813	−4.8396*
	(3.3828)	(4.8360)	(2.3400)	(3.3995)	(5.5293)	(2.3349)
Observations		2,467			2,467	

Robust standard errors are in parentheses; three natural cubic splines estimated but not shown.

** $p < 0.01$, * $p < 0.05$.

suggest. Political exclusion, or outright discrimination, of large ethnic groups increases the estimated risk of ethnic governmental conflict, and the effect is quite substantial. Holding all other covariates in Model 7.6 at median values, a shift in max discrimination from the 5th percentile value to the 95th percentile value yields a threefold increase in conflict risk.

The estimate for ethnopolitical exclusion suggests that it contributes to *reducing* the risk of ethnic territorial conflict at the country level, and a similar, if weaker, pattern is found for discrimination in Model 7.6. Although this appears puzzling at first, we believe that this primarily reflects the relationship between relative group size and capacity. Excluded groups that are large and relatively strong compared to incumbent ethnic groups are unlikely to settle for self-determination in a limited territory but instead are likely to perceive that they have a legitimate claim to central governmental power given their relative demographic size. Hypothesis 7.1 is thus supported, but only for the subset of civil wars that include interethnic competition for central governmental power.

Complementing the effect of horizontal political exclusion, we find that variation in economic marginalization of ethnic groups contributes to explaining ethnic territorial (but not ethnic governmental) conflict onset. Again, we believe this pattern is at least in part a function of the size of marginalized groups. Our proxy for horizontal income inequality compares the mean income for the poorest group in each country with the national average. Smaller groups are more likely to exhibit larger discrepancies from the mean as these groups will have little impact on national income statistics. Since very poor groups tend to be small relative to powerful ones, and also more likely to reside in peripheral areas of a country, increased autonomy or secession may be their only viable political objectives. These observations seem to fit well with contemporary insurgencies in Northeast India and the Philippines.

Most other covariates in the two models in Table 7.3 fail to yield significant coefficients within standard confidence intervals. This primarily reflects the short time span of the sample and the relatively few conflict observations for each outcome category. Nevertheless, in view of this limitation, it is even more remarkable that our inequality indicators seem to perform better than the standard covariates used in country-level studies of civil war, such as population size, per capita income, and ethnic fractionalization (see, e.g., Hegre and Sambanis 2006).

We use visualizations to further demonstrate the effects of intergroup inequalities on civil war onset. Figure 7.3 shows the estimated risk of ethnic governmental conflict as a function of political discrimination, with a confidence interval based on simulated data from estimates in Model 7.6. This makes it clear that states are much more likely to be challenged by nonstate actors as the relative size of the largest discriminated group increases. Likewise, Figure 7.4 plots the risk of ethnic territorial conflict over relative wealth gap between average national income and income per capita for the poorest ethnic group. Again, we see a clear positive association, although the substantive effect is smaller than for discrimination.

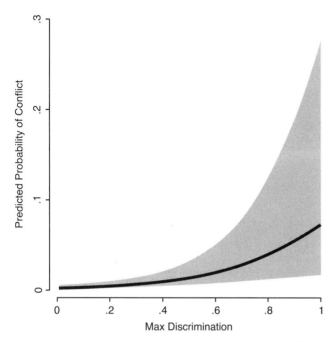

FIGURE 7.3. Estimated risk of ethnic governmental conflict as a function of extent of political discrimination (black line) with 90% confidence interval (gray area).

Since the effects in logit models are linear in the log-odds of outcomes, the exact shape of such effect plots – in this case ethnopolitical discrimination and horizontal economic inequality – will depend on the specific values of the other covariates in the underlying regression model that influence the baseline risk of conflict. In these plots we fixed all other variables in Model 7.6 at their means. However, the absolute risk scores would differ notably if we had considered a high-risk country profile, and it is clear that conflict-inducing factors often tend to go together (e.g., Buhaug and Gleditsch 2008).

We now examine if any particular cases are especially influential in driving these results, and whether the conflicts that "fit" the model in the sense of falling on the regression line plausibly can be linked to economic and political marginalization of ethnic groups, Put differently, can we replicate at the country level the patterns discussed for groups in earlier chapters, where politically excluded and discriminated groups (Chapter 4) as well as economically marginalized ethnic groups (Chapter 5) are significantly more likely to rebel against the state? In this regard, examining some of the conflict cases with high values on the inequality indicators may provide further insights. Table 7.4 lists the five countries with the highest scores of political and economic horizontal inequality, respectively.

For example, Russia appears to be one important case contributing to the main finding in Models 7.5 and 7.6 that economic inequality among ethnic

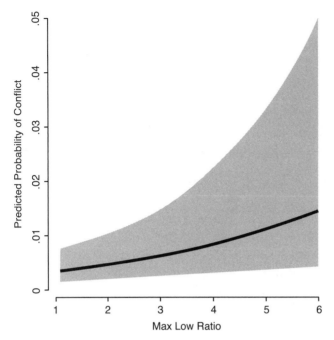

FIGURE 7.4. Estimated risk of ethnic territorial conflict as a function of extent of economic inequality (black line) with 90% confidence interval (gray area).

groups increases ethnic territorial conflict risk. Russia is the country in our data that has the highest level of income inequality (max low ratio = 6.8), and it hosted three onsets of ethnic separatist conflict, in Chechnya in 1994 and 1999 and in a larger part of the Caucasus in 2007. From the discussion in Chapter 5, it is clear that these conflicts are strongly rooted in local grievances related to the dismal economic situation relative to the national center. Likewise, the uprising against Saddam Hussein's regime in Iraq in 1991 was motivated in large part by the narrow concentration of political power, excluding the large Shia majority from participation and influence, and this political configuration is well captured by the country-aggregated exclusion indicator.

Out-of-Sample Prediction

Another way to assess model performance is to evaluate the ability to correctly predict new conflicts outside of the estimation sample. Sometimes a poor indicator of predictive power or theoretical leverage, statistical significance often favors more complex models that capture idiosyncrasies in the estimation sample but predict worse out of sample (Ward, Greenhill, and Bakke 2010). The regression results shown in Tables 7.1 and 7.2 provide strong evidence that inequalities that follow ethnic cleavages are more strongly associated with civil

TABLE 7.4. *High Horizontal Inequality in 1999 and Civil War Onset, 2000–9*

HI	Country	Max Exclusion 1999	Max Low Ratio 1999	Pr(onset) 2000–9
Max exclusion	Rwanda	0.85	1.00	0.47
	Iraq	0.77	1.06	0.78
	Niger	0.72	1.13	0.62
	Gunea	0.67	1.01	0.28
	Angola	0.59	1.15	0.62
Max low ratio	Russia	0.05	6.77	0.89
	Peru	0.40	2.06	0.38
	Central Afr. Rep.	0	1.78	0.31
	Turkey	0.19	1.74	0.33
	Israel	0.36	1.62	0.23

war onset in the post–Cold War period than inequalities unrelated to ethnicity. However, although this is the case for the current sample, it does not necessarily follow that horizontal inequalities can help improve our ability to predict where and when new conflicts will break out in the future.

Because of limitations in data for the group-based income inequality indicator, we have so far estimated empirical models for the post–Cold War period only. In order to obtain a reasonable training sample *and* a reasonable period for out-of-sample prediction, we relax this inclusion criterion. Based on the full global sample for all years since 1960, our prediction analysis is conducted in a number of steps. We start by estimating a horizontal inequality (HI) logit model of civil war onset (with a model specification identical to Model 7.4) for the period 1960–99. From this model we then calculate the accumulated predicted conflict risk for the subsequent decade, 2000–9, based on the observed country characteristics in the final year of observation (1999). We then estimate an alternative model on the same training sample 1960–99, substituting the intergroup inequality measures with our proxies for vertical inequality (VI) – democracy and the Gini coefficient of income dispersion. Following the procedures for the HI assessment, we calculate the compound conflict risk for the 10 year interval 2000–9, based on the model's prediction scores for 1999.[8] The final step compares our predictions with the record of observed civil wars for the period 2000–9 from the UCDP/PRIO Armed Conflict Data Set.

---

[8] If the annual conflict probability in 1999 is p, we can compute the compound probability over the ten-year period 2000–9 as $1-(1-p)^{10}$, based on the complement of peace in all the successive ten years.

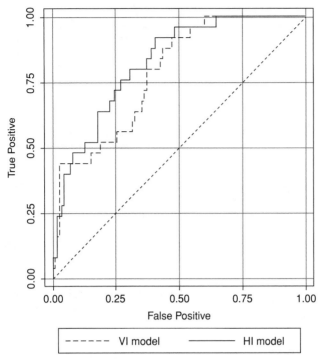

FIGURE 7.5. ROC plot of out-of-sample prediction, 2000–9.

As an illustration, we use a receiver operating characteristic (ROC) plot to compare the performance of the out-of-sample predictions in terms of the share of missed conflicts and false positives across the range of possible prediction thresholds. A better performing model would yield a higher ROC curve relative to an alternative model, reflecting a higher ratio of correct to false conflict predictions. As shown in Figure 7.5, the two models seem to perform quite well; when half of all countries (13 of 26) that experienced civil war onset during the first decade of the twenty-first century are correctly identified, less than 20% of the nonconflict observations are falsely predicted to host a new civil war. Overall, the model containing our group-based (HI) indices of economic inequality and political discrimination performs better than a similarly specified model based on individual-level inequality (VI) measures – especially when it comes to predicting some of the less obvious cases of civil war outbreak. The area under the curve (AUC) statistic provides a measure of overall predictive power that is useful for comparing models drawn from the same sample. The AUC scores for the HI and VI models are 0.822 and 0.783, respectively. The difference between these estimates, while less than massive, is statistically significant with a 5% margin of error. In other words, we have strong evidence to conclude

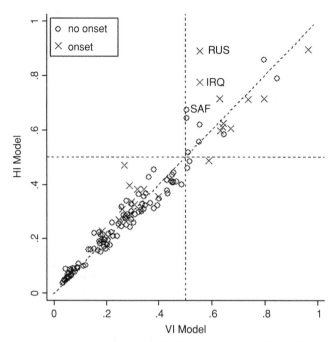

FIGURE 7.6. Scatter plot of individual out-of-sample predictions, 2000–9.

the HI model outperforms "standard" civil war models in terms of providing accurate predictions out-of-sample.

In a further evaluation of the prediction analysis, we consider the predictions for countries that had one or more civil war outbreak(s) between 2000 and 2009. Table 7.4 lists the five relevant countries with the highest exclusion and inequality scores, respectively, in the final year of the training period (1999). Quite tellingly, there is no overlap between these two lists; countries with very high ethnopolitical exclusion tend to score relatively low on the economic inequality indicator, and the reverse is equally true. The former group comprises states with highly exclusionary policies, where minority groups were politically dominant. Likewise, the civil war sample includes some countries with substantial interethnic economic differences, several of which have been discussed in earlier chapters.

Figure 7.6 provides a more complete overview of how the out-of-sample predictions match observed conflict outcomes for the VI and HI model. The top "true" predictions from Table 7.4 are easily detectable, but the plot also identifies one false positive, South Africa, which is considered at greater risk in the HI model than in the VI model. The relatively high prediction score is driven by South Africa's severe horizontal economic inequalities – only Russia scores higher on the max low ratio indicator.

TABLE 7.5. *High Horizontal Inequality in 2009 without Conflict, 1991–2009*

HI		Country	Max Exclusion 2009	Max Low Ratio 2009
Max exclusion		Syria	0.84	1.29
		Bahrain	0.70	1.00
		Bhutan	0.67	1.02
		Jordan	0.59	1.00
		Ecuador	0.42	1.05
Max low ratio		South Africa	<0.01	4.29
		Saud Arabia	0.19	2.06
		China	0.11	1.97
		Vietnam	0.02	1.75
		Namibia	0.03	1.71

A brief inspection of country characteristics for the final year with data may provide some insights for where new civil wars may be likely (see Table 7.5). When we focus on countries without a recent history of armed conflict (no conflict since 1990 until the end of 2009), we find the highest level of ethnopolitical exclusion in Syria, followed by Bahrain. The recent developments associated with the so-called Arab Spring in the Middle East 2011 would seem to add considerable credibility to this list. Yet, we should be cautious about making too strong claims here as the turmoil in Bahrain and the civil war in Syria clearly were influenced by preceding events, violent as well as nonviolent, in Tunisia, Egypt, and Libya, all of which have low values on the exclusion indicator as our present data are unable to capture nonethnic and nonspatial social inequalities.

Focusing on economic disparities, our model suggests that unless severe intergroup income inequalities are reduced, South Africa could see renewed violence and civil war, with the caveats noted previously.

Sensitivity Analysis

As in the other empirical chapters, we have conducted a number of additional sensitivity tests, with respect to sample inclusion criteria, variable operationalization, estimation technique, and potentially influential observations. These are documented in greater detail in the online supplementary material, and in this section we briefly synthesize the main tests.

In general, the results for ethnopolitical marginalization and horizontal economic inequality become stronger if we relax the stringent sample definition and extend our data to include the entire postcolonial period (1960–2009) or all years since 1946, the first year of the UCDP/PRIO conflict data.

A harder test is to replace the dependent variable by a separate data source. We reestimated all models with Fearon's (2010) updated civil war data,

TABLE 7.6. *Summary of Findings*

Hyp.	Prediction	Result
H7.1	political HI –> civil war	Yes, but only for ethnic governmental conflict; exclusion of large groups reduces risk of ethnic territorial conflict
H7.2	economic HI –> civil war	Yes, but only for ethnic territorial conflict; countries with poor, peripheral groups more likely to host self-determination conflicts
H7.3	political I –> civil war	Not confirmed; no robust association found
H7.4	economic VI –> civil war	Not confirmed; income dispersion weakly *negatively* associated with ethnic territorial conflict

classifying conflicts based on the original data set's coding of ethnic versus nonethnic and center versus exit wars. These data differ from the UCDP/PRIO data set by identifying only civil wars that caused at least 1,000 deaths in total, including at least 100 on each side, and with a yearly average of at least 100 deaths. Despite the considerable reduction in the number of civil war observations with these data, we are able to reproduce the distinct pattern of inequality and conflict, whereby exclusion or discrimination of large groups is associated with civil wars over governmental control while economic marginal-ization increases the risk of separatist claims (see the Online Appendix).

We have also evaluated the sensitivity of the main results to changes in the model specification, notably by modifying the sample inclusion criteria (time and space), by selection of control variables and the functional form of the grievance proxies, and by using rare events logit to correct for possible biases stemming from the rareness of civil war onset in our data (King and Zeng 2001). None of these modifications change the results substantively from those presented in this chapter.

Overall, these tests contribute to bolster our confidence in our overarching conclusion, namely that the risk of seeing civil war in a country should be con-sidered a function of collective grievances arising from political and economic inequalities across groups. By contrast, interpersonal differences seem largely unrelated to civil war (see Table 7.6).

Conclusions

In this chapter we have revisited the relationship between inequality, grievances, and civil war at the country level. We have previously criticized many exist-ing analyses that have tried to evaluate the relationship between inequality grievances and civil war for using measures with poor theoretical ground-ing, and argued that it is important to focus on group-specific inequality characteristics to understand the implications for grievances and conflict. However, although most previous analyses at the country level have dismissed the role of inequality, this is in our view primarily a result of the specific atheoretical measures used rather than due to the irrelevance of inequality or grievances per se. Nor does it follow that horizontal inequalities have no implication for the risk of conflict at the country level. In this chapter we have shown that it is possible to derive more informative country-level measures of horizontal inequality that specifically draw on underlying group-level data. When we compare these measures informed by our group-level theories to standard proxies for vertical economic and political inequalities, as represented by the Gini coefficient and democracy indices, we find strong empirical evidence in support of our approach highlighting the weakest link mechanism in relation to horizontal inequalities. Countries where the poorest ethnic groups are far below the national average income level face a significantly higher risk of civil war than more equal societies. Our evidence also suggests that ethnopolitical exclusion and discrimination are systematically related to a higher risk of civil war in the sense that countries with larger excluded groups with both plausible motivation and opportunity for conflict are more likely to see civil war. These findings show that there is no inherent level of analysis problem separating civil war studies at the country and the group level; using appropriate measures, it will often be possible to scale information up or down from one level to another. These findings lend strong support to our idea that risk of conflict depends on the worst-case scenario, or the weakest link, in the sense that risk is positively associated with extent of inequality for the most economically marginalized and/or largest excluded group. This analysis further demonstrates that it is entirely possible to create country-level profiles that reflect such variation at the group level.

The move to the country level also allows us to consider differences between types of civil war and how the risk of conflict for countries involving groups with plausible grievances compares to the risk of civil war in other countries that do not have ethnic cleavages. Distinguishing between types of conflict by actors and incompatibility in our view further strengthens the relevance of how grievances can arise over political and economic marginalization along ethnic lines. Our results clearly indicate that economic horizontal inequality above all tends to promote ethnic separatist conflict, where poorer groups seek to claim autonomy or separation from the state. This finding corresponds well with the patterns of contemporary conflicts, where separatist insurgencies typically involve small, economically disadvantaged groups and tend to be located in the peripheral hinterland of larger states. The physical distance from the group's homeland to the center of national politics – which often goes together with a substantial cultural divide – and the small size of a peripheral group will typically lead to political marginalization, even under more competitive political institutions. This, in turn, can imply that demanding full or partial self-determination may be perceived as the only viable option for groups dissatisfied with the status quo.

Distinguishing between specific incompatibilities also allows us to go further in terms of understanding the relationship between group characteristics and the specific demands or claims that groups are likely to pursue in violent conflicts. Whereas small marginalized groups are likely to seek secession or autonomy, large groups are more likely to demand control of the state itself. Our results strongly suggest that the risk of ethnic civil wars over control of the state increases with the size of the largest politically excluded group relative to the ethnic group(s) in power. Large marginalized groups can more easily make a plausible cause for demanding inclusion in national politics. Although such claims by themselves may not always be successful or overturn a restricted or minority rule, the sheer size of the excluded group means that it would constitute a potent military force if mobilized and hence is a clear threat. Cases like those in Iraq, Rwanda, and South Africa demonstrate the probabilistic rather than deterministic nature of this relationship, and strong ethnocratic regimes may be able to hold on to power for generations in the absence of a coordinated opposition.

Finally, the third form of civil war that we have considered in this chapter, namely nonethnic conflicts, comprises a more heterogeneous set of cases, and it appears that none of the standard suggested predictors of civil war explain much of the variation here (see also Buhaug 2006). The conventional indicators of vertical inequalities in economic and political privileges, the Gini coefficients of income dispersion and democracy, exhibit generally inconsistent and mostly trivial effects on the risk of civil war across all three conflict types. There are a number of possible interpretations that may be applicable here. Following on our previous analysis, one might argue that social inequalities at most are only weakly and inconsistently related to general civil conflict risk unless they follow important ethnic cleavages. This may, of course, be due to the low quality of the available data, and it is possible that more comprehensive and sophisticated data will give stronger results for the role of general social inequality in civil war (see, e.g., Boix 2008). However, this may also reflect another important component of agency, namely how mobilization does not follow directly from objective inequality or grievances per se, but requires entrepreneurs and organizations. This calls for further research into when specific organizations, such as Marxist ones, have been able to successfully mobilize or not in the face of large social inequalities. Although mobilization may be easier when groups can be mobilized along ethnic lines, organizations still play a mediating role between groups and resort to conflict, and we turn to this topic in the next chapter.

PART III

BEYOND CIVIL WAR ONSET

8

The Duration and Outcome of Civil Wars

The empirical chapters in Part II of this book have applied our grievance and inequality perspective to propositions on the initial outbreak of civil wars.[1] In this chapter, we consider the implications of exclusion and grievances for the duration and outcome of civil wars.

The duration of conflict is interesting in its own right, as the length and persistence vary dramatically across civil wars. Some civil wars can last as little as a single day. Many military coups that generate sufficient casualties to be considered civil wars in the UCDP/PRIO Armed Conflict Data Set or comparable data sets either fail or succeed within a very short time period (Gleditsch et al. 2002; Cunningham et al. 2009). For example, the coup by General Rodríguez against the Paraguayan dictator General Stroessner was limited to a five-hour military battle on 3 February 1989 (incidentally, Stroessner's daughter was married to Rodríguez's son, confirming the within-center character of the conflict).

Other civil wars, however, go on for decades. This, in particular, seems to be the case for many conflicts pitting the state or the political center against marginalized and excluded ethnic groups. For example, the armed conflict involving the Karen National Union in Myanmar, which first became active in 1966, has defied any kind of resolution or definite outcome. It was still considered ongoing at the end of 2011 in the UCDP database.

The fact that so many persistent conflicts seem to involve ethno-political cleavages have led many to argue that ethnic civil wars tend to be longer and more intractable than other civil conflicts. Researchers have emphasized how individuals are likely to harbor long-standing hatred against members of other

---

[1] This chapter draws on material from Cunningham et al. (2009) and Wucherpfennig, Metternich, Cederman, and Gleditsch (2012). We are grateful to David Cunningham, Nils Metternich, Idean Salehyan, and Julian Wucherpfennig for major conceptual and methodological contributions.

ethnic groups, as well as the role that opposing ethnic identities with competing claims can play in making compromise or agreement difficult, if at all possible.

However, looking only at a selection of durable ethnic conflicts can be misleading and may overstate the link between ethnicity and persistent conflict. As we will see in more detail later, existing comparative and large-N research has found little support for claims that ethnic conflicts or civil wars in more ethnically diverse countries tend to be systematically longer or more intractable than other civil wars.

We will argue that much of the existing conceptualization of ethnicity is misguided, highlighting ethnic distinctions and hatred between groups at the expense of the active role of the state in political exclusion and marginalizing ethnic groups. This political dimension of ethnic civil war, rather than ethnic diversity and cleavages per se, contributes to longer conflicts that defy resolution.

Before turning to the existing literature on ethnicity and duration, we briefly review some other important reasons for focusing on duration. Beyond its intrinsic interest, examining the dynamics of conflict in terms of duration and outcome is also helpful as it allows us to consider the actual actors involved in conflict and their observed characteristics. Likewise, studying ongoing conflict facilitates analysis of the relationship between groups and organizations and allows us to take seriously the possibility that ethnic groups may not be unitary actors and that rebel organizations can have a complex relationship to many ethnic groups. Moreover, we can consider the observed characteristics of organizations linked to ethnic groups in ongoing conflict, instead of relying on ex ante proxies, and evaluate whether the characteristics of actors and conflict dynamics actually correspond to the casual mechanisms highlighted as important for conflict.

In our analyses of conflict onset so far we have considered groups as unitary actors and used group features such as demographic size as proxies to approximate their expected power and ability to engage militarily with a government. The empirical chapters in Part II of this book show that these can be useful for identifying how group characteristics, and in particular political and economic configurations, influence the risk of civil conflict. However, in many cases a rebel organization may enjoy very limited support from its declared constituency, and in other cases there may be more than one organization claiming to represent an ethnic group. The actual mobilization and degree of resources held by different organizations within the same conflict or incompatibility can vary considerably. When we look at ongoing conflict, we do not face the same challenge in identifying potential groups and developing proxy measures for their possible resources in the event of a conflict. Instead, we can consider to what extent specific organizations claiming to represent ethnic groups actually can mobilize resources as well as their ability to take on the government's military in an armed conflict.

Consider the case of the Tamils in Sri Lanka, where no fewer than three organizations at various points have claimed to represent the ethnic group, namely the Liberation Tigers of Tamil Eelam (LTTE), the Tamil Eelam Liberation Organization (TELO), and the Eelam People's Revolutionary Liberation Front (EPRLF). These organizations also differed considerably in their size and military capacity. The LTTE had a substantial military capacity and it proved very difficult for the Sri Lankan government to defeat the organization since the onset of the armed conflict in 1984. Although the Sri Lankan Army eventually managed to crush the LTTE in the 2009 military offensive, it clearly required significant efforts to do so. By contrast, the EPRLF and TELO were much smaller organizations. Although all the groups in the Sri Lanka–Tamil conflict claimed to represent the Tamil ethnic group, the organizations spent a great deal of time fighting each other rather than fighting the Sri Lankan government. While the LTTE eventually rejected the 1987 Indo-Sri Lanka Accord, the EPRLF and TELO subsequently laid down their arms and eventually ended up joining forces with the government fighting the LTTE. Finally, only the LTTE received significant transnational and foreign support, including financial support from Indian Tamil communities and military training from the Indian government (Horowitz and Jayamaha 2007; Salehyan et al. 2011).

Previous studies focusing on civil war duration and outcome tend to consider outcomes at the level of countries, or lump organizations together as a "rebel" side (see Mason and Fett 1996; Mason, Weingarten, and Fett 1999; Walter 2002; DeRouen and Sobek 2004). Other studies examining conflict patterns using ethnic groups as the unit of analysis typically do not consider the specific organizations representing these groups and differences between competing organizations (see Gurr 1993a; Saideman and Ayres 2000; Toft 2003).

Although existing studies certainly have provided helpful insights about the duration and dynamics of civil wars, aggregating groups under the heading "rebels" and looking only at government or country-level characteristics ultimately leaves us unable to account for variation in conflict duration and outcome across organizations and their relationship to ethnic groups. In the Sri Lanka–Tamil conflict it would clearly be misleading to treat all of the Tamil organizations as a single actor. Moreover, since the organizations have different levels of resources and external support, we would also expect their ability to fight to differ notably, resulting in differences in tactics employed as well as expected durations and outcomes for the individual dyadic interactions between the government and the organizations.

In this chapter we adopt an organizational perspective and consider the characteristics of the actual organizations involved in conflict. We treat each of the named nonstate actors (NSA) or organizations in the in the UCDP/PRIO Armed Conflict Data Set as separate actors, and consider their interactions with the government in civil war organization dyads. We detect potential links between rebel organizations and ethnic groups in the EPR-ETH data, as well as their political status and possible involvement from transnational communities. Following the analysis in Chapter 7, we will also consider how organizational characteristics can be rescaled and inform analyses at other levels.

This chapter is structured as follows. We first review existing research on ethnicity and the duration of conflict. We then proceed to outline a theory on how ethnic exclusion influences conflict duration and the outcome of conflict, highlighting the effects of exclusion on recruitment and polarization. We then detail the data used for our empirical test and present the results and their implications.

Civil War Duration and Ethnicity

Most of the recent comparative research on civil war has focused exclusively on the initial onset of a violent conflict and has generally paid little attention to what happens in conflicts once they have broken out. This is puzzling, given the important role of expectations about fighting and outcomes in discussions of the resort to conflict, as well as potential influence in strategies used in ongoing conflict in shaping the outcomes. There is a long tradition of qualitative studies of individual conflicts that explore their dynamics, including duration and outcome. For example, civil wars between a state and insurgent nonstate groups tend to be asymmetric, which raises the puzzle of why conflicts start in the first place and why the state is not able to deter conflict or quickly achieve a decisive victory. Many studies have examined how particular insurgency strategies and favorable conditions for rebellion can allow weak parties to fight extended conflicts, and ultimately extract significant concessions from much stronger state opponents, if not fully prevail militarily (e.g., Mack 1975; Arreguin-Toft 2001).

More recently, there has been considerable interest in examining whether propositions on civil war onset can helpfully account for variation in the duration and outcome of conflict, as evidenced in particular by the special issue on civil war duration edited by Hegre (2004). An important source of inspiration for this research is the idea that the conditions under which wars end should reflect the factors that motivated resort to conflict in the first place. This argument is associated with Blainey's (1973) famous monograph synthesizing the causes of interstate wars. Studying the causes of war in the context of how wars end, for example by looking at timing or specific agreements where parties formalize an end to a civil war, has some advantages relative to studying onset (see, e.g., Wagner 1993). Considering what potential alternatives to war prior to outbreak might have been or identifying "close calls" where conflict was possible, but ultimately did not break out, involves difficult considerations about counterfactuals (see Tetlock and Belkin 1996). By contrast, we can easily compare successful conflict terminations with ongoing conflict. Other researchers argue that conditions at the initial outbreak of a conflict are likely to be closely associated with expected duration and outcomes, since parties make decisions at the outset based on the expected dynamics of conflict

TABLE 8.1. *Approaches to Civil War Dynamics/Duration*

		Non-State Actor	
		Ethnic Groups	Rebel Organizations
The State	*Passive*	(a) Security dilemma	(b) Rebel groups as firms
	Active	(c) Sons-of-the-soil	(d) War as a commitment problem; ethnic defection

(Wagner 2000). Finally, if war onset is associated with uncertainty between the actors and information is revealed through fighting, then we should see wars ending "when opponents learn enough about each other" (Slantchev 2003, p. 621).

From this perspective, the most remarkable feature of the recent literature on conflict duration is how many authors provide accounts for factors influencing conflict duration that are strikingly different from their suggested explanations for conflict onset. For example, even though Collier and Hoeffler (2004) give short shrift to grievances as an explanation for the onset of war based on their empirical analysis, Collier, Hoeffler, and Söderbom (2004) find greater income inequality to be associated with longer conflicts, and that the duration of civil war is longer in moderately ethnically fractionalized societies. They provide a valiant defense of why these results should be seen as consistent with their underlying opportunity-based model of conflict. However, they offer no direct explanation of why income inequality should be relevant to duration yet unrelated to conflict onset, beyond referring to their empirical findings suggesting that this is the case. More generally, it is unclear from this and most other studies why some factors should have similar effects on civil war outbreak and duration (e.g., GDP per capita) while others have differing effects on the two responses (e.g., inequality and ethnicity). Some studies even suggest that the initial origins of conflict are largely irrelevant to the prospects for civil war settlement, such as Walter's (2002) work on the need for external enforcers to overcome commitment problems in implementing peace settlements.

Although it is possible that the causes of civil war onset may differ from the factors making conflicts protracted or last longer, such differences call for an explanation. They can only be considered consistent with a theoretical framework with an adequate explanation of their differences. We strongly believe that the arguments offered earlier for how exclusion and inequality influence conflict onset also should provide insights into the dynamics of conflict, including duration and likely outcomes. However, we also acknowledge that the relationship between ethnicity and conflict dynamics is more complex than appreciated in much of the existing research.

Previous approaches to ethnicity and civil war dynamics can be classified by the simple 2 × 2 typology in Table 8.1. Here we differentiate between 1) whether the government's challenger is defined as an ethnic group or a rebel organization, and 2) whether the state is conceptualized as an active or passive actor. We classify existing approaches to civil war dynamics by identifying how they respond to the need to 1) theorize the linkage between ethnic groups and rebel organizations and 2) consider the state as an active agent in conflict.

By definition, civil wars pit a government against one (or more) rebel organization(s), challenging state authority through violent means, with the aim of overtaking the state's monopoly on legal use of force over either all or parts of its territory (see Sambanis 2004b for a discussion of different definitions of civil war). Civil wars differ from other types of violence, such as communal violence, in that the state by definition must be involved as an actor (Kalyvas 2006). Yet, many studies of civil war essentially disregard the state altogether when making predictions about the behavior of rebel organizations.

Definitions of civil war are usually less specific on how to conceptualize the challenger. Depending on the specific theoretical approach, researchers may highlight the nonstate actors as ethnic groups or rebel organizations. The conceptualization of actors and agency is crucial for understanding the dynamics of civil war, since it implicitly determines the locus of causation. As such, we need to go beyond the limited and somewhat disconnected existing literature on ethnic conflict duration, and consider their relationship to more general explanations of the dynamics within civil wars.

Many efforts seeking to understand the dramatic upsurge of civil wars during the early 1990s portrayed civil wars as conflicts fought between distinct ethnic groups, often using conflicts such as Yugoslavia or Rwanda as paradigmatic cases. Drawing on international relations theory, Posen (1993), for example, argues that these conflicts arose as the result of an ethnic security dilemma caused by state breakdown. We locate this approach in quadrant (a) in Table 8.1. This perspective sees ethnic groups as engaging in preemptive violence in weak state environments because they fear for their own survival under threats from other groups. The specific history of intergroup relations, as well as the physical and ethnic geography that groups face, are seen as the core determinants of the severity of the security dilemma (Posen 1993; Snyder and Jervis 1999; Toft 2003). This in turn has important implications for the expected duration of such conflicts. Although not all civil wars are ethnic, civil wars fought between ethnic groups are held to quickly become protracted and therefore endure much longer than nonethnic civil wars (Horowitz 1985; Kaufmann 1996; 1998; Rose 2000; Kaufman 2001; van Evera 2001; Kaufman 2006). This perspective tends to assert that ethnicity is fixed and immutable, thus distinguishing it from other ordering principles such as ideologies. According to Kaufmann (1996, p. 138),

[e]thnic conflicts are disputes between communities which see themselves as having distinct heritages, over the power relationship between the communities, while ideological civil wars are contests between factions within the same community over how that

community should be governed. The key difference is the flexibility of individual loyalties, which are quite fluid in ideological conflicts, but almost completely rigid in ethnic wars.

Moreover, battles, massacres, and other violent events in conflicts further harden these identities to the point where compromises become delegitimized (Kaufman 2006, p. 205). As a consequence, we see a "spiral of escalation" that renders these conflicts extremely difficult to resolve, if it is at all possible, without third party intervention (Walter 1997; Kaufman 2006). Indeed, some go as far as claiming that partition is the only possible solution to ethnic conflicts (Kaufmann 1996).

The opposing view – which we locate in quadrant (b) in Table 8.1 – argues that rebel organizations are the most appropriate unit of analysis (Kalyvas 2008a; Sinno 2008). Of course, rebel organizations are always present in civil wars, whether they are linked to ethnic groups or not (Cunningham et al. 2009). However, this approach more fundamentally questions the relevance of ethnic groups as theoretically meaningful actors in civil wars (Collier 2000; Fearon 2004b; Brandt et al. 2008; although see also Collier et al. 2004; Montalvo and Reynal-Querol 2010). This line of research argues that we should see rebel organizations as collectives or firms, which produce violence either for political aims or self-centered purposes or possibly some mix between the two, where ethnicity by itself usually has little importance, if any, for the mobilization or behavior of the organization (e.g., Collier and Hoeffler 2004; Mueller 2004; Kalyvas 2006).

Group-based approaches highlighting the security dilemma simply claim that ethnic wars tend to last longer, and offer illustrative case studies to support their claims. The "rebel groups as firms" perspective, by contrast, tends to highlight the problems of selection on the dependent variable and casual empiricism. Although case studies of long-lasting ethnic conflicts may seem to provide support for such claims, scholars in the rebel groups as firms approach challenge their conclusion by pointing to more systematic quantitative research indicating no significant relationship between ethnic diversity and conflict. Indeed, the claims relating the security dilemma and ethnicity to long conflicts usually rest on various untested theoretical assumptions, most fundamentally that the role of ethnicity in facilitating collective action is the only causal mechanism through which ethnic identities influence conflict.

The rebel group as firms perspective tends to downplay the role of political motivation in collective action, stressing the inherent risk of participating in conflict and how positive political outcomes from conflict tend to be public goods that cannot be withheld to contributors alone (Tullock 1971; Collier et al. 2004). Researchers such as Collier et al. (2004) instead stress the role of natural resources in facilitating collective actions and argue that opportunities for rents and personal wealth during conflict tend to lead to long and intractable civil wars.

Moreover, scholars in this line of research also downplay the role of ethnic groups in relation to rebel organizations. This is sometimes done with a reference to empirical studies disputing any link between conflict and common indicators of ethnic diversity such as ethno-linguistic fractionalization or polarization. From a more theoretical point of view, Mueller (2004) argues that individual beliefs and emotions, such as hatred, are not sufficiently stable to motivate long conflicts. Many, such as Brubaker (2004), argue that ethnic identities ("groupness") primarily are the result of violence, or merely an excuse, rather than a prior cause:

Although ... perceived groupness does not necessarily reflect what is felt and experienced by participants in an event, a compelling ex-post framing can exercise a powerful feedback effect, shaping subsequent experience and increasing levels of groupness (p. 16).

In the language of political economy approaches treating rebel groups as firms, Brubaker (2004) suggests that ethnic identities may be endogenous to conflict. Many researchers argue that "ethnic" warfare at best provides a cover story for criminal violence and predation (e.g., Fearon and Laitin 2003; Collier and Hoeffler 2004). Again, Brubaker (2004, p. 19) echoes many of the dominant political economic explanations for the onset of civil conflicts:

What is represented as ethnic conflict or ethnic war – such as violence in former Yugoslavia – may have as much or more to do with thuggery, warlordship, opportunistic looting, and black-market profiteering than with ethnicity.

Others do not necessarily dismiss the effect of ethnicity in regard to the onset of conflict, but argue that it has little influence on the dynamics of fighting. This is the case for researchers who stress both the fixed and fluid nature of ethnic identities. Walter (1997; 2002) argues that external enforcement is critical to the implementation of peace agreements in civil war, but insists that "ethnic differences ... have no predictive power in determining how civil wars end" and that they do not affect the likelihood of agreements or their eventual implementation (Walter 2002, p. 89). For example, Kalyvas (2008a, p. 1045) claims that "[e]ven when ethnic divisions cause the eruption of civil war in the first place, these identities do not always remain stable and fixed during the conflict; if they do change, they may soften rather than only harden." Thus, collective and/or individual preferences and identities are continuously reshaped during the course of a civil war, while master cleavages are frequently undermined by local cleavages (Kalyvas 2006; 2007). This argument runs directly counter to the claim that ethnic identities are fixed since it implies that they can be – and frequently are – transcended through the mechanism of ethnic defection, that is, fighting for ethnic "others" against members of one's own group. As such, Kalyvas (2008a) directly challenges Kaufmann's (2005, p. 183) conjecture that "cross-ethnic recruitment or defection is rare."

Finally, Weinstein (2007) lays out a theory of rebel behavior in which ethnicity represents an endowment from which rebel leaders choose to draw in the absence of more favorable economic resources, such as foreign sponsors or natural resources. Thus, rebel organizations are regarded as political entrepreneurs, whereas the presence of ethnic identities – just like lootable resources – represent an exogenously given endowment that has an effect on the organizational structure of a rebel organization (see also Beardsley and McQuinn 2009). However, social and economic endowments have a differential effect on the (self-)selection of fighters. Fighters recruited through ethnic identities are more committed than recruits motivated exclusively by personal benefits. By implication, the former should therefore be expected to fight longer and be less likely to defect.

Thus, save for Weinstein (2007), approaches focusing on rebel organizations tend to argue that ethnic identities have no predictable or uniform effect on the dynamics or duration of warfare. Whether fighting hardens or softens identities is largely irrelevant, either because the conditions of successful termination are largely unrelated to ethnic identities, or because rebel organizations, not ethnic groups, conduct the fighting. Indeed, if ethnic identities are variable, the presence of ethnic groups in an organization does not by itself yield any systematic implications for the dynamics of warfare.

Both the security dilemma and rebel groups as firms approaches tend to see the state as largely a passive actor or absent in civil war (we discuss notable exceptions below). Introducing the state as a relevant actor brings us to the lower row of Table 8.1. Approaches focusing on rebel organizations typically argue that these resort to violence for private benefits when state weakness makes such strategies feasible. Thus, the inability of the state to prevent violence by itself creates opportunity structures for rebellion. Similarly, group-based approaches frequently explain the occurrence of violence with a security dilemma that arises when the state cannot credibly provide security to groups due to structural weakness (Posen 1993; Snyder and Jervis 1999). The explanation also assumes away the state, and it is the absence of the state that provides an arena of "emerging anarchy" where ethnic conflicts can occur.

The state is an important actor in research on civil war termination as a commitment problem. Walter (1997; 2002) emphasizes the problems in settling civil wars relating to commitment problems, as the state has incentives to renege on agreements after rebels demobilize. This, in turn, can undermine either reaching or implementing peace agreements otherwise acceptable to the parties. However, ethnicity by itself is not relevant in the conventional approach to civil war termination as a commitment problem. A notable exception here is Fearon's (2004b) and Fearon and Laitin's (2011) analysis of the dynamics of so-called sons-of-the-soil conflicts, a subset of ethnic conflicts which we locate in quadrant (c) in Table 8.1. Following Weiner's (1978) original conceptualization, these are conflicts between a peripheral and geographically concentrated ethnic minority, that is, the sons of the soil, facing state-supported migration to its perceived homeland by a dominant ethnic group from the center. Scarcity of land and jobs generate strong grievances and local struggles. Importantly, these grievances are state-induced, since the migration is assumed to be at least partly orchestrated by the government. They are likely to escalate in situations where the state sides with migrants in order to appease its support base. The government is held to be unable to credibly commit to a peace agreement because migration is path dependent and it is in the government's interest to maintain such policies. Fearon (2004b) argues that this renders sons-of-the-soil conflicts especially difficult to end, thus prolonging armed struggle.

Kalyvas's (2008a) account of ethnic defection provides a rare example of active state behavior in the civil war literature. The problem of ethnic defection is put forward as a prime argument for why ethnic identities must be treated as fluid rather than fixed. Kalyvas (2008a, p. 1050) emphasizes how ethnic defection occurs when

(a) the incumbent state is willing and able to recruit members of the rebellious ethnic minority, (b) a substantial number of individuals collaborate with a political actor explicitly opposed to their own ethnic group, and (c) fighters and sympathizers switch sides from ethnic rebels to the state.

Although the theory postulates a variable effect of ethnicity, its relevance varies systematically based on what the state does. As Kalyvas (2008a, p. 1045) explains, "the behavioral potential of ethnicity is empirically variable . . . [and] a key determinant . . . is the willingness of incumbent states facing ethnic rebellion to recruit ethnic defectors, which in turn depends on their resources." Put differently, state strength, and in particular territorial control, is a systematic modifier of ethnic identities. Accordingly, we locate this approach in quadrant (d) in Table 8.1.

To recap, the effect of ethnicity on conflict dynamics remain disputed. Our overview here shows how many scholars treat ethnic identities as irrelevant to conflict while others argue that ethnic identities are relevant only in so far as they facilitate collective action. We strongly disagree with both of these claims. However, we also reject the idea that hatred between communities and the immutability of ethnic identities by itself makes conflicts involving ethnic groups longer and more intractable (see, e.g., Horowitz 1985; Kaufmann 1996; 1998; Kaufman 2001; 2006). Following Wucherpfennig et al. (2012), we argue instead that whether ethnicity leads to protracted conflict ultimately depends on the role of the state and whether ethnic groups are excluded. In the next section we develop a critique of the assumed nature of ethnic identities and identify the specific causal mechanisms through which ethnicity may operate.

A Theory of Ethno-Political Exclusion and Conflict Duration and Outcome

Clausewitz ([1831] 1984, p. 87) famously argued that "war is merely the continuation of politics by other means." We similarly highlight the political aims motivating both governments and nonstate challengers in civil wars and show how these shape their fighting behavior. We outline the costs and benefits of ethnic exclusion, both from the perspective of the state and from the perspective of rebel organizations, and highlight how state-induced patterns of ethnic exclusion condition the motivations, preferences, and constraints of actors, and thus the duration of civil war.

Ethnic exclusion is a political strategy enacted by leaders and groups controlling the state. It aims to secure their political, cultural, and economic interests through selectively excluding parts of the population from access to valuable political and economic goods based on ethnic affiliation. Excluding particular ethnic groups from access to state power has symbolic, material, and political advantages for incumbent governments. The most obvious benefit is that exclusion allows consolidating state power and its benefits for those that are included. State borders that leave ethnic groups without political representation through exclusionary policies violate the core principle of nationalism, which states that cultural and political boundaries need to coincide (Gellner 1983). Political representation and power status reinforce the subjective worth of one's group vis-à-vis other groups and legitimize their struggle for power and representation. Indeed, control over statehood ensures the ability to govern a "homeland," the freedom to speak the group's preferred language or to practice its religion.

Preferential treatment on an ethnic basis, through ascriptive marks, imposes categorical, rather than fluid, boundaries. Thus, unlike ideology, ethnicity is "sticky" and cannot easily be transcended. This makes it an ideal criterion for the *selective* provision of goods (Rothchild 1981, p. 222; see also Tilly 2006). Thanks to their relatively clear boundaries, ethnic groups are usually more serviceable groups than classes, and this has repercussions for war duration. For elites, nepotism and clientelism can secure a strong base of support and thus secure the political survival of leaders. Moreover, such practices frequently extend to recruitment into sensitive state agencies such as the police or armed forces, which in turn secures the group's survival in the long run (Rothchild 1981; Wimmer 2002).

Exclusion can also originate from direct security concerns. Roessler (2011) argues that ethnic exclusion can act as a strategy of threat displacement when there is a high probability of leadership turnover from within the state, that is, through coups. Rulers attempt to safeguard regimes through excluding co-conspirators. This can help avoid the commitment problem that arises when divided elites jointly control a state's coercive apparatus, but cannot guarantee that co-rulers will refrain from resorting to violence. Finally, in democracies and semidemocracies, governing elites may feel tempted to secure their positions through ethnic outbidding and diversionary war against a domestic minority (Tir and Jasinski 2008).

Exclusion benefits privileged groups but may come at a substantial cost as it tends to motivate challengers, and affected groups may resort to violence to change the status quo. Exclusion can backfire for a number of reasons. By its very nature, exclusion generates benefits for some at the expense of others, which is likely to generate grievances and make excluded groups fertile breeding grounds for rebellion (Gurr 1993a). Violations of norms of justice and equality typically arouse feelings of anger and resentment among members of the disadvantaged group (Petersen 2002; Williams 2003). Where exclusion is enduring and indiscriminate, collective grievances "reinforce the plausibility and justifiability of a radical political orientation or collective identity" (Goodwin 1997, p. 16), especially when institutional channels for political dissent resolution are perceived to be blocked (Hafez 2003). In the words of John F. Kennedy: "Those who make peaceful revolution impossible will make violent revolution inevitable."

Once established, exclusion tends to be taken for granted and legitimized by its beneficiaries. Rothchild (1981, p. 217) states that "favored ethnic groups come to take proprietary view of their traditional overrepresentation, or even monopoly position." However, the feelings of resentment and radicalism fostered by exclusion further raise the costs of political change. A fall from privilege becomes particularly unappealing when excluded groups threatening to seize power are likely to seek revenge when in power. This commitment problem is likely to be particularly severe under minority rule. Even if governments try to appease challengers, a further commitment problem arises when past experiences make such offers less credible. The case of Liberia powerfully illustrates these dynamics, where the 1980 coup headed by Master Sergeant Doe put an end to 133 years of minority rule by the Americo-Liberians and murdered or replaced many of the Americo-Liberian elites (Ballah and Abrokwaa 2003). Active discrimination against Americo-Liberians remained in place until Charles Taylor seized power in 1997.

Exclusion publicly signals a lack of willingness to compromise. By contrast, where political power is shared, the government has demonstrated at least minimal willingness to compromise, even if the actual arrangements are not always fully satisfactory in practice, as illustrated by the case of Burundi. Still, the mere fact that ethnic groups are not categorically excluded from public goods or even openly discriminated against demonstrates that compromise is possible and "discourages the sense that the state is unreformable . . . and needs to be fundamentally overhauled" (Goodwin 1997, p. 18).

Finally, ethnic groups in power in a context of ethnic exclusion may find themselves unable to grant partial concessions to challengers due to reputation concerns. Walter (2009b) argues that governments have incentives to deny settlements to initial challengers when facing other potential challengers in order to signal determination and avoid encouraging other challenges, since a slippery slide of concessions ultimately could erode the power of the central government.[2] In sum, ethnic exclusion is potentially very risky, and incumbent

---

[2] However, Forsberg (2013) finds no systematic evidence for such a domestic domino effect among minorities.

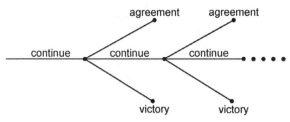

FIGURE 8.1. Sequential fighting in civil wars.

governments are, as a general rule, aware of this. Exclusion strategies must be enacted under the perception that the benefits outweigh likely costs.

Having outlined the logic of ethno-political exclusion, we are now ready to theorize its effect on the duration of civil wars. Many existing theories tend to be monadic or only theorize the actions of nonstate challengers. Other research on civil war termination focuses on the prospects for agreements and implementation, which only indirectly address the length or persistence of conflict. By contrast, our approach is explicit about the dyadic interaction between the state and nonstate actors pursuing distinct objectives, and how their interactions and relations influence conflict dynamics and duration (see Cunningham et al. 2009; Wucherpfennig 2011).

Our logic highlights a two-level game, where incumbent governments and non-state challengers also interact with their followers as they depend on their respective bases of support. Our core argument is that the combination of ascriptive ethnicity and political exclusion makes it difficult for both rebel groups fighting on behalf of excluded ethnic groups, as well as incumbent governments, to reach settlements that would allow for effective conflict resolution and lasting peace. The outcome more often is a protracted, durable conflict.

Our theoretical rationale is based on a *per-period logic* visualized in Figure 8.1. We conceptualize the dynamics of civil wars as sequential rounds of bargaining and fighting. During each round, there are three possible "outcomes": (1) the belligerents can reach a mutually acceptable agreement that terminates the fighting, (2) either side capitulates and accepts defeat, resulting in a winner and a loser, or (3) continued fighting if neither (1) nor (2) is possible. From our perspective, (1) and (2) both entail conflict settlements, although they obviously represent different distributions of the underlying incompatibility between the belligerents. We follow Wittman (1979) and Goemans (2000), who argue that conflict termination – short of complete eradication of the opponent, which is extremely rare – requires *both* parties to agree on a settlement, including losses as implicit settlements, since the other party would otherwise continue to fight.

Following this logic, explaining duration thus amounts to accounting for what prevents the belligerents from reaching a settlement during each round. In other words, if both victories and agreements are less likely, conflicts are more likely to continue, which will lead to longer conflict duration.

An obvious influence on conflict dynamics is the relative power balance. Cunningham et al. (2009) identify two distinct dimensions of dyadic power, which they argue are likely to have divergent effects on the dynamics and duration of conflict. The first one pertains to the conventional military capability of rebels relative to the government, or their ability to impose direct costs on a government. Conflicts should be shorter when nonstate actors have greater military strength, as the organization can be expected to be more likely to either prevail militarily in the contest or be offered some kind of concession by governments early on in a conflict, based on how well they fare in an armed conflict (Fearon 1994; Gartzke 1999). Although the ability of rebels to mobilize militarily conceivably may be underestimated prior to a conflict, such groups should quickly do relatively well on the battlefield or gain concessions. Empirical analyses confirm that strong or more capable rebels, who can pose a credible challenge to the government, tend to fight shorter wars and are more likely to see a favorable outcome (Buhaug, Gates, and Lujala 2009; Cunningham et al. 2009).

A second dyadic dimension of power is the ability of the rebels to resist or evade government repression. Groups that lack the capacity to pose a military challenge or impose significant costs on a government may have various logistic advantages that make it difficult for a government to defeat the group. Cunningham et al. (2009) argue that this leads to protracted, seemingly inefficient conflicts, often fought at low intensity in the periphery. Governments have few incentives to offer meaningful concessions to rebels, even though they may be unable to impose decisive military defeats on insurgent organizations. Since demobilization is dangerous and groups are at risk of retribution from the state if they lay down arms (see, e.g., Walter 1997), conflicts where rebels have a high capacity to resist are likely to become protracted and defy a decisive outcome, as, for example, in the Karen conflict in Burma/Myanmar.

Cunningham et al. (2009) discuss power in civil war dyads but do not consider the roles of ethnicity or transnational linkages or how these may affect relative strength. As we have seen previously, many arguments relate ethnic links to dyadic strength based on the effects of ethnicity on higher opportunities for collective action as well as greater resolve in conflicts pitting ethnic groups against one another. Although we also believe that rebel organizations with links to ethnic groups will differ systematically from other organizations, we seek to theorize their connection directly rather than proceed by assumption. We share Kalyvas's (2008a, p. 1063) concern that the "relation [of rebel organizations] to underlying populations must be the object of systematic theoretical and empirical investigation as opposed to mere assumption." Whereas many authors simply assert the putative irrelevance of ethnicity based on the varying connection to ethnicity in rebel groups, we take this concern seriously by focusing systematically on variation within the nexus between rebel organizations and ethnic groups and conflict duration. In brief, conceptualizing fighting in civil wars as violence between the state and nonstate actors, which may or may not be characterized by an explicit link to ethnic groups, allows us to capture a broad range of actor constellations.

We assume that rebel organizations are political entrepreneurs seeking to mobilize and sustain sufficient capacity to overthrow the government and challenge the government's force monopoly, either in the entire country or locally in some limited territory (Buhaug 2006). Rebel organizations face two key challenges. First, they need to *recruit* a sufficient number of people to challenge the government effectively (Gates 2002). Initial recruitment alone is insufficient to sustain armed conflict, and organizations must in equal measure provide incentives to *retain* recruits to fulfill the goals of the rebellion. In other words, rebel organizations need to create incentives to ensure that fighters do not abandon the rebellion.

We highlight two mechanisms that contribute to retaining fighters: greater cost tolerance and commitment, and increased group solidarity. These mechanisms are closely interrelated under ethno-political configurations involving exclusion and polarization. We first focus on mechanisms that emphasize how mobilizing and retaining fighters requires individual-level compensation. We argue that variation in the reward structure – time horizons in particular – helps explain why some organizations endure longer than others (Weinstein 2007). We extend this literature by emphasizing how reward structures are shaped by state-imposed ethno-political power configurations, in addition to the economic opportunities or fixed social networks emphasized by Weinstein (2007). This approach increases the causal depth over conventional approaches to war duration as we identify the specific conditions under which ethnicity matters.

In essence, we argue that state-induced ethnonationalist policies that exclude and discriminate against specific ethnic groups generate grievances within the affected groups. Rebel groups that claim to operate on behalf of such ethnic groups can attract fighters by the prospect of political representation or better economic access once the government is defeated. However, unlike immediate material payoffs, such a reward structure is associated with a great deal of uncertainty because it is conditional on the *future* success of the rebel organization. If recruitment and sustained combat are intricately linked to uncertain future rewards, then conflicts should be more likely to become persistent when opportunity costs are low. More specifically, whereas conventional approaches champion arguments about opportunity structures and generally downplay the actors (e.g., Fearon and Laitin 2003, Collier and Hoeffler 2004), we argue that the socioeconomic and ethno-political context of potential recruits jointly and directly shape individual and collective motivations to fight (Horowitz 1985). Aggrieved individuals are more likely to engage in and sustain fighting, independently of opportunity structures. Due to greater cost tolerance, claims about uncertain future benefits resonate particularly well in the presence of grievances. Although such grievances can arise in many scenarios, we focus on the ethnonationalist policies of the state. Challengers who are blocked from access to state institutions seek to escape the rule of dominant ethnic groups by seizing government control or seeking secession and are more likely to remain committed to such efforts.

Ethnic groups excluded from state power are deprived of political representation and likely to be disadvantaged in access to government services. Such exclusion manifests itself in everyday life, and members of excluded groups are often subject to humiliation and treated like second-class citizens. Individual and collective identities become interlinked, insofar as ethnic exclusion operates along categorical lines that are difficult to overcome at the level of the individual, "wrongs" by dominant groups, such as the aforementioned everyday humiliation, the systematic denial of state benefits, including being excluded from public goods, but also injuries and human losses suffered by fellow group members, are likely to be perceived collectively by members of the group. Oberschall (2007) labels this a "multiplier effect." Such dynamics are likely to result in reinforced group solidarity and collective grievances, which in turn also affect the level of grievances at the individual level. Fighters from excluded ethnic groups are therefore generally more cost tolerant and more committed. Moreover, precisely because ethnic exclusion operates along categorical boundaries, increased group solidarity is likely to raise the cost of free riding as group policing gains legitimacy (Hechter and Okamoto 2001). At the same time, these dynamics can also feed into the hands of extremists, who can exploit them to gain momentum and reinforce grievances (Hafez 2003).

At a systemic level, variation in the reward structure also implies systematic differences in vulnerability to exogenous shocks (see Fearon and Laitin 2007). Since rebel organizations composed of opportunistic fighters are heavily dependent on a steady cash flow, factors that impact their financial sources are likely to undermine the rebellion. For example, where rebellion is financed through lootable resources, losing control over relevant sites such as diamondiferous riverbeds and mines can have severe effects on the viability of the movement. By contrast, rebel organizations that rely on the hearts and minds of broader populations are less vulnerable to such shocks.

In sum, members of excluded ethnic groups are more likely to continue fighting than those who do not suffer from exclusion, which in turn allows rebel organizations to endure. To illustrate, it is no surprise that the African National Congress's (ANC's) efforts resonated well among excluded ethnic groups during Apartheid in South Africa. By contrast, members of groups included in the political process enjoy political rights and benefit from state provision. Moreover, since nonexcluded populations are not categorically disadvantaged, the grievance multiplier effect is less effective. As a consequence, organizations associated with ethnic groups in power are less inclined to endure very long periods of fighting, as are rebellions organized around classes or ideologies that do not benefit from categorical boundaries.

Thus far we have outlined why rebel organizations recruiting from excluded ethnic groups are better *able* to sustain long fighting. This by itself, however, does not suffice to account for long duration, since it does not explain why such organizations are less likely to reach settlements that can end the fighting, be it implicit through victory or conceding defeat, or explicitly in the form of a negotiated agreement. In other words, we need to show why rebel organizations associated with excluded ethnic groups are associated with lower probabilities for incumbent and challenger victories, as well as lower probabilities of negotiated agreements. Below, we address these three options.

We stipulate that the features that enable rebel organizations to recruit from excluded ethnic groups also render them harder to defeat for the government. Given the typically asymmetric nature of warfare in civil wars, there is nearly always a possibility for violence by spoilers (Stedman 1997). As we have argued above, ethnic exclusion plants the seeds for extremism and polarization. Moreover, deeply entrenched collective grievances, and a steady supply of fighters from a large pool that is characterized by strong group solidarity and high cost tolerance, can make it very difficult for the government to achieve decisive victory. For example, it took the Sri Lankan military forces nearly 26 years to defeat the Tamil Tigers, and ongoing separatist conflicts in Burma have lasted for more than half a century. By contrast, rebel organizations that draw from included ethnic groups, or do not claim or recruit along ethnic lines, cannot benefit from the same levels of collective grievances, since they lack the categorical division and solidarity that results from politicized ethnicity. To see this, consider the Eritrean Islamic Jihad Movement (EIJM) whose Muslim base is not excluded from central power along categorical lines, or various Marxist rebellions in Latin America, where organizations did not display explicit ethnic linkages.

Why do governments not reach an agreement with challengers to settle conflicts? As we have argued in the previous section, accepting something that will be perceived as a defeat is particularly risky in situations of politically induced grievances. Resentment and other emotional legacies raise the costs of turning the tables (Petersen 2002), since those who were previously in power may become excluded and discriminated against in the future. The ascriptive nature of ethnicity increases this problem, since members of a former group in power are easily detected. Thus, the categorical dividing lines of ethnicity provide a structure that allows for efforts to seek ethnic exclusion. Such arguments are generally less applicable to class or ideology, since such group delineations are less rigid and more susceptible to change (Rothchild 1981, p. 222; Tilly 1999; 2006).

More generally, as Walter (2009a) has forcefully argued, governments may face reputation costs when giving in to the challenger's demands, since doing so would signal weakness and invite other potential challengers to put forward similar demands. Even where the concept of rebel victory does not mean a change in the central government, but is confined to granting territorial autonomy or secession, incumbent governments will have strong reasons not to give in to challengers' demands. Furthermore, since members of ethnic groups in power frequently view their superior power status as just and legitimate, concessions may be hard to legitimize to the government's own constituency or ethnic group (Rothchild 1981).

Finally, we also argue that negotiated agreements are less likely when states engage in ethno-political exclusion and rebel organizations recruit and claim to operate on behalf of ethnic groups. Ethnic exclusion is likely to breed polarization and extremism and powerfully reinforces the subjective value of power status, territory, and statehood among both incumbent governments and ethno-nationalist challengers. The subjective characteristics of nationalist exclusion suggest that the state is not easily shared under competing nationalist claims, and sometimes even rendered indivisible. In other words, exclusion leads to a small (or nonexistent) bargaining range that makes compromise difficult. Toft (2003) and Goddard (2006) have laid out such arguments about indivisible territory, but a similar logic also applies to issues of statehood, representation, and redistribution. In addition, Roessler (2011) argues that incumbent governments may fear power-sharing arrangements, since co-conspirators may abuse their access to state forces in a coup d'état. Thus, we argue that agreements are particularly difficult to achieve between governments and rebel organizations linked to ethnic groups that have been excluded.

We can now state the main hypotheses that we will consider in the empirical analysis. Our first two hypotheses pertain to the role of power and strength in government-rebel interactions. It is important to consider the strength of an organization relative to the government jointly with ethnicity, since many excluded groups tend to have fewer resources, and evidence for ethnic linkages may reflect differences in resources. Moreover, territorial control – which Walter (2002) and Cunningham et al. (2009) promote as an indicator of a group's capacity to resist – is also highly relevant, since excluded ethnic groups often reside in peripheral geographic locations and may be more likely to gain territorial control, even if they are militarily weak.

H8.1. Rebel organizations with greater strength relative to the government will tend to fight shorter conflicts.

H8.2. Rebel organizations that control territory tend to fight longer conflicts.

Our next two hypotheses pertain to the effects of links between rebel organizations and excluded ethnic groups for duration and outcome. Based on our reasoning about ethnicity, recruitment, and polarization, we expect that ethnic exclusion affects the duration and outcome of civil wars as follows:

H8.3. Rebel organizations with a link to an excluded ethnic group will see longer conflicts with the state.

H8.4. Conflicts with the state where rebel organizations have a link to an excluded ethnic group are less likely to end in a decisive outcome.

Our next set of hypotheses pertains to the relationship between rebel organizations and excluded ethnic groups and the role of transnational ethnic kin linkages. Although ethnic dividing lines in civil war are often thought of as purely domestic, many ethnic groups extend beyond the boundaries of individual states. We have previously argued that the risk of civil wars is not determined exclusively by domestic factors, and that transnational linkages can have important influences on the onset of conflict (see Chapter 6). This is obviously also relevant for the duration and outcome of civil conflicts.

Walter (1997; 2002) stresses how external enforcement of peace agreements can increase the prospects for successful settlements. We do not wish to deny the potentially important role external actors may play in aiding conflict termination through enforcement. However, external parties may have many other motivations than simply ending civil wars, and most interventions are not focused on enforcing agreements that the main conflict antagonists have already reached. A number of studies have examined intervention in civil conflict more generally and found that intervention from other states tends to lengthen civil conflicts (e.g., Balch-Lindsay and Enterline 2000; Regan 2000). The most common interpretation of this finding sees interventions as lengthening conflict by shifting the military balance closer to parity between the parties, thereby preventing one side from achieving the expected default outcome sooner, and making protracted conflicts without decisive outcomes much more likely.

However, we believe that transnational linkages can do more than just shift the military balance. Although borders are just lines on the ground in a physical sense and not difficult to cross for insurgent groups, governments often face significant costs and risks of interstate conflict if violating international borders and pursuing rebels into neighboring states (see, e.g., Salehyan 2007; Gleditsch, Salehyan, and Schultz 2008; Salehyan 2009). Support originating from outside the state experiencing conflict is difficult to target for the government, since it involves actors and resources outside its sovereign territory where it may not be able to exercise much influence (see, e.g., Salehyan 2009). Moreover, it may be politically difficult for governments in other states to refuse shelter or deny support to coethnic rebel organizations. Gleditsch et al. (2008) find that ongoing civil wars notably increase the risk of militarized interstate conflict in neighboring countries, and present evidence from conflict description indicates that the civil war itself tends to generate contentious issues between countries. This suggests that transnational linkages will tend to increase the capacity to resist of rebel organizations and should thus be likely to be associated with longer conflicts

Moreover, transnational support may change the specific agenda of rebel organizations in ways that make the prospects for agreements more restrictive. From the perspective of organizations, Salehyan et al. (2011) consider external support for rebel groups from a principal-agent perspective. They argue that external support requires both a willingness from a potential patron to supply resources and willingness of the group to accept such assistance. Joint purposes such as ethnic ties or common enemies may increase the willingness to supply and accept transnational support. However, external supporters and rebel organizations may often have partly divergent motives, which can give rise to delegation problems from the perspective of supporters (e.g., rebels doing things they may not approve of), or strings attached to aid that rebels may be unwilling to accept, and these concerns may prevent potential aid from translating into actual support. Based on the possible goal displacement from principal agency relations and the argument that introducing new actors into conflict that can make conflict termination more complicated and less likely to be successful, we would expect conflicts where rebels receive transnational support to last longer than other conflicts (Cunningham 2006; 2011).

With regard to ethnic groups, in Chapter 6 we argued that we should expect to see a credible conflict-deterrent effect of transnational ethnic linkages on onset primarily when actors have links to included ethnic kin. Building on this logic, we should expect to see systematically longer conflicts in cases where a conflict actually breaks out when rebel organizations have links to transborder ethnic kin (TEK) that are included in other states, as these would tend to be able to mobilize and provide more resources.

We summarize our hypotheses on transnational linkages and conflict duration and outcomes with H8.5 and H8.6.

H8.5. Rebel organizations that receive support from TEK groups are likely to fight longer conflicts with the state.

H8.6. Rebel organizations that receive support from TEK groups controlling another state are likely to fight longer conflicts with the state.

Finally, our arguments about the role of inequality and grievances emphasize both the political and economic dimensions of inequality. Previous studies have found evidence suggesting that greater horizontal economic inequality tends to prolong conflict (Collier et al. 2004). Given the findings of Chapter 5 on inequality and conflict onset and our prior arguments about the effects of exclusion, it seems plausible to expect horizontal inequality to prolong conflict, especially in cases where it overlaps with ethnic exclusion. However, we are unable to evaluate this empirically here due to a lack of adequate data on inequality rates by group. The G-Econ data used to derive our spatial measure of inequality are available for 1990 only. It is difficult to defend the assumption that inequality remains constant for all groups actually involved in conflict and that the 1990 data can be extended back over several decades to 1945. Moreover, to use only post-1990 data would leave a short period and lead to problems of left truncation, since a large number of ongoing conflict started prior to this. Survey data such as the Demographic and Health Surveys (DHS) likewise tend to be available only for single years and do not provide a plausible alternative for examining horizontal inequalities over time. It is likely that horizontal and vertical income inequality would be correlated, and one could use measures of individual income inequality as a proxy for horizontal inequalities (indeed, existing research often resorts to such interpretations). However, this is a very strong assumption, and simply adopting it takes us away from our perspective emphasizing horizontal inequalities and the need for theory-measure correspondence. Besides, as shown in Chapter 7, country-aggregated measures of horizontal and vertical inequality are only moderately correlated, and many countries have high values on one dimension but not on the other (e.g., large interpersonal wealth differences unrelated to ethnicity). As such, we are unable to examine the implications of inequality for conflict duration empirically here. We note, however, that many temporal analyses for individual countries or conflicts with more detailed data suggest that conflict is often more persistent and severe in areas with higher inequality; see, for example, Murshed and Gates (2005) on the case of Nepal.

Data and Variables

Our data on conflict duration by rebel organizations are based on the Non-State Actors data, which in turn are based on the UCDP/PRIO Armed Conflict Data Set (Gleditsch et al. 2002; Cunningham et al. 2009). The ACD2EPR data allow us to consider the links between organizations and ethnic groups. The NSA data set provides information on the actual characteristics of organizations in terms of their size and military capacity as well as whether the group received support from transnational constituencies or other states. We exclude all colonial conflicts outside a country's core territory, as ethnic groups in colonies are not included in the EPR-ETH data. Cunningham et al. (2009) note that these conflicts have invariably ended in the eventual independence of the country. However, this is probably mainly due to the declining legitimacy of colonialism over time (Crawford 1993; Ravlo, Gleditsch, and Dorussen 2003), and we should thus not expect to see a strong relationship between the resources of the actors and duration and outcomes of conflict in colonial wars.

The start and end dates in our data derived from the UCDP/PRIO data set indicate the duration of conflicts, ignoring any intermittent periods of less than two calendar years with violence below the 25 deaths per calendar year threshold. In the Cox nonproportional hazard model we estimate here we are, strictly speaking, estimating the likelihood of termination given the covariates at some specific date rather than duration per se, as the hazard rate is not estimated parametrically in this model. However, observations that have a lower hazard of conflict termination will obviously be expected to last longer, as conflicts will become systematically screened out at different rates depending on the covariates of the model and their effects on the hazard rates. Hence, one can consider estimates of the effects of covariates on hazard rate in terms of relative differences in conflict length even if the model does not predict expected duration as such.

For the outcome of conflict we consider a subset of the categories identified in the UCDP Conflict Termination Data Set – that is, agreement (collapsing all agreement subtypes), government victory, rebel victory, or other outcomes, such as a conflict dropping below the 25 deaths threshold in a calendar year (see Kreutz 2010). We note that these data only identify explicit agreements at the end of a conflict. Thus, we are unable to consider empirically either implicit concessions, not ratified in a formal agreement, and efforts at peace agreements that fail to ensure an end to a conflict.[3]

In terms of our independent variables, we consider the military strength of a rebel organization relative to the government, and whether organizations control territory, based on the coding for individual organizations in the NSA data. We use the ACD2EPR data to establish whether organizations have a link to an ethnic group. This identifies whether each organization in the UCDP/PRIO and NSA data has an explicit claim to represent a particular group and recruits from a specific ethnic group in the EPR-ETH data. For example, the Karen National Union is linked to the Karen ethnic group in Burma/Myanmar, since the rebel organization advances explicit aims pertaining to the group as well as recruits soldiers from the group (see Kreutz 2007, p. 532). The data enable us to distinguish between links to excluded and included ethnic groups. This is important because our theory expects that conflicts will be longer primarily when rebel groups have links to excluded ethnic groups.

We use the NSA data to identify the specific transnational linkages between rebel groups and outside actors. In particular, we consider instances where rebels receive active assistance from a transnational constituency. Furthermore, the extended EPR-ETH data set tells us whether the transnational constituency is a TEK group that is marginalized or incumbent in a neighboring state. We expect to see longer conflicts primarily when organizations linked to excluded ethnic groups receive support from included transnational constituencies over and beyond the expected length from the domestic characteristics and dyadic balance. Most of the transnational constituencies coded as contributing explicit support in the NSA are ethnic, save for some examples of religious transnational networks such as al-Qaeda, which are not classified as ethnic in the EPR framework. Our measures here indicate if a group is included in one country. However, it is, of course, possible for a transnational group to be included in one country and marginalized in another, so the categories are not mutually exclusive at the transnational level.

We also consider whether rebels receive military support from a foreign government, as military support and intervention from governments are

---

[3] Walter (2002) also considers peace agreements that do not lead to conflict termination, but she does not consider duration or identify the timing of agreements. Moreover, her data build on the Correlates of War data and thus exclude conflicts that do not reach at least 1,000 battle deaths and often identify different start and end dates relative to the UCDP/PRIO Armed Conflict Data Set.

known to be associated with longer conflicts and support from transnational constituencies. Finally, we include various country-level control variables believed to influence the length of conflict which conceivably could be associated with our key explanatory variables, including the log of real GDP per capita, the log of population, and democracy, as reflected by the SIP measure developed by Gates et al. (2006).

Organizational-Level Analyses of Duration

Table 8.2 reports the results from our organizational-level analysis. The reported coefficients indicate the covariates' effects on the hazard of conflict termination, as estimated by a Cox nonproportional hazard model. A positive coefficient implies that a covariate increases the risk of conflict termination at time or makes conflict termination more likely and continued war less likely. By contrast, negative coefficients imply that a covariate increases the risk of continued and more persistent conflicts.

In Model 8.1 we study how the hazard of conflict termination for an organization depends on organization profiles, links to ethnic groups, as well as transnational linkages. Consistent with the results presented in Cunningham et al. (2009), our findings indicate that rebel organizations that have territorial control are much less likely to see conflict termination and tend to fight more protracted conflicts. By contrast, we find that rebel organizations that are relatively stronger or at parity with the state are more likely to see conflict termination, and tend to fight shorter conflicts. This provides strong support for hypotheses H8.1 and H8.2.

We now proceed to examine the effects of linkages between rebel organizations and ethnic groups. For Model 8.1 we find a negative coefficient for the term indicating whether rebel organizations have an explicit link to an ethnic group. This, in practice, means that such rebel organizations are less likely to see conflict termination, and that we are more likely to get protracted conflicts when organizations are linked to ethnic groups than when organizations do not have an ethnic base. Thus, there is strong support for Hypothesis 8.3, indicating that ethnically linked rebel organizations are more likely to see longer conflicts, even when we take into account the role of military strength and capacity to resist the rebel organization.

The results of Model 8.1 also strongly support our claim that transnational linkages can contribute to more protracted conflicts. As can be seen, both the terms for military support to the rebels and transnational constituency support are negative, indicating a decrease in the hazard of conflict termination or longer conflicts. However, we note that the coefficient for the transnational constituency support term is almost twice the size of the coefficient estimate for the impact of military support to the rebels from the government of another state. This suggests, in line with Hypothesis 8.5, that the role of ethnic linkages is important in its own right, beyond the general effect of increased resources.

TABLE 8.2. *Cox Proportional Hazard Regression Estimates of Termination,
1946–2009*

	Model 8.1	Model 8.2	Model 8.3	Model 8.4
Rebel organization variables				
Territorial control	−0.5005**	−0.5198**	−0.5182**	−0.5181**
	(0.1565)	(0.1552)	(0.1540)	(0.1594)
Rebels stronger	1.6676**	1.6858**	1.6707**	1.6810**
	(0.341)	(0.3027)	(0.3049)	(0.3069)
Rebels at parity	0.3310	0.3246	0.3106	0.3223
	(0.2573)	(0.2494)	(0.2489)	(0.2512)
Group claim link	−0.2798**			
	(0.1358)			
Excluded group link		−0.3448**	−0.3371**	−0.3584**
		(0.1376)	(0.1349)	(0.1367)
Included group link		0.2081		
		(0.2641)		
Sons-of-the-soil			−0.2361	
			(0.2217)	
Rebel external support	−0.3656**	−0.3557**	−0.3715**	−0.3823**
	(0.1298)	(0.1302)	(0.1349)	(0.1287)
Transnational constituency support	−0.4622**	−0.4450**	−0.4303**	
	(0.1638)	(0.1590)	(0.1604)	
Transnational support, excluded				−0.3878
				(0.2645)
Transnational support, included				−0.4457**
				(0.2221)
Country-level variables				
SIP²	−0.3983	−0.4074*	−0.3695	−0.4124**
	(0.1970)	(0.1986)	(0.2065)	(0.1979)
log(Real GDPpc)	−0.0212	−0.0208	−0.0216	−0.0332
	(0.0698)	(0.0690)	(0.0693)	(0.0695)
log(Population)	−0.1443**	−0.1412**	−0.1356**	−0.1413**
	(0.0537)	(0.0528)	(0.0531)	(0.0524)
Observations	1,717	1,717	1,717	1,717
Wald test (df)	87.77	89.34	97.97	83.38
	(df = 9)	(df = 10)	(df = 10)	(df = 10)

Robust standard errors in parentheses.
** $p < 0.01$, * $p < 0.05$.

Assessing Hypotheses 8.4 and 8.6 requires us to separate between included
and excluded groups. Before turning to the results for linkages to ethnic groups
by political status, we briefly comment on the results of the other control
variables in Model 8.1. The results are largely consistent with previous research:

Larger countries are less likely to see conflict termination and more likely to experience protracted conflict, while country per capita income does not have a significant influence on conflict duration, a finding that runs contrary to Collier et al. (2004). More democratic countries are less likely to see conflict termination. This finding has been replicated in many previous studies and appears to reflect some very long conflicts in democratic countries such as Israel and Colombia (Cunningham et al. 2009; Wucherpfennig 2011). The case of Israel is atypical, combining democratic institutions with a legacy of a displaced population largely outside the demos or defined citizens of the states but is generally consistent with our arguments regarding the role of exclusion for the duration and persistence of conflict.

We now proceed to examine how the effects of linkages between organizations and ethnic groups depend on the political status of groups. In Model 8.2 we separate between links to excluded groups and links to included groups, or ethnic groups in power. As can be seen, we find that the effects of links to groups on the hazard of conflict termination seems to be driven by the links to excluded groups, where we again continue to find a negative coefficient. By contrast, for organizations with links to included groups we have a nonsignificant and positive coefficient, suggesting that conflicts involving these organizations, if anything, seem more likely to come to an end rapidly than conflicts where organizations are not linked to ethnic groups. We believe that this strongly supports our claim that ethnicity per se is less relevant for conflict than political exclusion, in support of Hypothesis 8.4. The findings for the other covariates in Model 8.2 are largely similar to Model 8.1.

Building on Weiner's (1978) classical study, Fearon (2004b) has argued that sons-of-the-soil conflicts, where an indigenous community competes with settlers originating from the center, are likely to be particularly long, based on an argument that commitment problems will prevent the government from settling with the group or limiting future migration. We see this as a more restrictive special case of exclusion and less general than the theoretical framework based on exclusion and grievances that this book advances. However, it is important to consider this argument explicitly, since many conflicts that involve groups that fit the sons-of-the-soil category will also involve excluded groups. In Model 8.3 we add a term for an indicator of sons-of-the-soil conflicts in the ACD2EPR, based on the suggested criteria for such conflicts set forward by Fearon and Laitin (2011). As can be seen, adding this term does not alter the significant negative coefficient for conflicts with links to excluded groups. We find a negative coefficient for sons-of-the-soil conflicts, but this is not statistically significant. We interpret these findings as supporting our argument that sons-of-the-soil conflicts are best seen as a subset of conflicts where organizations have links to excluded groups. There are only two instances of organizations in sons-of-the-soil conflicts linked to groups considered included in the EPR-ETH data: the United Front for the Liberation of Assam

(UFLA) in India (linked to the Assamese) and the Movement of Democratic Forces of Casamance (MFDC) in Senegal (linked to Diola). Consequently, the sons-of-the-soil concept seems to us to contribute little added value, and we prefer the general explanation based on grievances and exclusion over the more narrow and highly specific explanation of conflict duration arising from a credible commitment problem offered by Fearon (2004b).

Organizational-Level Analyses of Outcome

So far we have focused only on termination without distinguishing between the different forms of conflict termination identified by the UCDP Conflict Termination Data Set. Although it is possible to estimate separate hazard rates for specific conflict terminations or outcomes, disregarding the other forms of termination, this assumes that the risks of different types of termination are independent (i.e., that the risk of an agreement, for example, is independent of the risk of termination by a decisive victory for one of the side). This seems implausible since agreements are likely to be entered into in the shadow of the battlefield. We instead opt for the simpler alternative of considering the likelihood of all the outcomes jointly as a function of time and the covariates, using a multinomial logit, using annual observations, and adding the duration of conflict as a right-hand-side term.

Testing our hypotheses about conflict outcomes involves a number of problematic issues. The agreement data only note if the conflict (in the sense of violent deaths) ended in a formal agreement, but do not classify the terms of agreements, how favorable these are to the actors, and to what extent these entail a shift from the status quo prior to the conflict. Many conflicts do not have any form of decisive outcome. Note that the modal outcome in the UCDP termination data is "low activity," without a formal agreement or a clear victory, and it is often ambiguous whether this is favorable to the government or rebels. Governments may be content with a rebel organization that ceases to engage in violence without a decisive defeat, and a rebel organization in the periphery may be content with a situation without direct challenges from the government.

Table 8.3 displays results from a multinomial logit model of how the log odds of each of the different termination outcomes (agreement, government victory, rebel victory, and low activity/other) change with the covariates (see Model 8.5). The first thing to note is that there are large differences in the coefficient for log(time), indicating that the likelihoods of specific outcomes differ notably over time. With regards to the coefficients for the covariates, militarily stronger rebels are much more likely to see rebel victory. With the exception of the agreement outcome, the estimated coefficients are always negative for the terms indicating that rebel organizations have a link to an excluded ethnic group, suggesting that conflicts with links to excluded groups are less likely to end in a decisive outcome, including eventual victory for the rebels. The terms for

TABLE 8.3. *Multinomial Logit by Outcome Type (to Conflict Continuation), 1946–2009*

	Model 8.5			
	Agreement	Gov. Victory	Rebel Victory	Low Activity
Intercept	3.0181	1.6006	4.6497	1.0981
	(1.7280)	(1.8400)	(2.5895)	(1.1941)
Rebel organization variables:				
log(time)	−0.2402**	−0.7251**	−0.5219**	−0.2753**
	(0.0930)	(0.0708)	(0.1173)	(0.0537)
Territorial control	−0.0149	−0.1331	−0.5576	−0.6371**
	(0.3360)	(0.3277)	(0.5057)	(0.2156)
Rebels stronger	−37.1727**	−1.1525	3.9553**	0.4093
	(0.754)	(1.1667)	(0.8243)	(0.9505)
Rebels at parity	0.1469	−0.6606	1.4207**	−0.1857
	(0.4070)	(0.7992)	(0.5838)	(0.4634)
Excluded group link	0.3465	−1.1700**	−2.5713**	−0.1546
	(0.3042)	(0.3790)	(0.5856)	(0.1931)
Rebel military support	−0.2188	−0.6595*	0.0738	−0.3728*
	(0.2432)	(0.3423)	(0.4610)	(0.2007)
Transnational support, included	0.2007	−0.7100	−0.1967	−0.6167*
	(0.4903)	(0.8866)	(1.0258)	(0.2709)
Country level variables:				
SIP^2	0.2783	−1.1425	−2.4609**	−0.4412
	(0.3919)	(0.6346)	(0.7723)	(0.2412)
log(Real GDPpc)	−0.0882	0.0601	−0.3092	−0.0597
	(0.1447)	(0.1694)	(0.2369)	(0.0970)
log(Population)	−0.4060**	0.0530	−0.1810	−0.0174
	(0.1254)	(0.1197)	(0.1963)	(0.0576)
Observations	1,920			
Wald test (df)	10544.54			
	(40)			

Robust standard errors in parentheses.
** $p < 0.01$, * $p < 0.05$.

support from an included transnational constituency likewise have negative estimated coefficients for all the outcomes, save for agreements.

Multinomial logit coefficients can be ambiguous to interpret directly, since the coefficient estimate indicates the effects of a covariate on the log odds of an outcome over the baseline (in this case, conflict continuation). However, the effect of covariate on an overall likelihood of one outcome depends not just on its effect on the relative odds of one outcome, but the baseline odds of other outcomes, and we must also consider the effect of the covariate on the likelihood of all the other outcomes. If the covariate has a relatively larger effect on other outcomes, the sign of an estimated coefficient does not need to reflect the impact on the overall probabilities. Hence, it is usually more instructive to look at the implied predictions for particular profiles and how these change with specific covariates.

In Figures 8.2–8.4 we plot how the likelihoods of the different outcomes vary over time for a median profile. Figure 8.2 shows the predicted likelihood for the different outcomes for a profile where a rebel organization has a link to an excluded ethnic group. In Figure 8.3, we display the predicted likelihood of the different outcomes for a profile where an organization has a link to an excluded group and has support from a transnational constituency that is a group controlling another state. Finally, Figure 8.4 shows the likelihood of the conflict outcomes for a rebel organization that has no link to an excluded ethnic group.

As can be seen in all of the profiles examined in Figures 8.2–8.4, government victory tends to be the most likely outcome early on in a conflict. However, the absolute likelihood of a government victory differs notably across the three organization profiles. For rebel organizations that have no ethnic link, or a link to an included group (which is a relatively rare outcome), government victories are substantially more likely, and the probability of such an outcome exceeds 0.5 until conflicts have lasted beyond a first full year. By comparison, for rebel organizations with links to excluded groups and links to excluded groups with support from transnational included kin, we find much lower probabilities of government victories. Moreover, the probability of a government victory quickly falls below that of other alternative outcomes as the conflict drags on.

Although outright rebel victories are rare outcomes for all the three profiles, the likelihood of agreements is substantially higher for rebel organizations with links to excluded groups and especially rebel organizations that have links to excluded groups and support from transnational ethnic communities that are included in other states. Agreements could come in many forms, but the simple fact that a government is willing to enter into an agreement with rebels at all will usually entail some concessions to their demands, at least in terms of recognizing the organization as a legitimate actor and negotiation partner. This finding is consistent with our notion that ethnic groups that have powerful state-controlling kin can mobilize more resources than would be expected because of their domestic characteristics alone, and that the features that we argued would be relevant for onset and deterring conflict indeed appear to be borne out by conflict dynamics. Although such transnational resources do not necessarily make organizations likely to win, they do appear to make organizations notably less likely to be defeated by governments.

In sum, the analysis of outcomes provides strong support for our previous arguments that conflicts involving rebel organizations not linked to excluded groups are consistently less likely to end in any settlement. The fact that the modal outcome in the UCDP termination data is "low activity" makes it difficult to establish general tendencies in whether outcomes are favorable to the

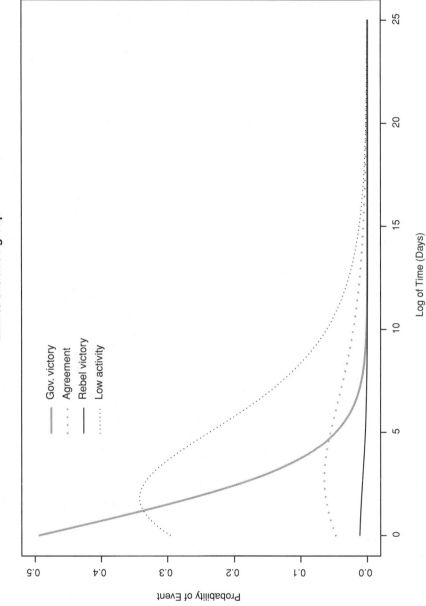

Link to excluded group

- Gov. victory
- Agreement
- Rebel victory
- Low activity

Probability of Event

Log of Time (Days)

FIGURE 8.2. Outcome probabilities by time, organizations with link to an excluded group.

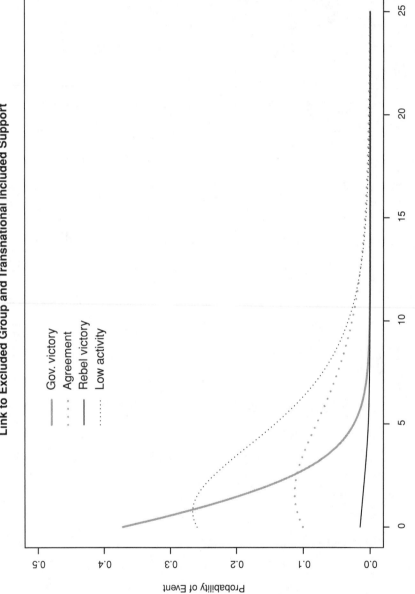

FIGURE 8.3. Outcome probabilities by time, organizations with link to an excluded group and support from a transnational constituency included in another state.

No Link to Excluded Group

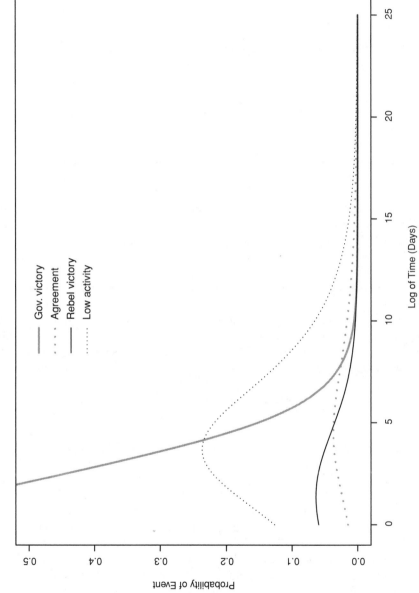

FIGURE 8.4 Outcome probabilities by time, organizations with no link to an excluded ethnic group.

government and the rebels. However, we view the fact that low activity outcomes are more likely for groups that have links to excluded groups as support for our claim that such conflicts are less likely to end in decisive outcomes.

Conflict-Level Analyses of Duration

Most research on civil wars tends to look at whether countries experience civil conflicts, while ignoring the specific organizations and links to ethnic groups. Skeptics may argue that our results could be an artifact of splitting up conflicts into individual rebel organizations, and possible double counting of multiple rebel organizations in specific conflicts. In particular, if ethnic conflicts are less likely to lead to fractionalization and the emergence of multiple organizations, it is possible that our analysis could involve comparing a few durable ethnically based organizations to many short-lived nonethnic rebel organizations.

We certainly do not agree that the conflict incompatibility is the inherently most appropriate level of analysis. More generally we believe that the appropriate level of analysis and degree of disaggregation must be considered relative to the specific research question (Cederman and Gleditsch 2009). However, we can actually examine the sensitivity of our results to the choice of level of analysis by rescaling the observations up to conflicts, while retaining information on the organizations active within the conflict.

In line with our previous arguments presented in Chapter 7, we see the risk of conflict as being determined by the weakest link, or the most war-prone organizational scenario in a conflict. This allows us to consider whether conflicts are likely to be more persistent if any one of the rebel organizations involved have links to excluded groups or transnational support from a group included in another state, but without double counting multiple organizations in the same conflict when assessing the effects of ethnic organization links on conflict. We also consider a term for the number of organizations in a conflict, as it is often argued that conflicts with multiple actors are more likely to become persistent as multiparty conflicts are much more challenging to solve (Cunningham 2006; 2011). The results of our Model 8.4 from Table 8.2, reestimated at the level of conflicts, are displayed in Table 8.4 (see Model 8.6).

The results in Table 8.4 yield very little support for the supposition that the previous results may be due to looking at organizations and the possible consequences of double counting multiple organizations in conflicts. We continue to find that conflicts with stronger rebels tend to be shorter, while conflicts where some rebels exercise territorial control tend to last longer. Moreover, we find that conflicts where at least one organization has a link to an excluded group tend to last longer, and this effect is further exacerbated if the organization receives support from a transnational constituency that is a politically privileged group in another state. Finally, consistent with Cunningham (2006; 2011), we find that conflicts with more organizations tend to last longer.

TABLE 8.4. *Cox Proportional Hazard Regression of Conflict Termination, Conflict Level, 1946–2009*

	Model 8.6
Rebel organization variables:	
Territorial control	−0.3839**
	(0.1496)
Rebels stronger	1.6783**
	(0.2893)
Rebels at parity	0.0637
	(0.2529)
Excluded group link	−0.3677**
	(0.1363)
Rebel military support	−0.5282**
	(0.1410)
Transnational support, included	−0.6154**
	(0.2347)
SIP^2	−0.4277**
	(0.1875)
log(Real GDPpc)	0.028
	(0.0574)
log(Population)	−0.0928**
	(0.0500)
No. organizations	−0.4565**
	(0.1288)
Observations	1,588
Wald test (df)	91.60
	(df = 10)

Robust standard errors are in parentheses.
** $p < 0.01$, * $p < 0.05$.

These results suggest that other analyses of conflict duration where researchers are not interested in organizations per se can still benefit from using more disaggregated information about the actors. Consistent with our argument in Chapter 7, we show again how it is possible to scale information from lower level units to generate more theoretically aggregate conflict profiles, and our results attest to how these can enhance standard country-level or aggregate conflict measures in analyses of conflict dynamics.

Conclusion

In this chapter we have applied our grievance, inequality, and exclusion approach to conflict dynamics. This chapter demonstrates how this generates clear expectations not just about the initial onset of conflict, but also the dynamics and outcome of conflicts. Since civil wars are dyadic phenomena, an understanding of conflict dynamics must consider both the state and rebel organizations. We have also illustrated the utility of looking at ongoing conflicts as we can consider additional information about the actors and their characteristics, such as the correspondence between rebel organizations and ethnic groups.

Contrary to common arguments, it is not the case that ethnic civil wars are generally longer than other conflicts due to the role of ethnic hatred. Nor do ethnic conflicts last longer because ethnic loyalties are rigid and difficult to transcend, or because ethnic identities per se help overcome collective action problems amongst the rebels. Rather, it is the political dimensions of ethnicity or exclusion that contribute to make such conflicts longer and more intractable. Ethnic exclusion strengthens the recruitment base and increases the stakes of conflicts and tolerance to carry costs of rebel organizations. It is this combination of ascriptive ethnic identities and state-enacted exclusion along such categorical lines rather than distinct ethnic identities per se that makes it easier to continue to fight and harder to settle ongoing civil war.

If exclusion is an important source that leads to persistent conflict and makes settlement difficult, institutions that introduce forms of ethnic power sharing through inclusion should help make violent conflict come to an end and prevent recurrence. In contrast to the essentialist view that deeply held ethnic identities drive such violence, we argue that grievances are by no means fixed and can be modified by removing policies of ethno-nationalist exclusion. The literature on power sharing highlights a number of pitfalls in power-sharing arrangements in post-conflict societies (e.g., Walter 2002; Rothchild and Roeder 2005). Still, representation at the political center could at least in principle be a powerful tool to alleviate grievances and thereby shorten armed conflicts. In particular, attention to the problematic aspects of power-sharing agreements and safeguarding the potential problems can help both solve conflicts and prevent recurrence, even if this may involve controversial aspects such as preserving the rights of privileged groups and amnesties (see, e.g., Melander 2009).

9

Conclusions for Theory and Policy

We are now ready to take stock of the findings of this book. The overall message is clear: group-level inequality and grievances matter for conflict. In contrast, much of the contemporary literature on within-state conflict has tended to brush aside ethnic grievances in favor of materialist interpretations that highlight individual economic incentives, natural resources, and state weakness, while overlooking the fundamental importance of group-level mechanisms. Once properly conceptualized and operationalized, horizontal inequality can be shown to have a strong impact on the outbreak and duration of civil war.

In this concluding chapter we first summarize our main findings and then discuss their theoretical significance, before turning to a discussion of past and future trends, as well as the policy relevance of our findings.

Summary of the Main Empirical Results

Throughout the book, we have highlighted access to state power as a pivotal factor strongly influencing both the risk of conflict and its duration. Our empirical investigations indicate that economic horizontal inequality contributes powerfully to the risk of civil war outbreak as well. Table 9.1 summarizes these findings by listing all hypotheses for which we have found solid empirical support.

Our first set of results pertains to political horizontal inequality. Perhaps the most important corroborated claim of the entire book is that excluded groups are more at risk of conflict (H4.1) together with its dynamic version relating to how downgrading increases the prospects of violent conflict (H4.2). We also found that the relative size of excluded groups has a positive influence on conflict risk (H4.3), as does the number of previous conflicts (H4.4). This set of relationships is exactly what you would expect given our theoretical framework and its postulated grievance mechanisms.

TABLE 9.1. *A Summary of the Confirmed Hypotheses of This Book*

Confirmed group-level hypotheses about conflict onset

H4.1. Ethnic groups that suffer from limited access to state power are more likely to experience conflict than those that enjoy full access.

H4.2. Groups that experienced recent loss of state power are especially likely to engage in internal conflict.

H4.3. Large excluded ethnic groups are more likely to experience conflict than are smaller excluded groups.

H4.4. Ethnic groups that have experiencd conflict in the past are more likely to experience conflict onset than those that have not.

H5.1. Relatively poor ethnic groups are more likely to experience civil war than those that are closer to the country average.

H5.3. Economic inequality makes less wealthy, excluded groups more likely to see civil war.

H6.3. The probability of conflict follows an inverted U-shape for the relative size of the TEK group in the secondary dyad.

H6.4. The conflict-dampening effect occurs for relatively large TEK groups that are included, and not for those that are excluded.

Confirmed country-level hypotheses about conflict onset

H7.1. Countries where large groups suffer from limited power access are more likely to experience conflict than those with lower levels of exclusion.

H7.2. Countries where the least wealthy groups fall far below the national average are more likely to experience conflict than those that are more equal.

Confirmed organization-level hypotheses about conflict duration and outcomes

H8.1. Rebel organizations with greater strength relative to the government will tend to fight shorter conflicts.

H8.2. Rebel organizations that control territory tend to fight longer conflicts.

H8.3. Rebel organizations with a link to an excluded ethnic group will see longer conflicts with the state.

H8.4. Conflicts with the state where rebel organizations have a link to an excluded ethnic group are less likely to end in a decisive outcome.

H8.5. Rebel organizations that receive support from TEK groups are likely to fight longer conflicts with the state.

H8.6. Rebel organizations that receive support from TEK groups controlling another state are likely to fight longer conflicts with the state.

However, it is not only political asymmetries among ethnic groups that matter, but also economic horizontal inequalities. Indeed, the poorer groups are compared to the country average, the higher the likelihood of civil war outbreak (H5.1). We have also established that this effect appears to worsen the prospects of sustained peace in cases that are already characterized by political inequality (H5.3). In this important sense, the conflict-inducing impact of economic horizontal inequality appears to hinge on there being some level of political grievances to start with. Thus, the combined effect of political and economic inequalities is not so much additive as conditional in the sense that the impact of the latter depends on the level of the former. In contrast, the evidence for the claim that wealthier groups are overrepresented in the conflict statistics is considerably weaker and cannot be statistically ascertained in general (see H5.2). However, we note that the results suggest a strong positive effect for wealthier and excluded groups, although the evidence here is somewhat less consistent, possibly due to the low number of such cases in the observed data.

Relaxing the closed-polity assumption, or that conflict risk can be satisfactorily assessed by considering domestic factors and conditions alone, we also studied the influence of transborder ethnic kin (TEK) and found that the risk of violent conflict is the highest in situations where the TEK group is of roughly equal size compared to the incumbent group(s) in the country in question (H6.3). However, there are important differences as regards the TEK group's own power status. Contrary to common fears about the dangers of irredentism, our results show that if transnational communities happen to control their respective states, this influence has a conflict-dampening impact for large groups (H6.4). Where the TEK group is stateless, however, one cannot count on such a reduction of conflict risk (H6.5).

Once we shift the focus from factors characterizing groups to those that influence the conflict risks of entire countries, we find very similar effects. We summarize the main results as the corroboration of two main hypotheses, each one corresponding to a dimension of horizontal inequality. Extending the claim of H4.1 to the country level, we found that countries with large excluded and discriminated groups are especially prone to governmental ethnic conflict (H7.1). Similarly, countries where some ethnic groups are severely disadvantaged in economic terms are significantly overrepresented among those experiencing territorial conflict (H7.2). In contrast, there is little evidence of greater vertical inequality increasing the risk of conflict, whether along political or economic lines.

Finally, we were able to derive a series of important results explaining why some rebel organizations fight civil wars that last longer than others, and why conflicts end in a particular way. Consistent with previous studies, it appears that rebel organizations that are relatively weak and are in control of their own territory are especially prone to endure longer conflict (H8.1 and H8.2, respectively). Returning to the main theme of the book, we detect a powerful influence of power status on conflict duration: excluded groups fight longer wars than those that enjoy privileged power access (H8.4). Such fights are also less likely to be decisive (H8.3). Finally, our analysis shows that rebel organizations that receive support from TEK groups will be involved in longer wars (H8.5), especially if the TEK groups control another state (H8.6).

Theoretical Consequences and Extensions

In view of the strong and coherent effect of both political and economic horizontal inequalities on internal conflict processes, which persists even when controlling for alternative explanations, we conclude that it is premature to write off grievances as causes of civil wars. Far from denying the importance of materialist interpretations, we argue that these often interact with grievance-related mechanisms. For example, our perspective is broadly compatible with Fearon and Laitin's (2003) emphasis on state weakness as a key factor increasing the risk of conflict. However, opposed to their account, we insist on measuring this weakness in relation to the strength of ethnonationalist challengers rather than treating it as merely a "technological" matter. Along the same lines, Hartzell, Hoddie, and Rothchild (2001) argue that state weakness is typically associated with state-led exclusion of entire ethnic groups from access to power. Far from being ethnically neutral, then, the lack of state capacity is intimately intertwined with issues relating to ethnicity and nationalism, and thus also to the emergence of ethnonationalist grievances.

We suspect that similar interactions between grievances and opportunities can be found with respect to the role of relative location, terrain, and natural resources as well. Indeed, it is not only the effectiveness of policing and military power that declines as one distances oneself from the center of government, but also the state's ethno-cultural penetration (Cederman 2008). Prominent studies in historical sociology demonstrate that reactive identity formation, opposing what is seen as the center's illegitimate incursion and exploitation, operates predominantly in geographically peripheral areas that have not been successfully assimilated by the power center (Rokkan in Flora 1999; Hechter 2001). Likewise, natural resources are not merely fought over by greedy individuals, but can also serve as a powerful source of grievances to the extent the state elites exploit them without sharing the riches with ethnically distinct local populations claiming them as their own property (e.g., Aspinall 2007). All these examples underline the futility of simplified bunching together and labeling of "proxies" as pertaining to this or the other side of abstract debates involving greed, opportunities, or grievances.

At this point, it is time to go back to the four weaknesses of the contemporary civil war literature that we listed in Chapter 1. There we identified deficits in mainstream, quantitative research as regards intermediate aggregation levels, motivational explanations, the underdeveloped role of the state, and theoretically relevant data resources.

Intermediate Disaggregation Rather Than Just Individual- or Country-Level Analysis

We have noted that much of the recent scholarship on internal conflict opts for micro-level research designs that highlight the role of individuals in conflict processes. Of course, this trend should be welcomed since it often strengthens causal inference by relying on a battery of methods including extensive archival research, interviews, surveys, and natural experiments (Kalyvas 2008b). However, something has been lost in the quest for internal validity. By leaping from country-level analysis to individual-level investigations, an entire class of phenomena involving group-level mechanisms has been left understudied. Despite the importance of private grudges and individual self-interest, we have argued that a large and important class of civil wars unfolds primarily in constellations featuring ethnic groups and governments. Social psychological theory offers compelling reasons why individuals identify with groups and act on their behalf (e.g., Turner 1987). Moreover, there is a vast empirical literature that proposes a number of conflict-inducing mechanisms at the group level. In particular, we have shown that Gurr and his colleagues have pioneered this type of investigation (Gurr 1993a; 2000b). Indeed, on the basis of our own data sets, we find patterns that strongly confirm the theoretical group-level postulates of this book.

This does not mean that we believe that groups constitute coherent "essences" or are the only relevant actors in conflict processes. Quite on the contrary, we have chosen to treat ethnic groups as our main units of analysis for pragmatic reasons, and we think that our empirical results confirm the usefulness of this choice. Nevertheless, ethnic identities vary from those that involve strong levels of identification and solidarity that justify talk of "groupness," to situations that are so fluid that ethnic groups cannot be said to exist at all. Yet, we part company from Brubaker (2004) as regards his wholesale rejection of identities and groups as approximations of a large set of phenomena. It would seem that tractability reasons speak for separating analytically blurred clusters of ethnic identities into recognizable units as long as one is conscious of the simplification underlying such analysis. However, as soon as the attention shifts from conflict onset to properties of conflicts, such as duration and outcome, it becomes possible to choose potentially more appropriate units of analysis. In Chapter 8, for example, we study how such patterns depend on the properties of rebel organizations and their relations to ethnic groups.

The limitations of exogenous and unitary ethnic group definitions are obvious, even if they are allowed to vary over time as is the case with the EPR-ETH data set. First, some important aspects of conflict processes hinge on internal tensions and strategic interactions among communities, subgroups, and organizations that are linked to the same ethnic category (e.g., Wucherpfennig 2011). Second, conflict processes can be seen as emanating from the very change of ethnic and nationalist boundaries (Cederman 1997). Statistical research based on panel data is inherently limited when it comes to handling such processes, especially in the case of mergers and splits of units (Abbott 2001). These limitations leave plenty of room for alternative methodologies, including historical, longitudinal studies and computational models that allow for a much more flexible way of handling identities and boundaries (Cederman 2002).

Motivational Rather than Merely Cognitive Mechanisms
The field of ethnicity and nationalism studies appears to have undergone a "cognitive turn" that privileges "cold" and "bloodless" accounts of conflict at the expense of those that accord emotions a central behavioral role (Brubaker 2009). Without denying the relevance of cognitive explanations, our focus on

grievances deviates from this trend at least to the extent that it brings attention to emotional reactions to inequality, including anger and resentment (see Chapter 3). For example, attempts have been made to emulate conflict situations in laboratories by cuing subjects with faces and symbols, but it remains doubtful whether the findings from such cognitive exercises can ever be properly generalized to real-world settings where life or death is at stake (e.g., Habyarimana et al. 2009). In fact, there is strong evidence, even within experimental settings, pointing to the essential role of emotional mechanisms in collective action processes. Indeed, prominent research in experimental economics has provided compelling reasons to believe that emotional reactions to unfair resource distributions help groups overcome collective-action dilemmas (Fehr and Gächter 2000).

Apart from brief references to selective cases in the empirical chapters, our book does not offer any direct evidence that emotions are involved, which is also difficult to demonstrate. Instead, we have relied mostly on indirect measures. However, we believe that grievance-based explanations gain credibility in light of these findings. In particular, the fact that loss of power is strongly associated with conflict outbreaks for groups could be seen as a clear sign that emotions, such as resentment and even outrage, may operate (see H4.2). In any case, it is hard to see how a purely cognitive approach could close the causal gap between horizontal inequality and conflict. We very much hope that future research will continue to investigate conflict mechanisms involving emotions explicitly. Major progress has been made by systematic investigations using case studies and other qualitative methods (e.g., Petersen 2002; 2011).

Ethnonationalism Rather than Merely Ethnicity

Running like a unifying theme throughout the chapters of this book, another critical line of reasoning targets the tendency of quantitative conflict researchers to reduce ethnicity to demographic aspects of "societies." Measures such as fractionalization and polarization pay no attention to the actual power relations that motivate challengers and incumbents in civil wars. After all, civil wars by definition do not merely confront individuals or groups with each other, but primarily feature the state and a specific incumbent government against one or more organized opposition actors. Thus, the state should be seen as both as a protagonist and a prize worth fighting over in internal conflict processes.

The reason for this oversight has a lot to do with the shift away from nationalism to ethnicity in recent conflict research (Cederman 2013). Limiting the focus to measurable aspects of ethnic politics within the "container" of the state has caused many researchers to lose sight of the institutional aspects of ethnicity, especially those associated with state organs and policies. Bunching ethnic and nationalist phenomena together into highly aggregated, primarily ethno-demographic indices that tap into societal and demographic properties such as diversity and polarity, many of these scholars have been keen on proving that there is nothing special about ethnicity and that it has no systematic or statistically discernible impact on collective violence.

Following in the footsteps of seminal studies by Horowitz (1985), Brass (1991), Hechter (2001), and Mann (2005), our analysis vindicates the value of adopting an institutional perspective on the link between ethnicity and conflict. Our analysis has also been directly inspired by the quantitative studies produced by Gurr and other scholars working with Minorities at Risk (MAR) data. As demonstrated in Chapter 2, this important stream of research in many ways anticipates our own theoretical framework by highlighting the relationship between ethnic groups and government. These studies have generally found that exclusive and discriminatory state policies tend to provoke grievances, thereby increasing the risk of political violence. Much of the grievance skepticism in the literature, including that of Fearon and Laitin (2003) and Collier and Hoeffler (2004), has targeted this research tradition. More recently, however, a number of scholars, who have followed up and improved on the earlier work on inequality and grievances, have found strong evidence of such effects (see, e.g., Regan and Norton 2005; Østby 2008b; Stewart 2008b; Østby et al. 2009; Goldstone et al. 2010). By further improving the data situation and offering a more comprehensive perspective than that of separate articles, the fact that this book confirms and further develops this recent wave of scholarship casts additional doubt on the attempts to downplay grievance-based explanations of civil war.

In fact, Fearon and Laitin now seem ready to at least partially abandon their previous, sweeping rejection of ethnic grievances as explanations of civil war. Indeed, their recent analysis of sons-of-the-soil conflicts features explicit frustrations on the part of cornered peripheral populations, who feel provoked by migratory flows typically consisting of members of the dominant ethnic group in the state (Fearon and Laitin 2011). Nevertheless, they treat this empirical pattern as a specific phenomenon rather than as a special case of grievance mechanisms. Moreover, they remain reluctant to open their theorizing to general patterns involving inequalities and grievances as causes of civil war onset, partly due to data problems associated with selection bias in the MAR data, and partly because of problems relating to endogeneity, as discussed at the end of Chapter 4. Our own duration analysis, presented in Chapter 8, suggests that sons-of-the-soil conflicts can be safely subsumed under the more general heading of political exclusion. Furthermore, our most recent research based on an instrumental-variable approach going back to the power access within the colonial empires indicates that there is indeed reverse causation, but this leads us to underestimate, rather than overestimate, the conflict-inducing impact of exclusion (see Wucherpfennig et al. 2012).

As illustrated by these observations, there is plenty of room for elaboration: future research will have to propose more innovative research designs that help us account for endogeneity while probing more deeply into the role of the state's suborganizations and political institutions as well as its activities and policies in areas such as policing and military affairs, law enforcement, tax collection, education, linguistic and religious rights, and cultural symbolism.

Theoretically Relevant Data and Measures, Rather than the Standard Toolbox

This book would not have been possible without a major investment in data collection. Rather than relying on existing data sources and measures, we have been involved in multiyear efforts to build and combine data sets on ethnic groups, their wealth, access to power and links to groups in neighboring countries, as well as their relations to rebel organizations. By addressing group-level properties, we believe that our measures are more directly linked to specific, conflict-related theoretical claims than most standard indices in the quantitative conflict researcher's "standard toolbox." Furthermore, they improve on existing data sources through their comprehensiveness in terms of sampling. Rather than restricting the sample to "minorities at risk," the EPR-ETH data project casts a wider net that also catches all privileged groups. Furthermore, our data offer systematic information about economic inequalities at the group level that go beyond what previous studies have been able to offer. Ultimately, these improvements allow us to draw firmer conclusions about the influence of inequalities, and indirectly grievances, on conflict.

In order to gather and combine the necessary information about hundreds of groups, organizations, and states around the world, we have relied on online surveys, geographic information systems, and relational databases. These computationally demanding procedures are made available to other researchers through a new integrated data portal called Geographic Research On War, Unified Platform, or GROW[up] for short.[1] This system integrates all relevant data used in this book and will also provide updates of our analyses as new data become available in the future.

Obviously, the empirical analysis of this book by no means exhausts what we want to know about ethnonationalist conflict. Indeed, the wish list of additional data sources is long. Future versions of the EPR-ETH Data set will offer information about different dimensions of ethnicity, including linguistic and religious categories. It would also be desirable to combine the spatial wealth estimates of Chapter 5 with information drawn from surveys and satellite data on nightlights emission. As mentioned above, more detailed information on institutional aspects of state organizations and their policies would also be very useful, as would more detailed information on the links between ethnic groups on the one hand and political parties and social movements on the other hand. Here we have only focused on civil wars that confront governments with nonstate challengers. Fortunately, systematic data are already available on other types of political violence, such as one-sided violence (Eck and Hultman 2007), communal (or nonstate) conflicts (Fjelde and von Uexkull 2012),

---

[1] See http://growup.ethz.ch.

interstate wars (Gleditsch 2004; Braithwaite 2010; Sarkees and Wayman 2010), and terrorism (Enders, Sandler, and Gaibulloev 2011). It is harder to find data that allow us to trace nonviolent conflict processes before they generate violence or entirely nonviolent processes (Chenoweth and Stephan 2011; Svensson and Lindgren 2011).

Inequality and Grievances in Time and Space

So far, we have discussed our results, as well as their theoretical significance and limitations, while assuming that they are universally valid both in time and space. However, such assumptions are most certainly too strong, as they conceal important contextual variation in terms of historical trends and geographic areas. Although it is beyond the scope of this book to model such spatiotemporal processes explicitly, we will here consider how different levels of inequality may affect the likelihood of conflict in terms of both the time period and the specific world region in question. This will help us identify the regions and countries most at risk when it comes to future outbreak of civil war.

Even though our analysis in Chapter 7 fails to detect any straightforward connection between political vertical inequality and internal conflict, we start by considering the evolution of governments' openness since WWII.[2] It is well known that the world has undergone a powerful democratization process at least since the 1970s (Gleditsch 2002; Gleditsch and Ward 2006). These regional "waves of democratization" started with the fall of the dictatorships of Southern Europe, followed by a series of democratic transitions in Latin American polities in the 1980s, culminating with the victory of democracy after the fall of the communist dictatorships in the early 1990s (Huntington 1991). In addition, Asia and even Sub-Saharan Africa have exhibited steady, if less dramatic, shifts toward democratic rule since the 1980s. Until 2009, which marks the end of our data set, the glaring exception from this trend was constituted by the Middle East and North Africa, a region that has recorded hardly any progress in this respect since the end of WWII.

As an illustration of these trends, we use data from the Polity Data set (Gurr 1993a) to plot the average level of democracy for six world regions on a scale from −10 to 10 (see Figure 9.1). The picture is striking: the three waves of democracy referred to above are clearly visible, especially the most dramatic one pertaining to "Eastern Europe" (which also includes the former Soviet Union). The Western world region, which includes Western Europe, the United States, Canada, Japan, Australia, and New Zeeland, exhibits very high levels

---

[2] Theories developed to account for the democratic peace imply that mutual democracy has a pacifying on interstate relations (see Chan 1997). However, the relationship between democracy and international conflict has long been acknowledged to be more complex (see, e.g., Gleditsch, Hegre, and Strand 2009).

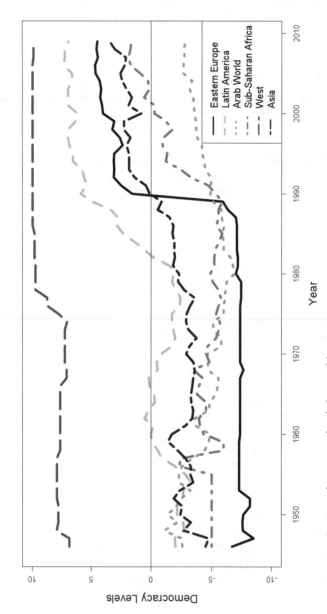

FIGURE 9.1. Average democracy levels by world region.

of democracy already after WWII. With the exception of the Middle East and North Africa, there is strong convergence of higher levels of democracy toward the end of the sample period. Obviously, the revolutions of 2011, commonly referred to as the "Arab Spring," may well change the status of this region as a laggard in terms of democratization, but at the moment of writing it is still too early to tell how fast, or whether, the global trend toward full democracy will include the countries of that region.

Whereas the general evolution toward democratization is by now well established as a major historical pattern, a lack of data on ethnic groups' access to power has prevented scholars from detecting a similar development in terms of ethno-political inclusion. Yet, this knowledge gap is of critical importance, especially in the light of this book's argument that horizontal, rather than vertical, inequality causes civil wars. Fortunately, the EPR-ETH Data set allows us to shed light on this important question. In parallel to the previous graph, Figure 9.2 traces the average level of ethnonationalist exclusion for the same world regions. Here exclusion is measured as the proportion of the population excluded from executive influence because the power access of their respective ethnic group is blocked.

Just as the degree of democracy has increased over the last couple of decades, a similar improving trend can be detected in terms of the power access of ethnic groups. The graph again reveals major differences across the globe. Whereas the Western states excluded a very small fraction of their population already in 1946 and have remained at that low level, other world regions have recorded a considerable decline in terms of exclusion since the late 1999s. As with democracy, however, there is still a major gap between the West and the least exclusive non-Western areas. Possibly as a reflection of normative pressure with global reach, the latter appear to be converging on an exclusion level of about 10–15% but could well continue to decline. Again, the Arab world and North Africa stand out as having recorded only modest improvements, such as the changes following after the US invasion and fall of Saddam Hussein in Iraq in 2003, but the level of exclusion remains about twice as high as most other parts of the world. The difference compared to the Western states is even more dramatic.

The findings of Chapter 4 indicate that discriminated groups are even more prone to experience violence than excluded ones, a finding that is reflected at the country level (see Chapter 7). We therefore turn to the development of ethnic discrimination by world region. The population that is discriminated represents a strict subset of our exclusion measure. Figure 9.3 plots regional averages of ethnically discriminated segments of each country's population. In this case, the Middle East and North Africa stand out even more clearly. In 2009, the level of discrimination for this part of the world amounted to around 15%, making it an order of magnitude more discriminatory than other world regions. The opposite pattern can be detected for Western countries, where the level of discrimination approaches zero over the years. In between, there is a

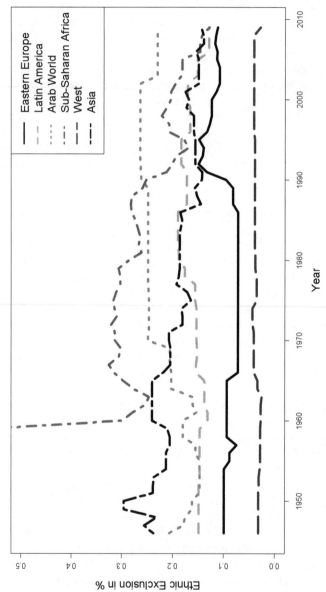

FIGURE 9.2. Ethnically excluded population by world region.

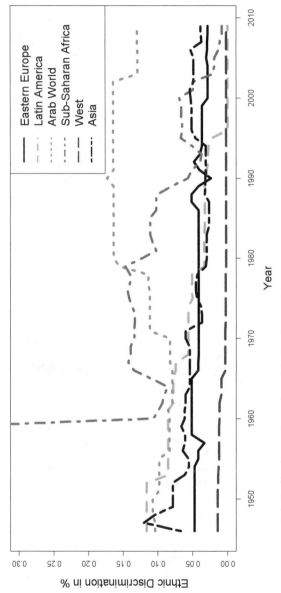

FIGURE 9.3. Ethnically discriminated population by world region.

converging trend to low levels below 5%, including a major decline in the case of Sub-Saharan Africa.[3]

Since the origins of exclusion and a full explanation of these patterns falls outside the scope of our book, we can only speculate about the reasons for the overall decline of exclusion and discrimination during the last couple of decades. According to Gurr (2000a), there are some signs that an international regime of conflict prevention and resolution may be emerging. Indeed, Gurr claims that since the mid-1990s, Western governments and international organizations have done much more to curb violence in troubled areas, and as a consequence, the incidence of new ethnic conflict has dropped significantly.

What does the nascent international regime consist of? Gurr (2000a) mentions four main pacifying developments that have characterized the post-Cold War period after its first turbulent half decade. First, increased attention has been paid to group rights rather than merely to individual human rights. In this respect the Organization of Security and Cooperation in Europe (OSCE) and the Council of Europe have played key roles. Second, ethnic pluralism and power sharing have become the expected modes of governance rather than confrontation and domination. Third, instead of resorting to an all-or-nothing strategy, parties in secessionist disputes now as a rule content themselves with compromise solutions, such as cultural autonomy. Finally, a key ingredient in the emerging regime depends on multilateral pressures orchestrated by international organizations, and a willingness to deploy more forceful policy instruments rather than letting regions descend into violence. Although this trend is not perfect, the international intervention in Libya in 2011 is a case in point. Ideally, coercive prevention should suffice to deter political leaders who may be tempted to escalate conflicts for ideological or opportunistic reasons.

Apart from the inherently normative attractiveness of this increasing pattern of ethnic inclusiveness, this book shows that the trend has potentially major pacifying effects as regards internal conflict. Despite these encouraging signs of progress, however, the contemporary world still exhibits considerable diversity as regards levels of ethnic exclusion and discrimination. In order to assess the prospects of conflict in these world regions, Figures 9.4 and 9.5 introduce maps of the share of the excluded and discriminated populations respectively for the year of 2009. The former figure tells us that the most important clusters of exclusive rule can be found in Sub-Saharan Africa, the Middle East, and North Africa, as well as in large parts of Asia. The exclusion levels are especially high in the Sudan, Rwanda, the Democratic Republic of Congo, Congo Brazzaville, and Angola. In the Middle East, Israel, Jordan, and Syria also exhibit extremely high levels. In the ranked societies of the Western Hemisphere, the difficulties experienced by native populations trying to participate in national politics are

---

[3] Our findings on discrimination confirm Asal and Pate's analysis in Marshall and Gurr (2005). Using data from Minorities at Risk, they report a strong declining trend in ethnic political discrimination around the world.

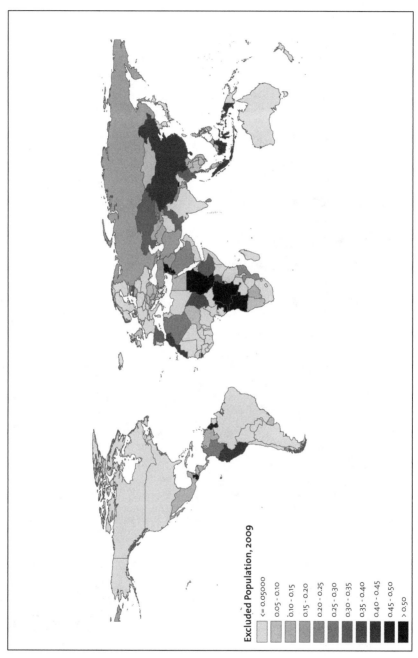

FIGURE 9.4. Share of excluded population by country in 2009.

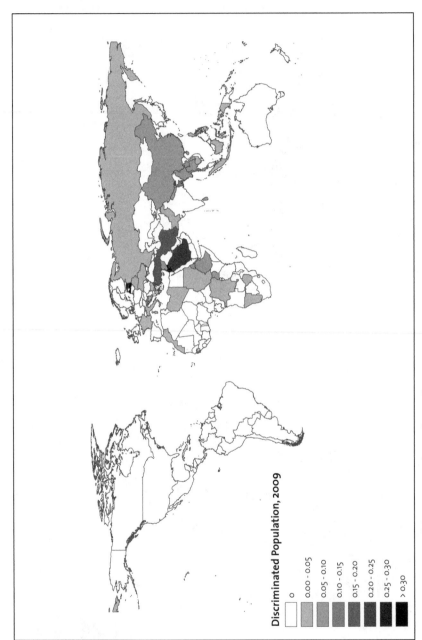

Discriminated Population, 2009

○

0.00 - 0.05

0.05 - 0.10

0.10 - 0.15

0.15 - 0.20

0.20 - 0.25

0.25 - 0.30

> 0.30

FIGURE 9.5. Share of discriminated population by country in 2009.

TABLE 9.2. *Top-Ten Countries with Largest Excluded and Discriminated Shares of the Population in 2009*

Country	Share of Excluded Population	Country	Share of Discriminated Population
Syria	87.6%	Bahrain	70%
Rwanda	84.8%	Jordan	59.2%
DR of Congo	80.2%	Latvia	37.6%
Sudan	75.4%	Israel	31.3%
Bhutan	75%	Estonia	29.9%
Congo	74.2%	Bhutan	25%
Angola	70.5%	Saudi Arabia	21.5%
Bahrain	70%	Turkey	19.9%
Jordan	59.2%	Iran	16.8%
Guatemala	52%	Bangladesh	11.1%

on ample display. Unsurprisingly, the Western countries are almost entirely free of exclusive policies.

When we turn to discriminated populations, the Middle East stands out. Israel, Jordan, Saudi Arabia, Bahrain, Turkey, and Iran belong to this category of states. In addition, two Baltic democracies, namely Estonia and Latvia, are also listed as exercising discrimination since they make political participation difficult for their Russian minorities by severely restricting naturalization along ethnic lines.

It is instructive to list the countries with the highest level of exclusion and discrimination. Introducing the first of these "exclusive" clubs, Table 9.2 reveals that Syria's ethnic minority rule reaches a staggering 87.6% of the population, closely followed by Rwanda with 84.8% and the Democratic Republic of the Congo at 80.2%. With the exception of Bhutan (75%) and Guatemala (52%), all of the top-ten cases can be found in Africa or the Middle East.

Interestingly, the African cases disappear from the list when we turn to outright discrimination (see the rightmost columns of Table 9.2). The Middle East, together with two cases in Eastern Europe and Asia, correspond to this category. At the very top, we find Bahrain and Jordan with 70% and 59% of the population, followed by Latvia, Israel, and Estonia (37.6%, 31.3%, and 29.9%, respectively).

Apparently democracy does not immunize countries against discrimination of large parts of the population. Whereas Guatemala is the only democratic country among the top-ten of the exclusion list, we find as many as four democracies among the most discriminatory regimes in 2009, namely Latvia, Israel, Estonia, and Turkey. It should be noted, however, that discrimination takes very different forms in these cases. As mentioned above, the two Baltic states were classified as discriminatory because of their restrictive citizenship rules, which in practice deprive the Russian minorities of even basic political rights

(Kelley 2004). In the case of Israel, long-standing and increasingly harsh discrimination in the occupied territories effectively blocks the Palestinians from taking part in the demos (Pappe 2004; Lustick 2008). Based on assimilatory principles in contrast to the Israeli approach, ethnic domination in the Turkish case does not prevent Kurdish individuals from participating even at the elite level as long as they are willing to assimilate to the dominant culture. However, up to 2009, the Kurds were exposed to discriminatory policies that prevented any Kurdish group-level influence over the executive.

What do these observations on the most egregious cases of exclusion and discrimination tell us about the risk of civil violence? In fact, three of the top-ten exclusion cases involve ethnonationalist conflict, namely Rwanda, which even experienced an outbreak that year, as well as the Sudan and Angola. Likewise, we find three conflict cases among the states that discriminate the largest populations. Within two years after these observations, the turbulence in the Middle East and North Africa triggered major conflict in Syria and Bahrain, both characterized by minority rule. Furthermore, tensions rose in Jordan for the same reasons, and even Saudi Arabia experienced trouble with its Shia minority in the east of the country. At the same time, the long-lasting conflicts in Israel and Iran showed no signs of being solved. In contrast, the Baltic states have remained peaceful, possibly in part thanks to the deterrent effect of their large transborder ethnic kin, as explained in Chapter 6. Going back to the trends displayed in Figures 9.2 and 9.3, the high levels of exclusion and discrimination in the Middle East and North Africa, if enduring, can be expected to generate conflict for years to come. Despite encouraging recent reductions of exclusion and discrimination in other parts of the world, such as Eastern Europe and the former Soviet Union, Asia, Sub-Saharan Africa, and Latin America, there is still considerable potential for ethnonationalist warfare in these world regions. In contrast, the Western World has been almost totally liberated from ethnonationalist conflict. After the settling of the armed conflict in Northern Ireland and promising steps toward a more comprehensive political settlement for the Basque region in Spain, few major risks of civil war remain among those countries.[4]

Policy Consequences

We ended Chapter 1 by offering some preliminary remarks on the policy relevance of our grievance-based perspective. Having now presented empirical

---

[4] Of course, there are still nasty cases of discrimination of the Roma populations, but their scattered settlement patterns make organized mobilization and civil conflict unlikely. It is conceivable that the economic crisis that started in 2008 could reverse some of this progress. There have been occasional ethnonationalist populist stirrings, such as the Hungarian government's irredentist gestures toward Hungarian populations in Slovakia, but domestic support for such moves has remained limited so far and the dense web of international institutions and norms within the Western world have generally helped keep such tendencies in check.

evidence in its favor, we return to the issue of what can be done to prevent and end civil wars. It is clear that those scholars who dismiss grievances will focus on different policy priorities than we do. In a pioneering article on theory and policy, Andrew Mack (2002, p. 522) explains how theoretical inferences have consequences for political decision making:

If grievances have nothing to do with the onset of war, then seeking to assuage them via preventive diplomacy, conflict resolution and confidence-building strategies will do nothing to reduce the risk of armed conflicts. If Collier & Hoeffler and Fearon & Laitin are correct, and what counts is not grievance but the relative capabilities of rebels versus the state, then strategies of "peace through strength," repression and deterrence would appear to be optimal prevention strategies.

Whether the explanatory approach diagnoses ruthless rebels or weak states as the main cause of conflict, most of the grievance critics can be expected to recommend a strengthening of the state's enforcement power. Ballentine and Nitzschke (2005, p. 4) summarize the prescriptive consequences of the "loot-seeking" paradigm:

The idea that civil war is driven by rebel greed was particularly appealing to some policy-makers, discouraged by the complexity and seeming intractability of "ethnic" and religious conflicts of the early 1990s. If many contemporary conflicts are driven by contests over economic resources, the "resource wars" should be more amenable to resolution than conflicts over such indivisible identity issues as ethnicity, religion, or ideology. The greed-thesis shaped politics as well as policy, as corrupt and repressive leaders in conflict countries found it a useful argument to deflect attention from their own wrong-doings by putting the blame for their countries' misery on "greedy rebels."

According to this view, what is needed is not compromise and diplomacy, but effective policing (van Creveld 1999). Summing up the experiences of Western interventions after the end of the Cold War, Mueller (2004, p. 139) argues that such efforts are relatively straightforward and effective in most cases: "The intimidating, opportunistic thugs have been successful mainly because they are the biggest bullies on the block. However, like most bullies (and sadists and torturers), they tend not to be particularly interested in engaging a formidable opponent." The disorganized and undisciplined thugs are no match for the professional armed forces of the developed countries. In sum, Mueller's conclusion for policy is strikingly opportunistic:

The record suggests, then, that it is possible to use policing wars to order the new world – or at least to eliminate many of the criminal regimes and to pacify many of the criminalized civil wars that are the main sources of unnatural death and deprivation in the world (p. 140).

Rationalist scholars have also argued in favor of outside intervention as a way to impose order on warring parties and pacify conflict zones. Anarchical conditions imply that governments and their challengers face difficulties in credibly committing to disarmament and political compromise (Fearon 1998; Walter

2009a). Provided they are forceful and sustained enough, third parties can provide the necessary credibility for agreements to stick. For example, Fearon and Laitin (2004) analyze the conditions under which "neo-trusteeships" will be able to stabilize postconflict situations.

From a more radical vantage point, some scholars assert that negotiated agreements often prevent strong states from emerging and even argue that the best option is to "give war a chance" (Luttwak 1999). In ethnonationalist conflicts, this could in practice amount to endorsing ethnic cleansing followed by ethnic dominance within each "purified" ethnic unit (Kaufmann 1996; 1998), or at least a more skeptical attitude toward compromise solutions secured through agreements (Toft 2010).

Without belittling the urgency of establishing order and strengthening law enforcement as a way to handle post-conflict situations, we believe that too much weight has been put on these functions at the expense of encouraging and pressuring conflict parties to accept compromises and political concessions. Nationality problems will not go away until the underlying issue has been resolved. In the absence of an equitable solution, resentment, and even hatred, may fester from generation to generation. In particular, in today's world of mass mobilization along ethnonationalist lines, it is very unlikely that "decisive victories" will guarantee long-term stability. Indeed, our results in Chapter 8 indicate that excluded groups are more likely to fight longer and less decisive civil wars than included ones (see H8.1 and H8.4, respectively). Furthermore, there is a danger that the wrong incentive structure for potential rebels or ruthless state rulers will result from excessive reliance on symptom treatment, such as external reinforcement, or on noninterference in the hope that this will create order through ethnic dominance. Instead, the best option is to address the root causes of the problem before violence erupts. Our book indicates the most obvious way to do so: if ethnic exclusion and inequality lead to conflict, then ethnic inclusion and a fairer distribution of public goods will offer the best prospects for conflict prevention.

Of course, power sharing is never an easy option and often fails, even without a history of prior conflict. It has often been remarked that most power-sharing experiments end in recurrent violence (Fearon and Laitin 2007; Toft 2010).[5] However, the argument that a conflict resolution method often fails is not a valid objection against it if conflict would have broken out sooner, or would be even more likely in its absence. Put differently, since power sharing is not randomly assigned, and in fact probably more likely in difficult cases where tensions are high or conflict has already occurred, then we cannot conclude that it causes more harm than good on the basis of simple static correlations. Failing to understand this logic of selection would lead us to identify hospitals

---

[5] Other scholars think that power sharing in its various guises worsens the prospects of peace by deepening cleavages and fueling mutual hostility (Rothchild and Roeder 2005; see also Roessler 2011).

as a threat against the patients' health, since more people are ill in hospitals than elsewhere.

Once we move beyond such naive analyses, things look quite different. Explicitly considering the conditions under which power sharing is invoked, Wucherpfennig (2011) models it as a result of the choices of strategic actors rather than as an exogenously occurring, random condition. Based on EPR data, he demonstrates that groups that are "upgraded" through improved access to governmental institutions are less likely to experience recurrence of conflict than those that are not accorded such concessions.

Of course, power sharing within the central executive is not the only way that ethnic inclusion can be implemented, as illustrated by Rothchild's (1997) extensive analysis of different approaches to the management of ethnic conflict in Africa. In some fortunate cases, elites' early choice of cooperative strategies put the development of their countries on a pacific path that allows "polyarchical" regimes to emerge. Such systems offer extensive opportunities to participate in political activities, both in parties and in civil society, regardless of one's ethnic identity (see also Horowitz 1985). In other cases, ethnic inclusion may rely extensively on political decentralization and ethnonationalist autonomy short of secession, although ethnic federalism has also been associated with the outbreak of ethnic conflict by accelerating centrifugal tendencies within decentralized regimes (see, e.g., Bunce 1999; Deiwiks et al. 2012).[6] However, as expected by Gurr's (2000a) analysis of declining ethnic warfare from the mid-1990s, the different strategies of ethnic inclusion appear to be more effective than non-cooperative policies based on ethnonationalist domination. Summing up his empirical investigation, Rothchild (1997, p. 19) concludes that

wherever Africa's ruling elites have encouraged inclusiveness or diffused power by means of electoral fine-tuning or territorial decentralization or have applied positive principles of proportionality and reciprocity in four key areas – political coalitions in central government politics, elite recruitment, public resource allocation, and group rights and protections – they have managed to reduce the intensity of state-ethnic conflicts.

In some difficult conflict cases, however, hostility and mutual suspicion may be so acute that power-sharing deals are simply not feasible and the only hope of stopping a conflict hinges on separation of the involved populations. Arguably, this is why Kosovo was allowed to secede and why a "two-state solution" to the Israeli-Palestinian conflict remains the predominant recommendation among scholars and politicians. However, in general, there are good reasons to be cautious in recommending such geopolitical "lobotomy," including the lack of a guarantee that the ensuing situation will remove all nationality

---

[6] Because ethno-federal institutions may lead to long-term fragmentation and even conflict, it is safer to introduce federalism in such a way that federal boundaries do not coincide with ethnic ones (Deiwiks 2011). However, it may be difficult to satisfy secessionist activists with less than partial sovereignty over ethnic matters, such as linguistic policies and religious institutions.

problems and prevent the parties from starting an interstate war (Sambanis and Schulhofer-Wohl 2009). Most importantly, careless encouragement of secessionism threatens to cause a problem of moral hazard that may undermine the stability of territorial borders and could ultimately reverse the gains made in terms of outlawing interstate warfare (Fearon 2004a). Instead, what is desperately needed is an international legal framework that stipulates clear conditions under which partitioning could be allowed to proceed.

Thus, wherever possible, challengers of the current political order should be encouraged to participate in the regime's politics by being granted governmental concessions through different types of power-sharing arrangements. In some cases this means sharing responsibility within the executive, and in others it entails offering minority rights and safeguards, and possibly regional autonomy in federal arrangements.

Here we cannot aspire to offer anything like a complete assessment of what specific types of institutions and policies stand the best chance of pacifying and possibly even transcending ethnonationalist conflict, despite the topic's obvious importance to policy making. Our goal has been much more modest and basic: we have attempted to offer a better understanding of the causes that trigger and prolong civil wars by removing arbitrary restrictions on what constitutes a good explanation. As we have shown, much of the extremely influential quantitative literature covering such conflicts has tended to brush aside grievances as matter of theoretical assumption and questionable empirical evidence. By improving data and measurements, we have been able to detect strong effects of both political and economic horizontal inequalities, thus strengthening the case of grievance-based interpretations. It is our hope that this book will contribute to a more lively and balanced debate about the causes and cures of civil wars, thus leaving more room for accounts that explicitly consider collective emotional reactions to maltreatment by oppressive and ethnically monopolistic governments.

References

Abbott, Andrew. 2001. *Time Matters: On Theory and Method.* Chicago, IL: University of Chicago Press.

Acemoglu, Daron and James A. Robinson. 2005. *Economic Origins of Dictatorship and Democracy.* Cambridge: Cambridge University Press.

Achen, Christopher H. and Duncan Snidal. 1989. "Rational Deterrence Theory and Comparative Case Studies." *World Politics* 41:143–69.

Agnew, John, Thomas W. Gillespie, Jorge Gonzales, and Brian Min. 2008. "Baghdad Nights: Evaluating the U.S. Military Surge Using Night Lights Signatures." *Environment and Planning A* 40:2285–95.

Alesina, Alberto and Eliana La Ferrara. 2005. "Ethnic Diversity and Economic Performance." *Journal of Economic Literature* 43:762–800.

Alesina, Alberto and Enrico Spolaore. 2005. "War, Peace, and the Size of Countries." *Journal of Public Economics* 89:1333–54.

Ali, Abdel Gadir, Ibrahim A. Elbadawi, and Atta El-Batahani. 2005. "Sudan's Civil War: Why Has It Prevails for So Long?" In *Understanding Civil War: Evidence and Analysis*, vol. 1, edited by Paul Collier and Nicholas Sambanis. Washington, DC: The World Bank.

Alschuler, Lawrence R. 1998–1999. "The Chiapas Rebellion: An Analysis According to the Structural Theory of Revolution." *Estudios Interdisciplinarios de América Latina y el Caribe* 10. http://www1.tau.ac.il/eial/index.php?option=com_content&task=blogsection&id=24&Itemid=235].

Anderson, Benedict. 1991. *Imagined Communities: Reflections on the Origin and Spread of Nationalism.* London: Verso.

Arreguin-Toft, Ivan. 2001. "How the Weak Win Wars: A Theory of Asymmetric Conflict." *International Security* 26:93–128.

Aspinall, Edward. 2007. "The Construction of Grievance: Natural Resources and Identity in a Separatist Conflict." *Journal of Conflict Resolution* 51:950–72.

Ayres, R. William. 2000. "A World Flying Apart? Violent Nationalist Conflict and the End of the Cold War." *Journal of Peace Research* 37:105–17.

Balch-Lindsay, Dylan and Andrew Enterline. 2000. "Killing Time: The World Politics of Civil War Duration." *International Studies Quarterly* 44:615–42.

Baldwin, Kate and John D. Huber. 2010. "Economic versus Cultural Differences: Forms of Ethnic Diversity and Public Goods Provision." *American Political Science Review* 104:644–62.

Ballah, Heneryatta and Clemente Abrokwaa. 2003. "Ethnicity, Politics and Social Conflict: The Quest for Peace in Liberia." *Penn State McNair Journal* 10:52–69.

Ballentine, Karen. 2003. "Beyond Greed and Grievance: Policy Lessons from Studies in the Political Economy of Armed Conflict." International Peace Academy, IPA Policy Report.

Ballentine, Karen and Heiko Nitzschke. 2005. "The Political Economy of Civil War and Conflict Transformation." Berghof Research Center for Constructive Conflict Management, Berlin.

Barbalet, Jack M. 1998. *Emotion, Social Theory, and Social Structure: A Macrosociological Approach*. Cambridge: Cambridge University Press.

Barkin, J. Samuel and Bruce Cronin. 1994. "The State and the Nation: Changing Norms and the Rules of Sovereignty in International Relations." *International Organization* 48:107–30.

Barrows, Walter L. 1976. "Ethnic Diversity and Political Stability in Black Africa." *Comparative Political Studies* 9:139–70.

Barth, Fredrik. 1969. "Introduction." In *Ethnic Groups and Boundaries: The Social Organization of Culture Difference*, edited by Fredrik Barth. Boston, MA: Little, Brown and Company.

Bass, Gary J. 2006. "What Really Causes Civil War?" *New York Times Magazine*, August 13. http://www.nytimes.com/2006/08/13/magazine/13wwln_idealab.html.

Bates, Robert H. 1983. *Essays on the Political Economy of Rural Africa*. Cambridge: Cambridge University Press.

Beardsley, Kyle and Brian McQuinn. 2009. "Rebel Groups as Predatory Organizations: The Political Effects of the 2004 Tsunami in Indonesia and Sri Lanka." *Journal of Conflict Resolution* 53:624–45.

Beck, Nathaniel, Jonathan N. Katz, and Richard Tucker. 1998. "Taking Time Seriously: Time-Series–Cross-Section Analysis with a Binary Dependent Variable." *American Journal of Political Science* 42:1260–88.

Beissinger, Mark R. 2002. *Nationalist Mobilization and the Collapse of the Soviet Union*. Cambridge: Cambridge University Press.

Benford, Robert D. and David A. Snow. 2000. "Framing Processes and Social Movements: An Overview and Assessment." *Annual Review of Sociology* 26:611–39.

Bhaumik, Subir. 2007. "Insurgencies in India's Northeast: Conflict, Co-option and Change." East-West Center, Washington DC.

Birnir, Jóhanna Kristín. 2007. *Ethnicity and Electoral Politics*. Cambridge: Cambridge University Press.

Blainey, Geoffrey. 1973. *The Causes of War*. New York, NY: Free Press.

Blattman, Christopher and Edward Miguel. 2010. "Civil War." *Journal of Economic Literature* 48:3–57.

Bøås, Morten. 2001. "Liberia and Sierra Leone – Dead Ringers? The Logic of Neopatrimonial Rule." *Third World Quarterly* 22:697–723.

Boix, Carles. 2008. "Economic Roots of Civil Wars and Revolutions in the Contemporary World." *World Politics* 60:390–437.

Bolt, Paul J. 2000. *China and Southeast Asia's Ethnic Chinese: State and Diaspora in Contemporary Asia*. Westport, CT: Praeger.

Booth, John A. 1991. "Socioeconomic and Political Roots of National Revolts in Central America." *Latin American Research Review* 26:33–73.

Bosker, Maarten and Joppe de Ree. 2010. "Ethnicity and the Spread of Civil War." *CEPR Discussion Paper* No. 8055.

Boswell, Terry and William J. Dixon. 1993. "Marx's Theory of Rebellion: A Cross-Nation Analysis of Class Exploitation, Economic Development, and Violent Revolt." *American Sociological Review* 58:681–702.

Bouquet, Christian. 2011. *Côte d'Ivoire: Le désespoir de Kourouma*. Paris: Armand Colin.

Braithwaite, Alex. 2010. "MIDLOC: Introducing the Militarized Interstate Dispute Location Data Set." *Journal of Peace Research* 47:91–8.

Brancati, Dawn. 2009. *Peace by Design: Managing Intrastate Conflict through Decentralization*. Oxford: Oxford University Press.

Brandt, Patrick T., T. David Mason, Mehmet Gurses, Nicolai Petrovsky, and Dagmar Radin. 2008. "When and How the Fighting Stops: Explaining the Duration and Outcome of Civil Wars." *Defence and Peace Economics* 6:415–434.

Brass, Paul. 1991. *Ethnicity and Nationalism: Theory and Comparison*. Newbury Park, CA: Sage.

Brown, David. 1994. *The State and Ethnic Politics in Southeast Asia*. London: Routledge.

Brown, Graham K. 2008. "Horizontal Inequalities and Separatism in Southeast Asia: A Comparative Perspective." In *Horizontal Inequalities and Conflict: Understanding Group Violence in Multiethnic Societies*, edited by Frances Stewart. Houndmills: Palgrave Macmillan.

Brubaker, Rogers. 1996. *Nationalism Reframed: Nationhood and the National Question in the New Europe*. Cambridge: Cambridge University Press.

———. 2004. *Ethnicity Without Groups*. Cambridge, MA: Harvard University Press.

———. 2009. "Ethnicity, Race, and Nationalism." *Annual Review of Sociology* 35:21–42.

Bruk, Solomon I. and V. S. Apenchenko. 1964. "Atlas Narodov Mira." Moscow: Glavnoe upravlenie geodezii i kartografii gosudarstvennogo geologicheskogo komiteta SSSR and Institut etnografii im. H. H. Miklukho-Maklaia, Akademiia nauk SSSR.

Brush, Stephen G. 1996. "Dynamics of Theory Change in the Social Sciences: Relative Deprivation and Collective Violence." *Journal of Conflict Resolution* 40:523–45.

Buhaug, Halvard. 2006. "Relative Capability and Rebel Objective in Civil War." *Journal of Peace Research* 43:691–708.

Buhaug, Halvard and Kristian Skrede Gleditsch. 2008. "Contagion or Confusion? Why Conflicts Cluster in Space." *International Studies Quarterly* 52:215–33.

Buhaug, Halvard and Päivi Lujala. 2005. "Accounting for Scale: Measuring Geography in Quantitative Studies of Civil War." *Political Geography* 24:399–418.

Buhaug, Halvard, Lars-Erik Cederman, and Kristian Skrede Gleditsch. Forthcoming. "Square Pegs in Round Holes: Inequalities, Grievances, and Civil War." *International Studies Quarterly*.

Buhaug, Halvard, Lars-Erik Cederman, and Jan Ketil Rød. 2008. "Disaggregating Ethno-Nationalist Civil Wars: A Dyadic Test of Exclusion Theory." *International Organization* 62:531–51.

Buhaug, Halvard, Scott Gates, and Päivi Lujala. 2009. "Geography, Rebel Capability, and the Duration of Civil Conflict." *Journal of Conflict Resolution* 53:544–69.

Buhaug, Halvard, Kristian Skrede Gleditsch, Helge Holtermann, Gudrun Østby, and Andreas Forø Tollefsen. 2011. "It's the Local Economy, Stupid! Geographic Wealth Dispersion and Conflict Outbrak Location." *Journal of Conflict Resolution* 55:814–40.

Bunce, Valerie. 1999. *Subversive Institutions: The Design and the Destruction of Socialism and the State*. Cambridge: Cambridge University Press.

Byman, Daniel and Jerrold Green. 1999. "The Enigma of Political Stability in the Persian Guld Monarchies." *Middle East Review of International Affairs* 3:20–37.

Calhoun, Craig. 1993. "Nationalism and Ethnicity." *Annual Review of Sociology* 19:211–39.

———. 1997. *Nationalism*. Minneapolis: University of Minnesota Press.

Callahan, Mary P. 2005. *Making Enemies: War and State-Buildling in Burma*. Ithaca, NY: Cornell University Press.

Campbell, Donald T. 1965. "Ethnocentric and Other Altruistic Motives." In *Nebraska Symposium on Motivation*, edited by David Levine. Lincoln: University of Nebraska Press.

Cederman, Lars-Erik. 1997. *Emergent Actors in World Politics: How States and Nations Develop and Dissolve*. Princeton, NJ: Princeton University Press.

———. 2002. "Endogenizing Geopolitical Boundaries with Agent-Based Modeling." *Proceedings of the National Academy of Sciences* 99:7296–303.

———. 2008. "Articulating the Geo-Cultural Logic of Nationalist Insurgency." In *Order, Conflict, and Violence*, edited by Stathis N. Kalyvas, Ian Shapiro, and Tarek Masoud, 242–70. Cambridge: Cambridge University Press.

———. 2013. "Nationalism and Ethnicity." In *The Handbook of International Relations*, edited by Walter Carlsnaes, Thomas Risse, and Beth Simmons. London: Sage.

Cederman, Lars-Erik and Luc Girardin. 2007. "Beyond Fractionalization: Mapping Ethnicity onto Nationalist Insurgencies." *American Political Science Review* 101:173–185.

Cederman, Lars-Erik and Kristian Skrede Gleditsch. 2009. "Introduction to Special Issue on 'Disaggregating Civil War.'" *Journal of Conflict Resolution* 53:487–95.

Cederman, Lars-Erik, Halvard Buhaug, and Jan Ketil Rød. 2009. "Ethno-Nationalist Dyads and Civil War: A GIS-Based Analysis." *Journal of Conflict Resolution* 53:496–525.

Cederman, Lars-Erik, Luc Girardin, and Kristian Skrede Gleditsch. 2009. "Ethnonationalist Triads: Assessing the Influence of Kin Groups on Civil Wars." *World Politics* 61:403–37.

Cederman, Lars-Erik, Kristian Skrede Gleditsch, Idean Salehyan, and Julian Wucherpfennig. 2013. "Transborder Ethnic Kin and Civil War." *International Organization* 67:389–410.

Cederman, Lars-Erik, T. Camber Warren, and Didider Sornette. 2011. "Testing Clausewitz: Nationalism, Mass Mobilization, and the Severity of War." *International Organization* 65:605–38.

Cederman, Lars-Erik, Nils B. Weidmann, and Kristian Skrede Gleditsch. 2011. "Horizontal Inequalities and Ethno-Nationalist Civil War: A Global Comparison." *American Political Science Review* 105:478–95.

Cederman, Lars-Erik, Andreas Wimmer, and Brian Min. 2010. "Why Do Ethnic Groups Rebel? New Data and Analysis." *World Politics* 62:87–119.

Cetinyan, Rupen. 2002. "Ethnic Bargaining in the Shadow of Third-Party Intervention." *International Organization* 56:645–77.

Chai, Sun-Ki. 2005. "Predicting Ethnic Boundaries." *European Sociological Review* 21:375–91.

Chan, Steve. 1997. "In Search of Democratic Peace: Problems and Promise." *Mershon International Studies Review* 41:59–91.

Chandra, Kanchan. 2006. "What Is Ethnic Identity and Does It Matter?" *Annual Review of Political Science* 9:397–424.

Chandra, Kanchan and Steven I. Wilkinson. 2008. "Measuring the Effect of 'Ethnicity.'" *Comparative Political Studies* 41:515–63.

Chazan, Naomi. 1991. "Irredentism and International Politics." Boulder, CO: Lynne Rienner.

Chen, Xi and William D. Nordhaus. 2011. "The Value of Luminosity Data as a Proxy for Economic Statistics." *Proceedings of the National Academy of Sciences* 108:8589–8594.

Chenoweth, Erica and Maria J. Stephan. 2011. *Why Civil Resinstance Works: The Strategic Logic of Nonviolent Conflict*. New York, NY: Columbia University Press.

Chua, Amy. 2003. *World on Fire: How Exporting Free Market Democracy Breeds Ethnic Hatred and Global Instability*. New York, NY: Doubleday.

Clark, John F. 2008. *The Faitlure of Democracy in the Republic of Congo*. Boulder, CO: Lynne Rienner.

Clausewitz, Carl von. [1831] 1984. *On War*. Princeton, NJ: Princeton University Press.

Coleman, James S. 1990. *Foundations of Social Theory*. Cambridge, MA: Harvard University Press.

Collier, Paul. 2000. "Doing Well out of War: An Economic Perspective." In *Greed and Grievance: Economic Agendas in Civil Wars*, edited by Mats Berdal and David M. Malone. Boulder, CO: Lynne Rienner.

———. 2007. *The Bottom Billion: Why the Poorest Countries Are Failing and What Can Be Done About It*. Oxford: Oxford University Press.

Collier, Paul and Anke Hoeffler. 2004. "Greed and Grievance in Civil Wars." *Oxford Economic Papers* 56:563–95.

Collier, Paul, Anke Hoeffler, and Dominic Rohner. 2009. "Beyond Greed and Grievance: Feasibility and Civil War." *Oxford Economic Papers* 61:1–27.

Collier, Paul, Anke Hoeffler, and Måns Söderbom. 2004. "On the Duration of Civil Wars." *Journal of Peace Research* 41:256–76.

Collier, Paul and Nicholas Sambanis. 2005. "Understanding Civil War: Evidence and Analysis." Washington, DC: The World Bank.

Connor, Walker. 1972. "Nation-Building or Nation-Destroying." *World Politics* 24:319–55.

———. 1994. *Ethnonationalism: The Quest for Understanding*. Princeton, NJ: Princeton University Press.

Cook, Karen S. and Karen A. Hegtvedt. 1983. "Distributive Justice, Equity, and Equality." *Annual Review of Sociology* 9:217–41.

Cornell, Svante E. 2002. "Autonomy as a Source of Conflict." *World Politics* 54:245–76.

Coronel Ferrer, Miriam. 2005. "The Moro and the Cordillera Conflicts in the Philippines and the Struggle for Autonomy." In *Ethnic Conflicts in Southeast Asia*, edited by Kusuma Snitwongsee and W. Scott Thompson. Singapore: ISEAS Publications.

Coser, Lewis A. 1964. *The Functions of Social Conflict*. New York: The Free Press.

Cramer, Christopher. 2006. *Civil War Is Not a Stupid Thing*. London: Hurst & Company.

Crawford, Neeta C. 1993. "Decolonization as an International Norm: The Evolution of Practices, Arguments, and Beliefs." In *Emerging Norms of Justified Intervention*, edited by Laura Reed and Carl Kaysen. Cambridge, MA: American Academy of Sciences.

Cuesta, José and Syed Monsoob Murshed. 2010. "On the Micro-Foundations of Contract versus Conflict with Implications for International Peace-Making." *International Journal of Development and Conflict* 1:11–24.

Cunningham, David E. 2006. "Veto Players and Civil War Duration." *American Journal of Political Science* 50:875–92.

———. 2011. *Barriers to Peace in Civil Wars*. Cambridge: Cambridge University Press.

Cunningham, David E., Kristian Skrede Gleditsch, and Idean Salehyan. 2009. "It Takes Two: A Dyadic Analysis of Civil War Duration and Outcome." *Journal of Conflict Resolution* 53:570–97.

Cunningham, Kathleen Gallagher. 2010. "Divide and Conquer or Divide and Concede: How Do States Respond to Internally Divided Separatists?" *American Political Science Review* 105:275–97.

Dahl, Robert A. 1971. *Polyarchy: Participation and Opposition*. New Haven, CT: Yale University Press.

Darden, Keith A. Forthcoming. *Resisting Occupation: Mass Schooling and the Creation of Durable National Loyalties*. Cambridge: Cambridge University Press.

Davies, James Chowning. 1962. "Toward a Theory of Revolution." *American Sociological Review* 6:5–19.

De Figuerido, Rui and Barry R. Weingast. 1999. "The Rationality of Fear: Political Opportunism and Ethnic Conflict." In *Civil Wars, Insecurity and Intervention*, edited by Barbara Walter and Jack Snyder. New York, NY: Columbia University Press.

Decalo, Samuel. 1996. *Historical Dictionary of Togo*. Lanham, MD: Scarecrow Press.

Deiwiks, Christa. 2011. "Ethnofederalism: A Slippery Slope Towards Secessionist Conflict?" PhD Dissertation Thesis, ETH Zürich.

Deiwiks, Christa, Lars-Erik Cederman, and Kristian Skrede Gleditsch. 2012. "Inequality and Conflict in Federations." *Journal of Peace Research* 49:289–304.

Derluguian, Georgi M. 2005. *Bourdieu's Secret Admirer in the Caucasus: A World-System Biography*. Chicago, IL: University of Chicago Press.

DeRouen, Karl R. Jr. and Jacob Bercovitch. 2008. "Enduring Internal Rivalries: A New Framework for the Study of Civil War." *Journal of Peace Research* 45:43–62.

DeRouen, Karl R. Jr. and David Sobek. 2004. "The Dynamics of Civil War Duration and Outcome." *Journal of Peace Research* 41:303–20.

Deutsch, Karl W. 1961. "Social Mobilization and Political Development." *American Political Science Review* 60:493–514.

Diamond, Larry. 1988. *Class, Ethnicity, and Democracy in Nigera: The Failure of the First Republic*. Syracuse, NY: Syracuse University Press.

Diehl, Paul F. and Gary Goertz. 2000. *War and Peace in International Rivalry*. Ann Arbor, MI: University of Michigan Press.

Eck, Kristine and Lisa Hultman. 2007. "Violence against Civilians in War: Insights from New Fatality Data." *Journal of Peace Research* 44:233–46.

Elias, Norbert. [1939] 1982. *The Civilizing Process: State Formation and Civilization*, vol. 2. Translated by Edmund Jephcott. Oxford: Basil Blackwell.

Ellingsen, Tanja. 2000. "Colorful Community or Ethnic Witches' Brew? Multiethnicity and Domestic Conflict During and After the Cold War." *Journal of Conflict Resolution* 44:228–49.

Elster, Jon. 1998. "A Plea for Mechanisms." In *Social Mechanisms: An Analytical Approach to Social Theory*, edited by P. Hedström and R. Swedberg. Cambridge: Cambridge University Press. 45–73.

Elvidge, Christopher D., Paul C. Sutton, Tilottama Ghosh, Bejamin T. Tuttle, Kimberly E. Baugh, Budhendra Bhaduri, and Edward Bright. 2009. "A Global Poverty Map Derived from Satellite Data." *Computers and Geosciences* 35:1652–60.

Emirbayer, Mustafa and Chad Alan Goldberg. 2005. "Pragmatism, Bourdieu, and Collective Emotions in Contentious Politics." *Theory and Society* 34:469–518.

Enders, Walter, Todd Sandler, and Khursrav Gaibulloev. 2011. "Domestic versus Transnational Terrorism: Data, Decomposition, and Dynamics." *Journal of Peace Research* 48:319–37.

Fearon, James D. 1994. "Ethnic War as a Commitment Problem." New York: Annual Meeting of the American Political Science Association.

———. 1995. "Rationalist Explanations for War." *International Organization* 49:379–414.

———. 1998. "Commitment Problems and the Spread of Ethnic Conflict." In *The International Spread of Ethnic Conflict*, edited by David A. Lake and Donald Rothchild. Princeton, NJ: Princeton University Press.

———. 2003. "Ethnic and Cultural Diversity by Country." *Journal of Economic Growth* 8:195–222.

———. 2004a. "Separatist Wars, Partition, and World Order." *Security Studies* 13:394–415.

———. 2004b. "Why Do Some Civil Wars Last So Much Longer Than Others?" *Journal of Peace Research* 41:275–301.

———. 2006. "Ethnic Mobilization and Ethnic Violence." In *The Oxford Handbook of Political Economy*, edited by Barry R. Weingast and Donald A. Wittman. Oxford: Oxford University Press.

———. 2011. "Governance and Civil War Onset." World Bank, World Development Report 2011, Washington, DC.

Fearon, James D. and David D. Laitin. 1996. "Explaining Interethnic Cooperation." *American Political Science Review* 90:715–35.

———. 2003. "Ethnicity, Insurgency, and Civil War." *American Political Science Review* 97:75–90.

———. 2004. "Neotrusteeship and the Problem of Weak States." *International Security* 28:5–43.

———. 2007. "Civil War Termination." Paper presented at the Annual Meeting of the American Political Science Association, Chicago, IL, USA.

———. 2011. "Sons of the Soil, Migrants, and Civil War." *World Development* 39:199–211.

Fearon, James D., Kimuli Kasara, and David D. Laitin. 2007. "Ethnic Minority Rule and Civil War Onset." *American Political Science Review* 101:187–93.

Fehr, Ernst and Simon Gächter. 2000. "Fairness and Retaliation: The Economics of Reciprocity." *Journal of Economic Perspectives* 14:159–81.

Femia, Joseph. 1975. "Hegemony and Consciousness in the Thought of Antonio Gramsci." *Political Studies* 23: 29–48.

Fjelde, Hanne and Nina von Uexkull. 2012. "Climate Triggers: Rainfall Anomalies, Vulnerability and Communal Conflict in Sub-Saharan Africa." *Political Geography* 31:444–53.

Flora, Peter. 1999. "State Formation, Nation-Building, and Mass Politics in Europe: The Theory of Stein Rokkan." Oxford: Oxford University Press.

Forsberg, Erika. 2013. "Do Ethnic Dominoes Fall? Evaluating Domino Effects of Granting Territorial Concessions to Separatist Groups." *International Studies Quarterly* 56:1–12.

Gagnon, Valère Philip Jr. 2004. *The Myth of Ethnic War: Serbia and Croatia in the 1990s*. Ithaca, NY: Cornell University Press.

Gall, Carlotta and Thomas de Waal. 1998. *Chechnya: Calamity in the Caucasus*. New York, NY: New York University Press.

Gamson, William. 1992. *Talking Politics*. New York, NY: Cambridge University Press.

Gartzke, Erik. 1999. "War Is in the Error Term." *International Organization* 22:567–87.

Gates, Scott. 2002. "Recruitment and Allegiance: The Microfoundations of Rebellion." *Journal of Conflict Resolution* 46:111–30.

Gates, Scott, Håvard Hegre, Mark P. Jones, and Håvard Strand. 2006. "Institutional Inconsistency and Political Instability: Polity Duration, 1800–2000." *American Journal of Political Science* 50:893–908.

Geller, Daniel. 1993. "Power Differentials and War in Rival Dyads." *International Studies Quarterly* 37:173–93.

Gellner, Ernest. 1964. *Thought and Change*. London: Widenfeld & Nicolson.

———. 1983. *Nations and Nationalism*. Ithaca, NY: Cornell University Press.

Gilley, Bruce. 2004. "Against the Concept of Ethnic Conflict." *Third World Quarterly* 25:1155–66.

Gilpin, Robert. 1981. *War and Change in World Politics*. Cambridge: Cambridge University Press.

Giuliano, Elise. 2011. *Constructing Grievance: Ethnic Nationalism in Russia's Republics*. Ithaca, NY: Cornell University Press.

Gleditsch, Kristian Skrede. 2002. *All International Politics is Local: The Diffusion of Conflict, Integration, and Democratization*. Ann Arbor, MI: University of Michigan Press.

———. 2004. "A Revised List of Wars between and within Independent States, 1816–2002." *International Interactions* 30:231–62.

———. 2007. "Transnational Dimensions of Civil War." *Journal of Peace Research* 44:293–309.

Gleditsch, Kristian Skrede and Michael D. Ward. 1999. "A Revised List of Independent States since 1816." *International Interactions* 25:393–413.

Gleditsch, Kristian Skrede and Michael D. Ward. 2006. "The Diffusion of Democracy and the International Context of Democratization." *International Organization* 60:911–33.

Gleditsch, Kristian Skrede, Idean Salehyan, and Ken Schultz. 2008. "Fighting at Home, Fighting Abroad: How Civil Wars Lead to International Dsputes." *Journal of Conflict Resolution* 52:479–506.

Gleditsch, Nils Petter, Håvard Hegre, and Håvard Strand. 2009. "Democracy and Civil War." In *Handbook of War Studies III: The Intrastate Dimension*, edited by Manus I. Midlarsky. Ann Arbor: University of Michigan Press.

Gleditsch, Nils Petter, Peter Wallensteen, Mikael Eriksson, Margareta Sollenberg, and Håvard Strand. 2002. "Armed Conflict 1946–2001: A New Data Set." *Journal of Peace Research* 39:615–37.

Goddard, Stacie E. 2006. "Uncommon Ground: Indivisible Territory and the Politics of Legitimacy." *International Organization* 60:35–68.

Goemans, Hein E. 2000. *War and Punishment: The Causes of War Termination and the First World War*. Princeton, NJ: Princeton University Press.

Goertz, Gary. 2007. *Social Science Concepts: A User's Guide*. Princeton, NJ: Princeton University Press.

Goldstone, Jack A. 1991. *Revolution and Rebellion in the Early Modern World*. Berkeley, CA: University of California Press.

———. 2001. "Toward a Fourth Generation of Revolutionary Theory." *Annual Review of Political Science* 4:139–87.

Goldstone, Jack A., Robert H. Bates, David L. Epstein, Ted Robert Gurr, Michael B. Lustik, Monty G. Marshall, Jay Ulfelder, and Mark Woodward. 2010. "A Global Model for Forecasting Political Instability." *American Journal of Political Science* 54:190–208.

González Casanova, Pablo. 1965. "Internal Colonialism and National Development." *Studies in Comparative International Development* 1:27–37.

Goodwin, Jeff. 1997. "State-Centered Approaches to Social Revolutions: Strengths and Limitations of a Theoretical Tradition." In *Theorizing Revolutions*, edited by John Foran. London: Routledge.

———. 2001. *No Other Way Out: States an Revolutionary Movements, 1945–1991*. Cambridge: Cambridge University Press.

Goodwin, Jeff and Steven Pfaff. 2001. "Emotion Work in High-Risk Social Movements: Managing Fear in the U.S. and East German Civil Rights Movements." In *Passionate Politics: Emotions and Social Movements*, edited by Jeff Goodwin, James M. Jasper, and Francesca Polletta. Chicago, IL: University of Chicago Press.

Goodwin, Jeff, James M. Jasper, and Francesca Polletta. 2001a. "Introduction: Why Emotions Matter." In *Passionate Politics: Emotions and Social Movements*, edited by Jeff Goodwin, James M. Jasper, and Francesca Polletta. Chicago, IL: University of Chicago Press.

———. 2001b. "The Return of the Repressed: The Fall and Rise of Emotions in Social Movement Theory." *Mobilization: An International Journal* 5:65–83.

Gourevitch, Peter. 1979. "The Re-Emergence of 'Peripheral Nationalisms': Some Comparative Speculations on the Spatial Distribution of Political Leadership and Economic Growth." *Comparative Studies in Society and History* 21.

Gunes, Cengiz. 2012. *The Kurdish National Movement in Turkey: From Protest to Resistance*. London: Routledge.

Gunter, Michael. 2008. *The Kurds Ascending: the Evolving Solution to the Kurdish Problem in Iraq and Turkey*. New York, NY: Palgrave Macmillan.

Gurr, Ted Robert. 1970. *Why Men Rebel*. Princeton, NJ: Princeton University Press.

———. 1993a. *Minorities at Risk: A Global View of Ethnopolitical Conflicts.* Washington, DC: United States Institute of Peace Press.

———. 1993b. "Why Minorities Rebel: A Global Analysis of Communal Mobilization and Conflict since 1945." *International Political Science Review* 14:161–201.

———. 2000a. "Ethnic Warfare on the Wane." *Foreign Affairs* 79:52–64.

———. 2000b. *Peoples versus States: Minorities at Risk in the New Century.* Washington, DC: United States Institute of Peace Press.

Gurr, Ted Robert and Raymond Duvall. 1973. "Civil Conflict in the 1960s: A Reciprocal System with Parameter Estimates." *Comparative Political Studies* 6:135–69.

Habyarimana, James, Macartan Humphreys, Daniel N. Posner, and Jeremy M. Weinstein. 2009. *Coethnicity: Diversity and the Dilemmas of Collective Action.* New York: Russell Sage Foundation.

Hafez, Mohammed M. 2003. *Why Muslims Rebel.* Boulder, CO: Lynne Rienner.

Hale, Henry E. 2008. *The Foundations of Ethnic Politics: Separatism of States and Nations in Eurasia and the World.* Cambridge: Cambridge University Press.

Hale, Henry E. and Rein Taagepera. 2002. "Russia: Consolidation or Collapse?" *Europe-Asia Studies* 54:1101–25.

Hall, Rodney Bruce. 1999. *National Collective Identity: Social Constructs and International Systems.* New York, NY: Columbia University Press.

Hannan, Michael T. 1979. "The Dynamics of Ethnic Boundaries in Modern States." In *National Development and the World System,* edited by John W. Meyer and Michael T. Hannan, 253–75. Chicago, IL: University of Chicago Press.

Hardin, Russell. 1995. *One For All: the Logic of Group Conflict.* Princeton, NJ: Princeton University Press.

Hartzell, Caroline, Matthew Hoddie, and Donald Rothchild. 2001. "Stabilizing the Peace after Civil War: An Investigation of Some Key Variables." *International Organization* 55:183–208.

Hechter, Michael. 1975. *Internal Colonialism: The Celtic Fringe in British National Development, 1536–1966.* London: Routledge and Kegan Paul.

———. 1978. "Group Formation and the Cultural Division of Labor." *American Journal of Sociology* 84.

———. 1987. *Principles of Group Solidarity.* Berkeley and Los Angeles, CA: University of California Press.

———. 2001. *Containing Nationalism.* Oxford: Oxford University Press.

Hechter, Michael and Dina Okamoto. 2001. "Political Consequences of Minority Group Formation." *Annual Review of Political Science* 4:189–215.

Hedström, Peter and Peter Bearman. 2009. *The Oxford Handbook of Analytical Sociology.* Oxford: Oxford University Press.

Hedström, Peter and Richard Swedberg. 1998. "Social Mechanisms: An Analytical Approach to Social Theory." Cambridge: Cambridge University Press.

Heger, Lindsay and Idean Salehyan. 2007. "Ruthless Rulers: Coalition Size and the Severity of Civil Conflict." *International Studies Quarterly* 51:385–403.

Hegre, Håvard. 2004. "The Duration and Termination of Civil War (Introduction to special issue)." *Journal of Peace Research* 41:243–52.

Hegre, Håvard and Nicholas Sambanis. 2006. "Sensitivity Analysis of Empirical Results on Civil War Onset." *Journal of Conflict Resolution* 50:508–35.

Hegre, Håvard, Tanja Ellingsen, Scott Gates, and Nils Petter Gleditsch. 2001. "Toward a Democratic Civil Peace? Democracy, Political Change, and Civil War, 1816–1992." *American Political Science Review* 95:33–48.

Hegre, Håvard, Gudrun Østby, and Clionadh Raleigh. 2009. "Poverty and Civil War Events A Disaggregated Study of Liberia." *Journal of Conflict Resolution* 53:598–623.

Heraclides, Alexis. 1990. "Secessionist Minorities and External Involvement." *International Organization* 44:341–78.

Herrera, Yoshiko M. 2005. *Imagined Economies: The Sources of Russian Regionalism.* Cambridge: Cambridge University Press.

Heston, Alan, Robert Summers, and Bettina Aten. 2011. "Penn World Table Version 7.0." Philadelphia, PA: Center for International Comparisons of Production, Income and Prices, University of Pennsylvania.

Hintze, Otto. 1975. "Military Organization and the Organizatoin of the State." In *The Historical Essays of Otto Hintze*, edited by Felix Gilbert. New York: Oxford University Press.

Hirshleifer, Jack. 1983. "From Weakest-Link to Best-Shot." *Public Choice* 41:371–86.

Hogg, Michael A. and Dominic Abrams. 1988. *Social Identifications: A Social Psychology of Intergroup Relations and Group Processes.* London: Routledge.

Holbrooke, Richard. 1998. *To End a War.* New York: Random House.

Holsti, Kalevi J. 1996. *The State, War, and the State of War.* Cambridge: Cambridge University Press.

Horowitz, Donald L. 1985. *Ethnic Groups in Conflict.* Berkeley, CA: University of California Press.

_____. 2002. *The Deadly Ethnic Riot.* Berkeley and Los Angeles, CA: University of California Press.

Horowitz, Shale and Buddhika Jayamaha. 2007. "Sri Lanka (1972–Present)." In *Civil Wars of the World: Major Conflicts since World War II*, edited by Karl R. DeRouen Jr. and Uk Heo. Santa Barbara, CA: CLIO.

Howard, Michael. 1976. *War in European History.* Oxford: Oxford University Press.

Hroch, Miroslav. 1985. *Social Preconditions of National Revival in Europe: A Comparative Analysis of the Social Composition of Patriotic Groups among the Smaller European Nations.* Cambridge: Cambridge University Press.

Hug, Simon. 2003. "Selection Bias in Comparative Research: The Case of Incomplete Data Sets." *Political Analysis* 11:255–74.

_____. 2013. "Use and Misuse of MAR." *Annual Review of Political Science* 13 (in press).

Humphreys, Macartan and Habaye ag Mohamed. 2005. "Senegal and Mali." In *Understanding Civil War: Evidence and Analysis*, vol. 1, edited by Paul Collier and Nicholas Sambanis. Washington, DC: The World Bank.

Humphreys, Macartan and Jeremy Weinstein. 2006. "Handling and Manhandling Civilians in Civil War." *American Political Science Review* 99:61–74.

Huntington, Samuel P. 1968. *Political Order in Changing Society.* New Haven, CT: Yale University Press.

———. 1991. *The Third Wave: Democratization in the Late Twenthieth Century*. Norman, OK: University of Oklahoma Press.

Huth, Paul K. 1988. *Extended Deterrence and the Prevention of War*. New Haven, CT: Yale University Press.

Ibrahim, Jibrin. 1994. "Political exclusion, Democratisation and Dynamics of Ethnicity in Niger." *Africa Today* 41.

Ige, Bola. 1995. *People, Politics and Politicians of Nigeria (1940–1979)*. Ibadan: Heinemann Educational Books.

Jackson, Robert H. 1990. *QuasiStates: Sovereignty, International Relations, and the Third World*. Cambridge: Cambridge University Press.

Jaggers, Keith and Ted Robert Gurr. 1995. "Transitions to Democracy: Tracking Democracy's Third Wave with the Polity III Data." *Journal of Peace Research* 32:469–82.

Jasper, James M. 1998. "The Emotions of Protest: Affective and Reactive Emotions in and around Social Movements." *Sociological Forum* 13:397–424.

Jenkins, Richards. 1997. *Rethinking Ethnicity: Arguments and Explorations*. London: Sage.

Jenne, Erin K. 2007. *Ethnic Bargaining: The Paradox of Minority Empowerment*. Ithaca, NY: Cornell University Press.

Jervis, Robert. 1989. "Rational Deterrence: Theory and Evidence." *World Politics* 41:183–207.

Kalyvas, Stathis N. 2001. "'New' and 'Old' Civil Wars: A Valid Distinction?" *World Politics* 54:99–118.

———. 2003. "The Ontology of 'Political Violence': Action and Identity in Civil Wars." *Perspectives on Politics* 1:475–94.

———. 2006. *The Logic of Violence in Civil War*. Cambridge: Cambridge University Press.

———. 2007. "Civil Wars." In *The Oxford Handbook of Comparative Politics*, edited by Carles Boix and Susan C. Stokes. Oxford: Oxford University Press.

———. 2008a. "Ethnic Defection in Civil War." *Comparative Political Studies* 41:1043–68.

———. 2008b. "Promises and Pitfalls of an Emerging Research Program: The Microdynamics of Civil War." In *Order, Conflict, and Violence*, edited by Stathis N. Kalyvas, Ian Shapiro, and Tarek Masoud, 397–421. Cambridge: Cambridge University Press.

Kalyvas, Stathis N. and Matthew Adam Kocher. 2007. "How 'Free' Is Free Riding in Civil Wars? Violence, Insurgency, and the Collective Action Problem." *World Politics* 59:177–216.

Kanbur, Ravi, Prem kumar Rajaram, and Ashutosh Varshney. 2010. "Ethnic Diversity and Ethnic Strife: An Interdisciplinary Perspective." *World Development* 39:147–58.

Kaufman, Stuart J. 2001. *Modern Hatreds: The Symbolic Politics of Ethnic War*. Ithaca, NY: Cornell University Press.

———. 2006. "Symbolic Politics or Rational Choice? Testing Theories of Extreme Ethnic Violence." *International Security* 30:45–86.

———. 2011. "Symbols, Frames, and Violence: Studying Ethnic War in the Philippines." *International Studies Quarterly* 55:937–58.

Kaufmann, Chaim D. 1996. "Possible and Impossible Solutions to Ethnic Civil Wars." *International Security* 20:136–75.

_____. 1998. "When All Else Fails: Ethnic Population Transfers and Partitions in the Twentieth Century." *International Security* 23:120–56.

_____. 2005. "Rational Choice and Progress in the Study of Ethnic Conflict: A Review Essay." *Security Studies* 14:178–207.

Kaysen, Carl. 1990. "Is War Obsolete? A Review Essay." *International Security* 14:42–64.

Kelley, Judith G. 2004. *Ethnic Politics in Europe: The Power of Norms and Incentives.* Princeton, NJ: Princeton University Press.

Kemper, Theodore D. 1978. *A Social Interaction Theory of Emotions.* New York: John Wiley.

Khalidi, Raja. 2008. "Sixty Years After the UN Partition Resolution: What Future for the Arab Economy in Israel?" *Journal of Palestine Studies* 37:6–22.

Kinder, Donald R. and D. Roderick Kiewiet. 1979. "Economic Discontent and Political Behavior: Role of Personal Grievances and Collective Economic Judgments in Congressional Voting." *American Journal of Political Science* 23:495–527.

King, Charles. 2001. "The Myth of Ethnic Warfare." *Foreign Affairs* 80:687–706.

King, Charles and Neil J. Melvin. 1999/2000. "Diaspora Politics: Ethnic Linkages, Foreign Policy, and Security in Eurasia." *International Security* 24:108–38.

King, Gary and Langche Zeng. 2001. "Logistic Regression in Rare Events Data." *Political Analysis* 9:137–163.

Kirisci, Kemal and Gareth M. Winrow. 1997. *The Kurdish Question in Turkey: An Example of a Trans-State Ethnic Conflict.* London: Frank Cass.

Koktsidis, Pavlos-Ioannis and Caspar Ten Dam. 2008. "A Success Story? Analysing Albanian Ethno-Nationalist Extremism in the Balkans." *East European Quarterly* 42.

Kolstoe, Paul. 1995. *Russians in the Former Soviet Republics.* Bloomington: Indiana University Press.

Kornprobst, Markus. 2002. "The Management of Border Disputes in African Regional Sub-Systems: Comparing West Africa and the Horn of Africa." *Journal of Modern African Studies* 40:369–93.

Kreutz, Joakim. 2007. "Myanmar/Burma (1968–1995)." In *Civil Wars of the World: Major Conflicts Since World War II,* edited by Karl R. DeRouen Jr. and Uk Heo. Santa Barbara, CA: CLIO.

_____. 2010. "How and When Armed Conflicts End: Introducing the UCDP Conflict Termination Data Set." *Journal of Peace Research* 47:243–50.

Krings, Thomas. 1995. "Marginalisation and Revolt among the Tuareg in Mali and Niger." *GeoJournal* 36:57–63.

Laitin, David D. 1986. *Hegemony and Culture: Politics and Religious Change among the Yoruba.* Chicago, IL: University of Chicago Press.

Laitin, David D. 1998. *Identity in Formation: The Russian-Speaking Populations in the Near Abroad.* Ithaca, NY: Cornell University Press.

_____. 2007. *Nations, States and Violence.* Oxford: Oxford University Press.

Lang, Nicholas R. 1975. "The Dialectics of Decentralization: Economic Reform and Regional Inequality in Yugoslavia." *World Politics* 27:309–35.

Langer, Arnim. 2005. "Horizontal Inequalities and Violent Group Mobilization in Côte d'Ivoire." *Oxford Development Studies* 33:25–44.

Le Bon, Gustave. 1913. *The Psychology of Revolution.* New York, NY: Putnam.

Lemarchand, René. 1994. *Burundi: Ethnic Conflict and Genocide*. Cambridge: Cambridge University Press.

———. 2004. "Exclusion, Marginalization, and Political Mobilization: The Road to Hell in the Great Lakes." In *Facing Ethnic Conlicts: Toward a New Realism*, edited by Andreas Wimmer, Richard J. Goldstone, Donald L. Horowitz, Ulrike Joras, and Conrad Schetter. Lanham, MD: Rowman and Littlefield.

Lemke, Douglas and Suzanne Werner. 1996. "Power Parity, Commitment to Change, and War." *International Studies Quarterly* 40:235–60.

LeVine, Robert A. and Donald T. Campbell. 1972. *Ethnocentrism: Theories of Conflict, Ethnic Attitudes, and Group Behavior*. New York, NY: J. Wiley & Sons.

Lichbach, Mark Irving. 1989. "An Evaluation of 'Does Economic Inequality Breed Political Conflict?'" *World Politics* 41:431–70.

———. 1995. *The Rebel's Dilemma*. Ann Arbor: University of Michigan Press.

Lindemann, Stefan. 2011. "Just Another Change of Guard? Broad-Based Politics and Civil War in Museveni's Uganda." *African Affairs* 110:387–416.

Liow, Joseph Chinyong. 2006. "Muslim Resistance in Southern Thailand and Southern Philippines: Religion, Ideology, and Politics." East-West Center, Policy Studies, Washington, DC.

Lloyd, Peter C. 1970. "The Ethnic Background to the Nigerian Crisis." In *Nigerian Politics and Military Rule: Prelude to the Civil War*, edited by Simone K. Panter-Brick. London: University of London.

Lund, Christian. 2001. "Precarious Democratization and Local Dynamics in Niger: Micro-Politics in Zinder." *Development and Change* 32:845–69.

Lustick, Ian S. 2008. "Abandoning the Iron Wall: Israel and 'The Middle Eastern Muck.'" *Middle East Policy* 15.

Luttwak, Edward N. 1999. "Give War a Chance." *Foreign Affairs* 784:36–44.

Mack, Andrew. 1975. "Why Big Nations Lose Small Wars: The Politics of Asymmetric Conflict." *World Politics* 27:175–200.

———. 2002. "Civil War: Academic Research and the Policy Community." *Journal of Peace Research* 39:515–25.

Malaquias, Assis. 2000. "Ethnicity and Conflict in Angola: Prospects for Reconciliation." In *Angola's War Economy: The Role of Oil and Diamonds*, edited by Jakkie Cilliers and Christian Dietrich. Pretoria: Institute of Security Studies.

Malesevic, Sinisa. 2010. *The Sociology of War and Violence*. Cambridge: Cambridge University Press.

Mancini, Luca, Frances Stewart, and Graham K. Brown. 2008. "Approaches to the Measurement of Horizontal Inequalities." In *Horizontal Inequalities and Conflict: Understanding Group Violence in Multiethnic Societies*, edited by Frances Stewart. Houndmills: Palgrave Macmillan.

Mann, Michael. 1986. *The Sources of Social Power: A History of Power From the Beginning to A.D. 1760*. Cambridge: Cambridge University Press.

———. 2005. *The Dark Side of Democracy: Explaining Ethnic Cleansing*. Cambridge: Cambridge University Press.

Marcus, Aliza. 2007. *Bood and Belief: The PKK and the Kursish Fight for Independence*. New York, NY: New York University Press.

Martin, Terry. 2001. *The Affirmative Action Empire: Nations and Nationalism in the Soviet Union, 1923–1939*. Ithaca, NY: Cornell University Press.

Markowsky, Barry. 1985. "Toward a Multilevel Distributive Justice Theory." *American Sociological Review* 50:822–39.

Marshall, Monty G., Keith Jaggers, and Ted Robert Gurr. 2011. "Polity IV Project: Data Set Users' Manual." Vienna, VA: Center for Systemic Peace.

Marshall, Monty G. and Ted Robert Gurr. 2005. "Peace and Conflict: A Global Survey of Armed Conflicts, Self-Determination Movements, and Democracy." Center for International Development and Conflict Management, University of Maryland, College Park, MD.

Mason, T. David. 2009. "The Evolution of Theory on Civil War and Revolution." In *Handbook of War Studies III: The Intrastate Dimension*, edited by Manus I. Midlarsky. Ann Arbor, MI: University of Michigan Press.

Mason, T. David and Patrick J. Fett. 1996. "How Civil Wars End: A Rational Choice Approach." *Journal of Conflict Resolution* 40:546–68.

Mason, T. David, Joseph P. Weingarten, and Patrick J. Fett. 1999. "Win, Lose, or Draw: Predicting the Outcome of Civil Wars." *Political Research Quarterly* 52:239–68.

McAdam, Doug, John D. McCarthy, and Mayer N. Zald. 1988. "Social Movements." In *The Handbook of Sociology*, edited by Neil Smelser. Beverly Hills, CA: Sage.

McAdam, Doug, Sidney Tarrow, and Charles Tilly. 2001. *Dynamics of Contention*. Cambridge: Cambridge University Press.

McDowall, David. 2005. *A Modern History of the Kurds*. New York: IB Tauris.

McGovern, Mike. 2011. *Making War in Côte d'Ivoire*. Chicago, IL: University of Chicago Press.

Melander, Erik. 2009. "Justice or Peace? A Statistical Study of the Relationship between Amnesties and Durable Peace." Lund University, JAD-PdP Working Paper. http://www.lu.se/upload/LUPDF/Samhallsvetenskap/Just_and_Durable_Peace/Workingpaper4.pdf.

Mercer, Jonathan. 2005. "Rationality and Psychology in International Politics." *International Organization* 59:77–106.

Miller, Benjamin. 2007. *States, Nations, and the Great Powers: The Sources of Regional War and Peace*. Cambridge: Cambridge University Press.

Miodownik, Dan, Ravi Bhavnani, and Hyun-Jin Choi. 2011. "Violence and Control in Civil Conflict: Israel, the West Bank, and Gaza." *Comparative Politics* 44:61–80.

Mitra, Subrata K. 1995. "The Rational Politics of Cultural Nationalism: Subnational Movements of South Asia in Comparative Perspective." *British Journal of Political Science* 25:57–77.

Montalvo, José G. and Marta Reynal-Querol. 2005. "Ethnic Polarization, Potential Conflict, and Civil Wars." *American Economic Review* 95(3):796–816.

———. 2010. "Ethnic Polarization and the Duration of Civil Wars." *Economics of Governance* 11:123–43.

Moore, Barrington Jr. 1966. *Social Origins of Dictatorship and Democracy*. Boston, MA: Beacon Press.

———. 1978. *Injustice: The Social Bases of Obedience and Revolt*. London: Macmillan.

Moore, Will H. and David R. Davis. 1997. "Ethnicity Matters: Transnational Ethnic Alliances and Foreign Policy Behavior." *International Studies Quarterly* 41:171–84.

———. 1998. "Ties that Bind? Domestic and International Conflict Behavior in Zaire." *Comparative Political Studies* 31:45–71.

Morrison, Donald G., Robert C. Mitchell, and John N. Paden. 1972. "Black Africa: A Comparative Handbook." New York, NY: The Free Press.

Mousseau, Demet Yalcin. 2001. "Democratizing with Ethnic Divisions: A Source of Conflict." *Journal of Peace Research* 38:547–67.

Mueller, John E. 2000. "The Banality of 'Ethnic War.'" *International Security* 25:42–70.

———. 2004. *The Remnants of War*. Ithaca, NY: Cornell University Press.

Muller, Edward N. 1985. "Income Inequality, Regime Repressiveness, and Political Violence." *American Sociological Review* 50:47–61.

Muller, Edward N. and Mitchell A. Seligson. 1987. "Inequality and Insurgency." *American Political Science Review* 81:425–51.

Murshed, S. Mansoob and Scott Gates. 2005. "Spatial-Horizontal Inequality and the Maoist Insurgency in Nepal." *Review of Development Economics* 9:121–34.

Nordhaus, William D. 2006. "Geography and Macroeconomics: New Data and New Findings." *Proceedings of the National Academy of Sciences* 103:3510–17.

Nordhaus, William D. and Xi Chen. 2009. "Geography: Grahics and Economics." *B. E. Journal of Economic Analysis and Policy* 9. http://www.bepress.com/bejeap/vol9/iss2/art1.

Oberschall, Anthony. 1978. "Theories of Social Conflict." *Annual Review of Sociology* 4:291–315.

———. 1993. *Social Movements: Ideologies, Interests, and Identities*. New Brunswick, NJ: Transaction Publichers.

———. 2007. *Conflict and Peace Building in Divided Societies: Responses to Ethnic Violence*. London: Routledge.

Olson, Mancur. 1965. *The Logic of Collective Action: Public Goods and the Theory of Groups*. Cambridge, MA: Harvard University Press.

Olzak, Susan. 2006. *The Global Dynamics of Racial and Ethnic Mobilization*. Stanford, CA: Stanford University press.

Opp, Karl-Dieter. 2009. *Theories of Political Protest and Social Movements: A Multi-disciplinary Introduction, Critique, and Synthesis*. Abingdon: Routledge.

Østby, Gudrun. 2008a. "Inequalities, the Political Environment and Civil Conflict: Evidence from 55 Developing Countries." In *Horizontal Inequalities and Conflict: Understanding Group Violence in Multiethnic Societies*, edited by Frances Stewart. Houndmills: Palgrave Macmillan.

———. 2008b. "Polarization, Horizontal Inequalities and Violent Civil Conflict." *Journal of Peace Research* 45:143–62.

Østby, Gudrun, Ragnhild Nordås, and Jan Ketil Rød. 2009. "Regional Inequalities and Civil Conflict in Sub-Saharan Africa." *International Studies Quarterly* 53:301–24.

Outram, Quentin. 1999. "Liberia: Roots and Fruits of the Emergency." *Third World Quarterly* 20:163–73.

Paige, Jeffrey M. 1975. *Agrarian Revolution: Social Movements and Export Agriculture in the Underdeveloped World*. New York, NY: Free Press.

Pappe, Ilan. 2004. *A History of Modern Palestine: One Land, Two Peoples*. Cambridge: Cambridge University Press.

Parekh, Bhikhu. 2008. *A New Politics of Identity: Political Principles for an Interdependent World*. Basingstoke: Palgrave Macmillan.

Paxton, Pamela. 2000. "Women's Suffrage in the Measurement of Democracy: Problems of Perationalization." *Studies in Comparative International Development* 35:92–111.

Petersen, Roger. 2002. *Understanding Ethnic Violence: Fear, Hatred, and Resentment in Twentieth-Century Eastern Europe*. Cambridge: Cambridge University Press.

———. 2011. *Western Intervention in the Balkans: The Strategic Use of Emotion in Conflict*. Cambridge: Cambridge University Press.

Pettifer, James and Miranda Vickers. 2007. *The Albanian Question: Reshaping the Balkans*. London: I. B. Taurus.

Phillips, John. 2004. *Macedonia: Warlords and Rebels in the Balkans*. New Haven, CT: Yale University Press.

Piven, Frances Fox and Richard A. Cloward. 1991. "Collective Protest: A Critique of Resource Mobilization Theory." *International Journal of Politics, Culture and Society* 4:435–58.

Polletta, Francesca. 1998. "'It Was Like a Fever': Narrative and Identity in Social Protest." *Social Problems* 45:137–59.

Polletta, Francesca and James M. Jasper. 2001. "Collective Identity and Social Movements." *Annual Review of Sociology* 27:283–305.

Popkin, Samuel L. 1979. *The Rational Peasant: The Political Economy of Rural Society in Vietnam*. Berkeley and Los Angeles, CA: University of California Press.

Posen, Barry R. 1993. "The Security Dilemma and Ethnic Conflict." In *Ethnic Conflict and International Security*, edited by Michael E. Brown. Princeton, NJ: Princeton University Press.

Posner, Daniel N. 2004. "Measuring Ethnic Fractionalization in Africa." *American Journal of Political Science* 48:849–63.

———. 2005. *Institutions and Ethnic Politics in Africa*. Cambridge: Cambridge University Press.

Prunier, Gérard. 1995. *The Rwanda Crisis: History of a Genocide*. New York, NY: Columbia University Press.

———. 2005. *Darfur: The Ambiguous Genocide*. Ithaca, NY: Cornell University Press.

———. 2009. *Africa's World War: Congo, the Rwandan Genocide, and the Making of a Continental Catastrophe*. Oxford: Oxford University Press.

Rabushka, Alvin and Kenneth A. Shepsle. 1972. *Politics in Plural Societies: A Theory of Democratic Instability*. Columbus, OH: Charles. E. Merrill.

Ravlo, Hilde, Nils Petter Gleditsch, and Han Dorussen. 2003. "Colonial War and the Democratic Peace." *Journal of Conflict Resolution* 47:520–48.

Reed, Jean-Pierre and John Foran. 2002. "Political Cultures of Opposition: Exploring Idioms, Ideologies, and Revolutionary Agency in the Case of Nicaragua." *Critical Sociology* 28:335–70.

Regan, Patrick M. 2000. *Civil Wars and Foreign Powers: Interventions and Intrastate Conflict*. Ann Arbor, MI: University of Michigan Press.

Regan, Patrick M. and Daniel Norton. 2005. "Greed, Grievance, and Mobilization in Civil Wars." *Journal of Conflict Resolution* 49:319–36.

Reiter, Dan. 2003. "Exploring the Bargaining Model of War." *Perspectives on Politics* 1:27–43.

Robinson, William S. 1950. "Ecological Correlations and the Behavior of Individuals." *American Sociological Review* 15:351–7.

Roessler, Philip G. 2011. "The Enemy From Within: Personal Rule, Coups, and Civil Wars in Africa." *World Politics* 53:300–46.

Rose, William. 2000. "The Security Dilemma and Ethnic Conflict: Some New Hypotheses." *Security Studies* 9(4):1–51.

Rosecrance, Richard. 1986. *The Rise of the Trading State: Commerce and Conquest in the Modern World*. New York, NY: Basic Books.

Ross, Michael L. 2005. "Resources and Rebellion in Aceh, Indonesia." In *Understanding Civil War: Evidence and Analysis*, vol. 2, edited by Paul Collier and Nicholas Sambanis. Washington, DC: The World Bank.

_____. 2012. *The Oil Curse: How Petroleum Wealth Shapes the Development of Nations*. Princeton, NJ: Princeton University Press.

Rothchild, Donald. 1997. *Managing Ethnic Conflict in Africa: Pressures and Incentives for Cooperation*. Washington, DC: Brookings Institution Press.

Rothchild, Donald and Philip G. Roeder. 2005. "Power Sharing as an Impediment to Peace and Democracy." In *Sustainable Peace: Power and Democracy After Civil Wars*, edited by Philip G. Roeder and Donald Rothchild. Ithaca, NY: Cornell Unversity Press.

Rothchild, Joseph. 1981. *Ethnopolitics*. New York, NY: Columbia University Press.

Rubenzer, Trevor. 2007. "South Africa (1976–1994)." In *Civil Wars of the World: Major Conflicts since World War II*, vol. 2, edited by Karl R. DeRouen Jr. and Uk Heo. Santa Barbara, CA: CLIO.

Runciman, William. 1966. *Relative Deprivation and Social Justice*. London: Routledge and Kegan Paul.

Russett, Bruce M. 1964. "Inequality and Instability: The Relation of Land Tenure to Politics." *World Politics* 16:442–54.

Saideman, Stephen M. 2001. *The Ties That Divide: Ethnic Politics, Foreign Policy, and International Conflict*. New York, NY: Columbia University Press.

Saideman, Stephen M. and R. William Ayres. 2000. "Determining the Causes of Irredentism: Logit Analyses of Minorities at Risk Data from the 1980s and 1990s." *Journal of Politics* 62:1126–44.

_____. 2008. *For Kin or Country: Xenophobia, Nationalism, and War*. New York, NY: Columbia University Press.

Salehyan, Idean. 2007. "Transnational Rebels: Neighboring States as Sanctuary for Rebel Groups." *World Politics* 59:217–42.

_____. 2009. *Rebels Without Borders: Transnational Insurgencies in World Politics* Ithaca, NY: Cornell University Press.

Salehyan, Idean and Kristian Skrede Gleditsch. 2006. "Refugees and the Spread of Civil War." *International Organization* 60:335–66.

Salehyan, Idean, Kristian Skrede Gleditsch, and David E. Cunningham. 2011. "Explaining External Support for Insurgent Groups." *International Organization* 65:709–44.

Sambanis, Nicholas. 2001. "Do Ethnic and Nonethnic Civil Wars Have the Same Causes? A Theoretical and Empirical Inquiry." *Journal of Conflict Resolution* 45:259–82.

_____. 2004a. "Using Case Studies to Expand Economic Models of Civil War." *Perspectives on Politics* 2:259–79.

_____. 2004b. "What is Civil War? Conceptual and Empirical Complexities of an Operational Definition." *Journal of Conflict Resolution* 48:814–58.

_____. 2005. "Conclusion: Using Case Studies to Refine and Expand the Theory of Civil War." In *Understanding Civil War: Evidence and Analysis*, vol. 2, edited by Paul Collier and Nicholas Sambanis. Washington, DC: The World Bank.

Sambanis, Nicholas and Branko Milanovic. 2011. "Explaning the Demand for Sovereignty." World Bank, Policy Research Working Paper 5888.

Sambanis, Nicholas and Jonah Schulhofer-Wohl. 2009. "What's in a Line? Is Partition a Solution to Civil War?" *International Security* 34:82–118.

Sarkees, Meredith Reid and Frank Wayman. 2010. *Resort to War: 1816–2007*. Washington, DC: Congressional Quarterly.

Scarritt, James R. 1993. "Communal Conflict and Contention for Power in Africa South of the Sahara." In *Minorities at Risk: A Global View of Ethnopolitical Conflicts*, by Ted R. Gurr. Washington, DC: United States Institute of Peace Press.

Schock, Kurt. 1996. "A Conjunctural Model of Political Conflict: The Impact of Political Opportunities on the Relationship between Economic Inequality and Violent Political Conflict." *Journal of Conflict Resolution* 40:98–133.

Scott, James C. 1976. *The Moral Economy of the Peasant: Rebellion and Subsistence in Southeast Asia*. New Haven, CT: Yale University Press.

———. 2009. *The Art of Not Being Governed: An Anarchist History of Upland Southeast Asia*. New Haven, CT: Yale University Press.

Selbin, Eric. 2010. *Revolution, Rebellion, Resistance: The Power of Story*. London: Zed Books.

Shain, Yossi and Aharon Barth. 2003. "Diasporas and International Relations Theory." *International Organization* 57:449–79.

Shelef, Nadav G. 2010. *Evolving Nationalism: Homeland, Identity, and Religion in Israel, 1925–2005*. Cambridge: Cambridge University Press.

Sherif, Muzafer and Carolyn Wood Sherif. 1953. *Groups in Harmony and Tension*. New York, NY: Harper.

Shindler, Colin. 2002. *The Land Beyond Promise: Israel, Likud and the Zionist Dream*. London: I.B. Tauris.

Shlaim, Avi. 2009. *Israel and Palestians: Reappraisals, Revisions, Refutations*. London: Verso.

Shlapentokh, Vladimir, Munir Sendich, and Emil Payin. 1994. *The New Russian Diaspora*. New York, NY: ME Sharpe.

Sidanius, James and Felcia Pratto. 1999. *Social Dominance: An Intergroup Theory of Social Hierarchy and Opression*. Cambridge: Cambridge University Press.

Simmel, Georg. 1955. *Conflict and the Web of Group-Affiliations*. Translated by Reinhard Bendix. New York, NY: Free Press.

———. [1908] 1971. "How is Society Possible." In *Georg Simmel: On Individuality and Social Forms*, edited by Donald N. Levine. Chicago: University of Chicago Press.

Simpson, Brent and Michael W. Macy. 2004. "Power, Identity, and Collective Action in Social Exchange." *Social Forces* 82:1373–409.

Sinno, Abdulkader H. 2008. *Organizations at War in Afghanistan and Beyond*. Ithaca, NY: Cornell University Press.

Skocpol, Theda. 1979. *States and Social Revolutions: A Comparative Analysis of France, Russia, and China*. Cambridge: Cambridge University Press.

Slantchev, Branislav L. 2003. "The Principle of Convergence in Wartime Negotiations." *American Political Science Review* 87:621–32.

Smith, Anthony D. 2009. *Ethno-symbolism and Nationalism: A Cultural Approach* London: Routledge.

Snyder, David and Charles Tilly. 1972. "Hardship and Collective Violence in France, 1830 to 1960." *American Sociological Review* 37:520–32.

Snyder, Jack and Robert Jervis. 1999. "Civil War and the Security Dilemma." In *Civil Wars, Insecurity, and Intervention*, edited by Barbara F. Walter and Jack Snyder. New York, NY: Columbia University Press.

Stedman, Stephen John. 1997. "Spoiler Problems in Peace Processes." *International Security* 22:5–53.

Stein, Janice Gross. 2002. "Psychological Explanations of International Conflict." In *The Handbook of International Relations*, edited by Walter Carlsnaes, Thomas Risse, and Beth Simmons. London: Sage.

Stewart, Frances. 2000. "The Root Causes of Humantiarian Emergencies." In *War, Hunger, and Displacement: The Origins of Humanitarian Emergencies*, edited by E. Wayne Nafziger, Frances Stewart, and Raimo Väyrynen. Oxford: Oxford University Press.

———. 2008a. "Horizontal Inequalities and Conflict: An Introduction and Some Hypotheses." In *Horizontal Inequalities and Conflict: Understanding Group Violence in Multiethnic Societies*, edited by Frances Stewart. Houndmills: Palgrave Macmillan.

———. editor. 2008b. *Horizontal Inequalities and Conflict: Understanding Group Violence in Multiethnic Societies*. Houndmills: Palgrave Macmillan.

Stewart, Frances, Graham K. Brown, and Arnim Langer. 2008. "Major Findings and Conclusions on the Relationship Between Horizontal Inequalities and Conflict." In *Horizontal Inequalities and Conflict: Understanding Group Violence in Multiethnic Societies*, edited by Frances Stewart. Houndmills: Palgrave Macmillan.

Sukma, Rizal. 2005. "Ethnic Conflict in Indonesia: Causes and the Quest for Solution." In *Ethnic Conflicts in Southeast Asia*, edited by Kusuma Snitwongsee and W. Scott Thompson. Singapore: ISEAS Publications.

Sundberg, Ralph, Kristine Eck, and Joakim Kreutz. 2012. "Introducing the UCDP Non-State Conflict Data Set." *Journal of Peace Research* 49:351–62.

Svensson, Isak and Mathilda Lindgren. 2011. "Community and Consent? Exploring Unarmed Insurgencies in Non-democracies." *European Journal of International Relations* 17:97–120.

Tajfel, Henri and John C. Turner. 1979. "An Integrative Theory of Intergroup Conflict." In *The Social Psychology of Intergroup Relations*, edited by W. G. Austin and S. Worchel. Monterey, CA: Brooks Cole.

Tarrow, Sidney. 1994. *Power in Movement: Social Movements and Contentious Politics*. Cambridge: Cambridge University Press.

———. 2007. "Inside Insurgencies: Politics and Violence in an Age of Civil War." *Perspectives on Politics* 5:587–600.

Taylor, A. J. P. 1948. *The Habsburg Monarchy: A History of the Austrian Empire and Austria-Hungary*. London: Harper and Row.

Tetlock, Philip E. and Aaron Belkin. 1996. "Counterfactual Thought Experiments in World Politics: Logical, Methodological, and Psychological Perspectives." Princeton, NJ: Princeton University Press.

Themnér, Lotta and Peter Wallensteen. 2011. "Armed Conflict, 1946–2010." *Journal of Peace Research* 48:525–36.

Thyne, Clayton. 2007. "Cheap Signals with Costly Consequences: The Effect of Interstate Relations on Civil War." *Journal of Conflict Resolution* 50:937–61.

Tilly, Charles. 1973. "Does Modernization Breed Revolution?" *Comparative Politics* 5:425–48.

———. 1978. *From Mobilization to Revolution*. New York, NY: McGraw-Hill.

———. 1999. *Durable Inequality*. Berkeley and Los Angeles, CA: University of California Press.

———. 2006. "Poverty and the Politics of Exclusion." In *Background Paper for World Bank Study: Moving Out of Poverty*. Washington, DC: World Bank.

Tir, Jaroslav and Michael Jasinski. 2008. "Domestic-Level Diversionary Theory of War." *Journal of Conflict Resolution* 52:641–64.

Tocqueville, Alexis de. [1856] 1956. *The Old Regime and the French Revolution*. Translated by Stuart Gilbert. New York, NY: Anchor Books.

Toft, Monica Duffy. 2003. *The Geography of Ethnic Violence: Identity, Interests, and the Indivisibility of Territory*. Princeton, NJ: Princeton University Press.

———. 2010. *Securing the Peace: The Durable Settlemet of Civil Wars*. Princeton, NJ: Princeton University Press.

Treisman, Daniel S. 1999. *After the Deluge: Regional Crises and Political Consolidation in Russia*. Ann Arbor, MI: University of Michigan Press.

Tullock, Gordon. 1971. "The Paradox of Revolution." *Public Choice* 11:89–99.

Turner, John C. 1987. *Rediscovering the Social Group: A Self-Categorization Theory*. Oxford: Basil Blackwell.

Turner, Jonathan H. and Jan E. Stets. 2005. *The Sociology of Emotions*. Cambridge: Cambridge University Press.

UNU-WIDER. 2008. "World Income Inequality Database version 2.0c." United Nations University, http://www.wider.unu.edu/research/Database/en_GB/database/.

Van Creveld, Martin. 1999. "The Future of War." In *Security in a Post-Cold War World*, edited by Robert G. Patman. New York, NY: St. Martin's.

Van Evera, Stephen. 1994. "Hypotheses on Nationalism and War." *International Security* 18:5–39.

———. 2001. "Primordialism Lives." *APSA-CP: Newsletter of the Organized Section in Comparative Politics of the American Political Science Association* 12:20–22.

Van Houten, Pieter. 1998. "The Role of a Minority's Reference State in Ethnic Relations." *Archives européennes de sociologie* 39:110–46.

Vanhanen, Tatu. 1999. "Domestic Ethnic Conflict and Ethnic Nepotism: A Comparative Analysis." *Journal of Peace Research* 36:55–73.

———. 2000. "A New Data Set for Measuring Democracy, 1810–1998." *Journal of Peace Research* 37:251–65.

Varshney, Ashutosh. 2003. "Nationalism, Ethnic Conflict, and Rationality." *Perspectives on Politics* 1:86–99.

Vogt, Manuel. 2007. "Ethnic Exclusion and Ethno-Nationalist Conflicts. How the Struggle over Access to the State Can Escalate: A Quantitative and Qualitative Analysis of West Africa." University of Zürich, NCCR Democracy 21 Working Paper.

Vreeland, James Raymond. 2008. "The Effect of Political Regime on Civil War: Unpacking Anocracy." *Journal of Conflict Resolution* 52:401–25.

Wagner, R. Harrison. 1993. "The Causes of Peace." In *Stopping the Killing: How Civil Wars End*, edited by Roy Licklider. New York: New York University Press.

———. 2000. "Bargaining and War." *American Journal of Political Science* 44:469–84.

Walter, Barbara F. 1997. "The Critical Barrier to Civil War Settlement." *International Organization* 51:335–64.

———. 2002. *Commiting to Peace: The Successful Settlement of Civil Wars*. Princeton, NJ: Princeton University Press.

———. 2006. "Information, Uncertainty, and the Decision to Secede." *International Organization* 60:105–35.

———. 2009a. "Bargaining Failures and Civil War." *Annual Review of Political Science* 12:243–61.

———. 2009b. *Reputation and Civil War: Why Separatist Conflicts Are So Violent*. Cambridge: Cambridge University Press.

Ward, Michael D., Brian Greenhill, and Kristin Bakke. 2010. "The Perils of Policy by *p*-value: Predicting Civil Conflicts." *Journal of Peace Research* 46:363–75.

Weber, Max. 1946. *From Max Weber: Essays in Sociology*. Edited by H. H. Gerth and C. W. Mills. New York, NY: Oxford University Press.

Weede, Erich. 1987. "Some New Evidence on Correlates of Political Violence: Income Inequality, Regime Repressiveness, and Economic Development." *European Sociological Review* 3:97–108.

Weidmann, Nils B., Doreen Kuse, and Kristian Skrede Gleditsch. 2010. "The Geography of the International System: The CShapes Data Set." *International Interactions* 36:86–106.

Weidmann, Nils B., Jan Ketil Rød, and Lars-Erik Cederman. 2010. "Representing Ethnic Groups in Space: A New Data Set." *Journal of Peace Research* 47:87–119.

Weiner, Myron. 1971. "The Macedonian Syndrome: An Historical Model of International Relations and Political Development." *World Politics* 23:665–83.

———. 1978. *Sons of the Soil: Migration and Ethnic Conflict in India*. Princeton, NJ: Princeton University Press.

Weingast, Barry R. 1998. "Constructing Trust: The Political and Economic Roots of Ethnic and Regional Conflict." In *Institutions and Social Order*, edited by Karol Soltan, Eric M. Uslaner, and Virginia Haufler. Ann Arbor, MI: University of Michigan Press.

Weinstein, Jeremy. 2007. *Inside Rebellion: The Politics of Insurgent Violence*. Cambridge: Cambridge University Press.

Wilkinson, Steven I. 2009. "Riots." *Annual Review of Political Science* 12:329–43.

Williams, Robin M. Jr. 2003. *The Wars Within: Peoples and States in Conflict*. Ithaca, NY: Cornell University Press.

Wimmer, Andreas. 2002. *Nationalist Exclusion and Ethnic Conflict: Shadows of Modernity*. Cambridge: Cambridge University Press.

Wimmer, Andreas, Lars-Erik Cederman, and Brian Min. 2009. "Ethnic Politics and Armed Conflict: A Configurational Analysis of a New Global Data Set." *American Sociological Review* 74:316–37.

Wittman, Donald. 1979. "How a War Ends." *Journal of Conflict Resolution* 23:743–63.

Wood, Elisabeth Jean. 2003. *Insurgent Collective Action and Civil War in El Salvador*. Cambridge: Cambridge Unversity Press.

Woodward, Susan L. 1995. *Balkan Tragedy: Chaos and Dissolution After the Cold War*. Washington DC: Brookings.

Woodwell, Douglas. 2004. "Unwelcome Neighbors: Shared Ethnicity and International Conflict During the Cold War." *International Studies Quarterly* 48:197–223.

Wucherpfennig, Julian. 2011. "Fighting for Change: Onset, Duration, and Recurrence of Ethnic Conflict." Doctoral Dissertation Thesis, ETH Zürich.

Wucherpfennig, Julian, Philipp Hunziker, and Lars-Erik Cederman. 2012. "Who Inherits the State? Colonial Rule and Post-Colonial Conflict." Unpublished paper, ETH Zürich.

Wucherpfennig, Julian, Nils W. Metternich, Lars-Erik Cederman, and Kristian Skrede Gleditsch. 2012. "Ethnicity, the State, and the Duration of Civil War." *World Politics* 64:79–115.

Wucherpfennig, Julian, Nils B. Weidmann, Luc Girardin, Lars-Erik Cederman, and Andreas Wimmer. 2012. "Politically Relevant Ethnic Groups across Space and Time: Introducing the GeoEPR Data Set." *Conflict Management and Peace Science* 28: 423–37.

Ye, Min. 2007. "China." In *Civil Wars of the World: Major Conflicts Since World War II*, vol. 1, edited by Karl R. DeRouen Jr. and Uk Heo. Santa Barbara, CA: CLIO.

Yildiz, Kerim. 2004. *The Kurds in Iraq: The Past, Present and Future*. London: Pluto Press.

Ylönen, Aleksi. 2005. "Grievances and the Roots of Insurgencies: Southern Sudan and Darfur." *Peace, Conflict and Development* 7, available at http://www.bradford.ac.uk/ssis/peace-conflict-and-development.issue-7/Roots-of-insurgencies.pdf

Young, John. 1996. "Ethnicity and Power in Ethiopia." *Review of African Political Economy* 70:531–42.

Zacher, Mark W. 2001. "The Territorial Integrity Norm: International Boundaries and the Use of Force." *International Organization* 55:215–50.

Zevelev, Igor. 2001. *Russia and Its New Diasporas*. Washington, DC: United States Institute of Peace.

Zinn, Annalisa J. 2005. "Theory versus Reality: Civil War Onset and Avoidance in Nigeria since 1960." In *Understanding Civil War: Evidence and Analysis*, vol. 1, edited by Paul Collier and Nicholas Sambanis. Washington, DC: The World Bank.

Zürcher, Christoph. 2007. *The Post-Soviet Wars: Rebellion, Ethnic Conflict, and Nationhood in the Caucasus*. New York, NY: New York University Press.

Index

Series list continued from page iii